A Guide to Hitler's Munich

D1616192

A Guide to Hitler's Munich

David Mathieson

PEN & SWORD
HISTORY

AN IMPRINT OF PEN & SWORD BOOKS LTD.
YORKSHIRE - PHILADELPHIA

First published in Great Britain in 2019 by
Pen and Sword History
An imprint of
Pen & Sword Books Ltd
Yorkshire - Philadelphia

First published in hardback in 2019, this edition published 2020.

ISBN: 9781526766250

Typeset in 11.5/14 Ehrhardt by Vman Infotech Pvt. Ltd.

Printed and bound in the UK by CPI Group (UK) Ltd., Croydon, CR0 4YY

Pen & Sword Books Ltd incorporates the Imprints of Pen & Sword Books
Archaeology, Atlas, Aviation, Battleground, Discovery, Family History, History,
Maritime, Military, Naval, Politics, Railways, Select, Transport, True Crime,
Fiction, Frontline Books, Leo Cooper, Praetorian Press, Seaforth Publishing,
Wharncliffe and White Owl.

For a complete list of Pen & Sword titles please contact

PEN & SWORD BOOKS LIMITED
47 Church Street, Barnsley, South Yorkshire, S70 2AS, England
E-mail: enquiries@pen-and-sword.co.uk
Website: www.pen-and-sword.co.uk

or

PEN AND SWORD BOOKS
1950 Lawrence Rd, Havertown, PA 19083, USA
E-mail: Uspen-and-sword@casematepublishers.com
Website: www.penandswordbooks.com

Contents

In Memory of my parents, Flight Sergeant Reginald Mathieson, who fought with the RAF in the Second World War, and Molly, who lived through the Blitz in south London.

'Those who cannot remember the past are condemned to repeat it'.
—*George Santayana*

Preface

by Mike Gapes MP

In the 1920s Munich was the cradle of Nazism, a force which, over the next twenty-five years, engulfed Germany and brought untold destruction to the whole of Europe. This timely book puts some of that dark history in context by guiding today's traveller to Munich step by step through the old city. It explores many of the places where the most important events of the tragic saga unfolded: from Hitler's arrival in Munich as a transient artist, through the rowdy beer-hall meetings and the Munich *Putsch*, to the Nazis' pharaonic plans for the city, which they called the 'Capital of the Movement'. This book is a guide to the what, where and, most importantly, why history unfolded as it did in Munich.

Many people said that the events described here could never happen. But they did. It would be comforting to believe now that the evil bred in Munich then could be consigned to history, a traumatic episode which will never be repeated. As this invaluable guidebook shows, however, that history was the result of decisions taken, often by ordinary individuals, and in real places which can still be visited. These locations are a standing reminder to us that our choices and our words matter as much now as the decisions people made then.

The great American writer Mark Twain said that 'history does not repeat itself – but it does rhyme.' It is impossible to believe that what happened in Munich in the 1920s will ever recur in identical form. Nevertheless, some of the challenges which people faced in the last century are similar to those of our own age – and we too must decide how to meet them. Countries can choose between the pursuit of narrow, nationalist self-interest or opt for greater cooperation between neighbours for the benefit of all. Communities can choose between racism and xenophobia or tolerance and integration. And as individuals, we can choose to remain silent or raise our voice to promote the kind of world we want for ourselves and our families.

Some in the 1920s and 30s thought that they could duck the challenges in the hope that problems would solve themselves or simply go away. It was not a viable path to take then, nor is it a practicable course now. Across Europe and North America we can see the resurgence of nationalist, right-wing populism. Politicians ready to blame 'others' and offer quick-fix solutions to complex global problems are once again on the march. The message of this book is that we, too, have choices to make. By revisiting, reflecting and understanding the mistakes made in the 1920s and 1930s we stand a better chance of not repeating them in our own age.

House of Commons,
London
2019

Chapter One

Hitler, Munich and the Nazis:
A Brief Background

Hitler, Nazism and the Third Reich are some of the most trawled over subjects in history and there are many excellent books which relate the whole appalling saga. This guide explores events in just one corner – Munich – but at least some of the wider picture is nevertheless necessary to put that story in its proper place. This quick introduction answers some of the general questions that come up most often and provide a brief background to the different chapters in the rest of this book.

Who was Adolf Hitler?

This is not such a simple question as it might sound. Hitler's family was rooted in a semi-literate rural peasantry and their nineteenth-century civic records are somewhat sketchy. Hitler's father, Alois, appears to have been an illegitimate child born in 1837. Whilst Alois' mother was called Schicklgruber, the man assumed to be his father went by the surname Hiedler. At some subsequent point the name Hiedler then morphed into Hitler. By 1876, Alois had taken the surname Hitler and this was also the name given to his baby boy, Adolf, who was born on 20 April 1889. During the Second World War some allied propaganda portrayed the Führer as a phony and – to Anglo Saxon ears – a rather more ridiculous sounding character, by repeatedly calling him 'Herr Schicklgruber'.

What was Germany?

This is another tricky puzzle. Despite independence movements in Scotland and Wales, the British have an easy answer to the question: what is Britain? Being an island surrounded by the sea makes it easy to fix external borders. The shape of Germany, by contrast, has changed repeatedly over the past century or more and given rise to a great deal of angst. The fraught questions of what Germany was, where it began, where it ended and, crucially, who it included were at the forefront of heated political debates throughout the late nineteenth century. The various answers were a key to understanding the rise of Nazism in the twentieth. It was only in 1871 that Chancellor Otto von Bismarck, managed to weld together dozens of smaller states and principalities in a process known as German unification. The borders of the new state were effectively fixed by the Baltic Sea in the north and by the Alps in the south. But on either side, in east and west, were German-speaking communities not included in the new state or territories which had, historically, been German. For Hitler, the vexed question of territorial integrity and a unification of German-speaking peoples was unfinished business at the core of his political creed.

What were the origins of the city of Munich?

Munich began to develop in the medieval period as a stop-off point on the trade route between Italy in the south and other commercial centres in the north of Europe. During the nineteenth century, Munich grew rapidly from being a market town of some 30,000 people to the capital of the state of Bavaria with over half a million inhabitants. Bavaria is a region which has always boasted its own distinct style and culture (as say, Scotland does within the UK or Catalonia within Spain). The region was largely rural and Roman Catholic. But with the unification of Germany in 1871, Bavaria went from being a proud sovereign state to a satellite dominated by the much larger northern state of Prussia. Many thought that German unification was little more than a euphemism for Prussian domination and Munich, in turn, became the poorer relation of well-heeled cities of the north like Berlin and Hamburg. The cultural differences between the militaristic swagger of Protestant northerners and the more relaxed Catholic southerners, who lived in the shadow of the Italian Alps, sat uncomfortably within the unified Germany and these tensions were exacerbated by the First World War. Religion continued to be an important fault line within Germany after the war: in 1933 some six out of ten Germans described themselves as Protestant and three out of ten were Catholic. But in Bavaria the figure was almost the reverse; seventy per cent of people were Catholic and just under thirty per cent Protestant.

What was Munich like after The First World War?

By the 1920s Munich had a population of almost three-quarters of a million and was by far the largest city in Bavaria. Nuremberg was the region's next largest city with a population of just over 400,000. The population of Bavaria, with some eight million people, was mainly rural. A plethora of small and medium-sized companies dominated the local economy – a feature of southern Germany still – so that it was, according to one commentator, 'very much the land of small industry characterized by workshops run by independent craftsmen'. Industrial behemoths like the BMW car plant in Munich grew, but still employed only a tiny fraction of the overall workforce.

Was Hitler from Munich?

No. Hitler was not even German by birth. He was actually born in Braunau am Inn, a quaint provincial town on the Austrian side of the border from Germany. Hitler's domineering and frequently drunken father worked there as a customs inspector for the Austro-Hungarian authorities. He went to school in the Austrian city of Linz and attempted to study art in Vienna. Later in life Hitler tried to make a virtue of the fact that he was not born a German national by claiming that his birthplace was a 'providential' sign of unity between Germanic peoples. One of Hitler's main goals was to unite the two countries and this he achieved with the *Anschluss* and invasion of Austria in 1938 (see Chapter 9). Hitler only arrived in Munich in the spring of 1913 and immediately felt at home in the city. He was, he wrote, more attached to Munich 'than any other spot on earth,' and it 'remains inseparably bound up with the development of my own life.' He described Munich as the 'Capital of the movement' and came to use the city as his power base.

What did Hitler do in the First World War?

When war broke out in the summer of 1914, Hitler joined the Bavarian infantry and held the rank of corporal. He was a runner, carrying messages from commanders to frontline troops and won the Iron Cross medal for his service. Unlike many of his company, however, he survived relatively unscathed until the final days of the war. In October 1918 Hitler was caught in a gas attack. Temporarily blind and bewildered, he was led from the trenches to recover at a hospital in the Pasewalk in Pomerania, in the north east of Germany. It was the end of the war for him and a month later the shattered Germany surrendered.

How did Germany react to the defeat of the First World War?

The German Emperor, Kaiser Wilhelm II, embarked on the war in 1914, confident that the conflict would enhance German authority on the international stage, promote cohesion at home and bolster his image everywhere. But none of these aims were realised and the defeat was a national calamity. Wilhelm was forced to abdicate and immediately fled to Holland. The Kaiser's flight left a power vacuum in which old antagonisms between social classes and the different regions surfaced in the most virulent forms. Traumatised by war and defeat, the country appeared to be on the point of total political, social and economic collapse while millions of Germans sank into abject poverty.

What was the Weimar Republic?

With the disintegration of the old order, German leaders agreed a new constitution for the country when they met in the northern town of Weimar in the summer of 1919. But the 'Weimar Republic', as it was known, was little loved and much criticised by powerful political forces across the political spectrum, one wit describing it as 'a Republic without Republicans'. The fledgling state was buffeted by immensely powerful external forces and lacked the strong foundations it needed to remain stable. The artist George Grosz, later pilloried by the Nazis (see Chapter 4) wrote: 'There were speakers on every street corner and songs of hatred everywhere. Everybody was hated: the Jews, the capitalists, the gentry, the communists, the military, the landlords, the workers, the unemployed … the Allied control commissioners, the politicians, the department stores, and again the Jews. It was a real orgy of incitement and the Republic so weak … It all had to end with an awful crash.' And so it did. Weimar lasted for just fourteen years, during which time there were apparently endless elections and twenty changes of government. Then, in 1933, the Nazis came to power and put an end to the ailing republic and to democracy.

Why was the Treaty of Versailles so important?

Retribution against Germany swiftly followed the armistice that brought an end to the First World War on 11 November 1918. Lop-sided negotiations – in which the Germans came off badly – followed the peace and an international conference was convened at the Palace of Versailles, just outside Paris, to sign off the agreement. The resulting Treaty of Versailles was presented as a done deal to a horrified German nation and commonly known as the *Diktat*. The country was humiliated: its borders were redrawn, the military was emasculated and the country was stripped of all its overseas colonies. Worst of all, Germany was forced to make payments to compensate the Allies. Called 'reparations', and totaling just under half a trillion US dollars at today's prices, these repayments further crippled the German economy. The terms of the Versailles treaty were condemned across the political spectrum as unjust and degrading. It was the Nazis, however, who were most skillful in exploiting the general grievances about the Treaty. They dubbed the German leaders who had been obliged to sign the treaty as the 'November Traitors' and helped fan the myth that the valiant military had never been defeated but 'stabbed in the back' by perfidious politicians. It was a narrative eagerly seized upon by an army's officer class which sought to blame anyone but themselves for the defeat.

What were the Freikorps?

German politics became increasingly unstable after 1918. Street violence and assassinations were common as different groups clashed in their attempts to take control. Paramilitary bands known as the *Freikorps* (Free Corps) were in the vanguard of the fighting. These gangs of army veterans, brutalised by conflict, had been discharged from formal military discipline but were unable to demobilise psychologically from the war and became the shock troops of the political right. The Free Corps were used, along with the traditional bodies of police and army, to topple revolutionary left-wing administrations that sprang up briefly in cities like Munich and Berlin. But this effectively legitimised the role of non-state paramilitary groups in street politics and the consequences unfolded with devastating effects. The violent culture of the Free Corps effectively became embedded in German politics and the public mind. Exiled journalist Sebastian Haffner wrote that they 'resembled the Nazi storm troops which most of them later joined. They certainly had the same outlook, behaviour and fighting methods.' They frequently shot prisoners against a wall without questions, or 'whilst attempting to escape', and honed methods of torture. 'All that was lacking,' wrote Haffner, 'was a theory to justify the practice. That would be provided by Hitler'.

What was the *Völkisch* movement?

The tendrils of Nazi ideology were many but those of the *Völkisch* or ethnic movement ran deepest. The leading Nazi newspaper, for example, was called the *Völkisch Beobachter* (the Völkisch Observer). The *Völkisch* movement arose in Germany at the end of the nineteenth century and was a reaction to the intellectual forces behind the French Revolution, the Enlightenment, liberal democracy and socialism. Race was at the centre of the creed. As Hitler wrote in *Mein Kampf,* 'The *Völkicsh* view recognizes the importance of the racial subdivisions ... it sees the state only a means to an end and it considers the preservation of the race ... as the end.' It was scarcely necessary for him to add that he 'by no means believes in the equality of all races'. Some volkisch theory was widely shared elsewhere; a belief in racially determined superiority, eugenics and a Darwinian struggle for survival were far from unique to Germany. Nevertheless, *Völkisch* theory twisted these with other ideas into an especially toxic brew. The *Völkisch* movement regarded the German language as a sacred transmission belt. As one theorist put it, 'The moral and spiritual salvation of mankind depends on things German ... science, philosophy and religion can today make no step forward except in the German language'. Discipline, order, duty, unity, hierarchy and national welfare were also core values of the *Völkisch* ideal. Individual liberty, the cornerstone of Western liberals, was rejected out of hand as an illusion. Another bug-bear of *Völkisch* thought was democracy, which was held to be disruptive, divisive and a corrosive enemy of the revered national 'whole'. In the fractious years of the Weimar republic, the prospect of trading individual liberty for greater national cohesion gained some traction and was eagerly seized upon by the Nazis as a justification for their totalitarian state.

Why was Hitler's Regime called the Third Reich?

The word Reich means 'empire' and prior to Hitler there had been two already. Charlemagne forged the Holy Roman Empire and created the First Reich in the early Middle Ages. This amorphous power block survived in various forms but was finally ended by Napoleon in the early nineteenth century. Otto Von Bismarck created the Second Reich under Kaiser Wilhelm with the unification of Germany in 1871. The concept of a Third Reich was coined by a *Völkisch* writer after the First World War and had a mystic undertone which harked back to the medieval glories of Charlemagne. The number 'three' was also particularly valued by *Völkisch* folklore as being a synthesis of opposites. The symbolism was adopted with alacrity by Hitler who boasted that his Third Reich would last for 'a thousand years'. In fact, it survived for just twelve.

Timeline of German History 1871–1948

1871   Unification of Germany, founding of German Empire and Second Reich under Chancellor Otto von Bismarck.

1888   Wilhelm II becomes German Kaiser.

1889   Adolf Hitler born in Braunau am Inn, Austria.

1899   Houston Stewart Chamberlain, social Darwinist and ideologue of the racist *Völkischer* movement, publishes his influential book *Foundations of the 19th Century* in Munich.

1913   *May*: Hitler arrives in Munich from Vienna.

1914   *June*: Archduke Franz Ferdinand of Austria assassinated, triggering the First World War. October: Hitler enlists in the Bavarian Infantry and leaves Munich for the front.

1918   *November*: First World War ends. The Kaiser Wilhelm abdicates and Weimar Republic is declared. Hitler returns to Munich. Revolution in Bavaria.

1919   *January*: Anton Drexler and others found the German Workers Party DAP (*Deutsch Arbieterpartei*) in Munich. June: Treaty of Versailles is signed. September: Adolf Hitler is sent to inform on the DAP but is so impressed with their ideas that he becomes a member.

1920   *February*: DAP adopts its '25-point programme' and subsequently changes name to the National Socialist German Workers Party (NSDAP), or Nazi for short.

1921   *July*: Hitler becomes leader of NSDAP. November: The *Sturm Abteilung* (SA), the party militia, is formed.

1922   *October*: Mussolini organises the 'March on Rome' to take control of the Italian state.

1923   *November*: Beer Hall *Putsch* in Munich attempts to overthrow German government and Weimar Republic.

1924   *February*: Hitler tried in Munich for High Treason and jailed for his part in the Beer Hall *Putsch*.

1925   *July*: first volume of *Mein Kampf* published in Munich.
       November: The *Schutzstaffel* (SS) 'protection squadron' is formed from Hitler's bodyguard.

1927   *August*: first annual party conference held at Nuremberg.

1928   *May*: Nazi party wins just 2.6 per cent of vote and twelve Reichstag seats in the General Election.

1929   *October*: start of the Wall Street Crash and global economic depression

1930   *September*: Nazis win eighteen per cent of the vote in the Reichstag elections and become the second largest party.

1932   *July*: Nazis win thirty-seven per cent of the vote in the Reichstag elections and become largest party.
       November: Nazis lose thirty-five seats and Communists gain seats in Reichstag elections.

1933   *January:* Hitler appointed chancellor and head of a coalition cabinet.
       February: Hitler announces foreign policy goal of *lebensraum*

(living space); Reichstag fire happens and Communist Party (KPD) is banned;

March: Nazis gain forty-four per cent of votes in rigged Reichstag elections; Enabling Act passed which allows Hitler to rule by decree and suspends civil liberties; the first official concentration camp is opened in Dachau, just outside Munich;

April: Gestapo secret police established;

May: trade unions banned; burning of 'un-German books' takes place in university towns across Germany including Munich;

July: Nazis become the only party recognized by law;

October: Germany withdraws from League of Nations;

1934 *June*: Ernst Röhm, other SA leaders and opponents are murdered during the 'Night of the Long Knives';

August: President Hindenburg dies; Hitler assumes office of both President and Chancellor and declares himself Führer.

1935 *January*: Plebiscite in the Saar region declares ninety-one per cent vote in favour of reunion with Germany;

February: German Luftwaffe (airforce) established in defiance of Versailles Treaty;

March: German army expansion plans announced and introduction of conscription;

September: Nuremberg laws define racial purity and further measures to discriminate against Jews.

1936 *March*: Germany reoccupies Rhineland in defiance of Versailles Treaty;

July: Spanish military botch their attempt to overthrow Republican government in Madrid and civil war breaks out;

August: Berlin Olympic games provide propaganda boost for Nazi regime;

October: Axis alliance between Germany and Italy settled;

November: Anti-communist alliance between Germany and Japan settled;

December: Hitler Youth membership becomes compulsory for young people.

1938   *March*: *Anschluss* with Austria; German troops – and Hitler – make triumphant entry into Vienna;

September: Munich agreement surrenders Sudetenland region of Czechoslovakia to Germany;

November: *Kristallnacht* destroys Jewish property and Jewish community is fined. Mass detention of Jews.

1939   *March*: Britain issues statement to guarantee inviolability of Poland;

August: Ribbentrop-Molotov pact between Germany and USSR guarantees mutual assistance in the event of attack;

September: Germany invades Poland; Second World War breaks out.

1940   *April*: Denmark and Norway invaded by Germany;

May: France invaded by Germany;

July: Battle of Britain to defend UK;

October: London and other UK cities Blitzed.

1941   *April*: Germany invades Yugoslavia and Greece;

June: Germany invades Russia (Operation Barbarossa);

December: Japanese attack Pearl Harbour and Germany declares war on USA.

1942   *January*: Wannsee conference approves plans for 'Final Solution' of Jews;

September: German troops reach Stalingrad but are surrounded in November;

October: – British 8th Army forces German retreat at El Alamein in North Africa;

November: Germans occupy Vichy France.

1943   *February*: White Rose members arrested in Munich; Goebbels declares 'total war' in Berlin;

April: Warsaw Ghetto uprising is suppressed with great brutality;

July: Allied troops land in Sicily. Mussolini deposed and Italians sue for peace.

1944   *June*: Allied troops take Rome; D-Day landings in Normandy; Allied troops liberate Paris;

November: gassing operations end at Auschwitz.

1945   *February*: Churchill, Stalin and Roosevelt meet at Yalta to agree on post-war division of Germany;

April: Mussolini executed in Milan; Hitler commits suicide in Berlin;

May: Germany declares unconditional surrender;

November: Nuremberg war crimes trials begin.

1947   *June*: General George Marshall unveils European Recovery Programme to rebuild European economy.

1948   *June*: Soviets block western access to Berlin.

1949   *May*: Federal Republic of Germany created with Konrad Adenauer as first chancellor.

Chapter Two

Hitler's Early Life in Munich:
From Bohemia to Germania

O n the sunny afternoon of Sunday, 25 May 1913, a callow young
man carrying a suitcase made his way up the platform of Munich's
Hauptbahnhof (central station). Adolf Hitler had arrived for the
first time and was immediately seized by the Bavarian capital. 'The city,'
he enthused, 'was as familiar to me as if I had lived for years within its
walls.' He subsequently claimed to have arrived in the spring of 1912 – a
year before he actually did – and he remained rooted in Munich for the
rest of his life. It was here that he would make his home, meet his wife
and create a base for one of the most destructive movements in human
history.

Hitler reveled in the traditional Bavarian culture of Munich but
was apparently oblivious to the fact that he had stepped into one of
Europe's most Bohemian cities. Prior to the First World War, Munich
was synonymous with intellectual freedom, vibrant creativity and
artistic exploration. Along with Berlin, Paris and Vienna, the city was
a cauldron of innovation and home to pioneers of modernist art. None
then would have predicted that the down-at-heel young foreigner would
turn the free-wheeling Munich into the crucible of a rigid and repressive
totalitarian regime.

'Adi' Comes to Town

When he first arrived in Munich looking to make a new life for himself,
Hitler was accompanied by his companion from the Vienna dosshouse
he had just left, Rudiger Häusler. They call each other 'Adi' and 'Rudi'.
Häusler was the black sheep of a middle-class Vienna family; his father
disowned him and slung him out of the family home following his expulsion
from school.

The two loafers walked the streets of Munich looking for lodgings until they saw a sign, 'Room to Rent', above a small tailor's shop in **Schleissheimerstrasse 34**.[1] (By coincidence, the exiled Vladimir Lenin had lodged briefly in the same street, at number 106, just a decade before). Frau Popp, the landlady, showed him to a small room on the third floor. A deal was struck and the two lodgers agreed to rent the single room for three Marks per week. In his scrawling handwriting, Hitler signed the registration form as 'Adolf Hitler, architectural painter from Vienna'.

Once settled in Schleissheimerstrasse, Hitler lived pretty much as he had done in Vienna. His fantasies about winning design competitions to become a great architect foundered on the rocks of routine and discipline. In the shared, sparsely furnished room, Hitler's existence was one notch above that of the dosser's life of the Viennese hostel. Never an early riser, he wandered the city painting chocolate-box images of its famous buildings, which he then tried to sell in beer gardens or door to door. One of his first sketches of Munich was of the small playground opposite his flat. He also whiled away time in the **Bayerische Staatsbibliothek** (Bavaria's state library) in **Ludwigstrasse**, reading up on a range of topics such as German history and political theory.[2] This was not, however, a scholarly quest in pursuit of truth: books were seldom selected to broaden or challenge Hitler's views but chosen to reinforce those opinions which had already gelled in his mind.

He seems to have got along well enough with the Popps whenever he met them and their two young children, Josef and Elsie, living on the floors below, but any deeper relationship was beyond him; and remained so throughout his life. In somewhat jumbled recollections, Frau Popp later said that she had 'never met a man with such good manners,' but, strangely, could not recall a single visitor calling to see her insular lodger in the two years of the tenancy. There were, apparently, no friends, no women, no drinking; just an irregular lifestyle, living hand to mouth by whatever he could sell to supplement the dwindling legacy of his dead parents. Hitler would read with the light on half the night or, worse still, talk in seemingly endless, exhausting diatribes. Häusler quickly became fed up with his room-mate's moodiness and singular timetable and, after just a few months, he moved out to find some peace and quiet.

Hitler was now twenty-four years old, almost completely alone and adrift. His paintings seem to have sold reasonably well for those of a jobbing artist but were never going to bring either wealth or fame. One Dr Hans Schirmer recalled sitting with a glass of beer on the shady patio of the **Hofbräuhaus**, one of Munich's most venerated beer halls and a favourite haunt of locals since it was founded in 1589. Schirmer soon became aware of a 'very shabby looking man' wending his way amongst the tables.[3] The impecunious artist was trying to sell a picture to the seated drinkers but without success. At around ten in the evening the young man still had not sold the picture and the doctor called him over, 'I asked him, being touched by his predicament from a purely human point of view, whether he would be willing to sell the picture.' They settled on a price but, after an evening's drinking, the doctor did not have enough cash on him to pay there and then so they agreed to meet the next day.

When Hitler called on the doctor to deliver the picture called *Der Abend* (the evening) and take payment, the artist and client began to talk more. The doctor sensed that, although 'having a hard time of it', the young artist was too proud to accept charity. Hitler then offered to paint more pictures for the doctor and these were delivered 'within a week'. But the doctor was not rich and could not afford to buy more work so the painter and the patron did not meet again.

Hitler did, however, have better luck with other clients. A jeweler called Kerber bought some twenty paintings from him, between 1913 and 1914, and a soap manufacturer called Schnell also liked his work. Schnell was something of a patron of young artists and must have been important to Hitler. Long after he came to power in the 1930s, Hitler invited Schnell to meet him in Munich's plush Vier Jahreszeiten (Four Seasons) hotel, one of his favourite haunts on the opulent Maximilianstrasse. The two talked over old times and Hitler, ever concerned about his paintings, quizzed the doctor about their state of preservation.

Most other sales, however, seem to have been to one-off buyers. It is estimated that Hitler turned out up to two thousand pictures between 1905 and 1920, and after 1933 the Nazis set about tracking them down. Hitler effectively attempted to nationalise his own body of work; functionaries were instructed to repurchase some of the paintings and insist on a memorandum of where and how the owner had actually met the Führer. Even today there is a mawkish demand for Hitler's art: one of his watercolours recently sold for a hefty six figure sum.

The City of a Thousand Artists

While Hitler was hawking his own rather pedestrian, conservative watercolours, others in the city were joining an artistic revolution. Munich had been a hub of trade since medieval times but creativity was central to its growth. The city boasted an Academy of Fine Arts; founded in the eighteenth century this was one of the pre-eminent teaching centres of central Europe. As the capital of Bavaria, King Ludwig II had adorned the city with so many neoclassical buildings, columns and arches that Munich was dubbed 'Athens on the Isar', the name of the river which runs through the city. The world-famous Neue Pinakothek, a gallery founded in the 1850s by Ludwig I, is still home to a very fine collection of nineteenth-century works, mainly by non-German artists.

In 1892 a municipal committee reported that, 'Munich owes its outstanding importance amongst German cities to art and artists, however highly one may rate other factors in its development.' The thriving cultural scene boomed and at the turn of the twentieth century there were well over a thousand painters registered as living in the city more than Berlin which had a population four times that of Munich. One English painter who visited the city in the 1880s observed that in Munich painters 'had the status of generals'. Close to Italy, Munich had a reputation as being less buttoned-up than Prussian Berlin and there was a strong sense of pushing artistic convention to its limit. At the turn of the twentieth century, author Thomas Mann observed that 'Munich was radiant … Young artists with little round hats on their heads … carefree bachelors who paid for their lodgings with colour sketches.' There were, said Mann, an endless number 'of little shops which sold picture frames, sculptures and antiques,' with owners 'who spoke of Mino de Fiesole or Donatello as though he had received the rights of reproduction from them personally.'

Central to the lively pre-war city life was the *Neue Kunstlervereinigung Munchen* (Munich New Artists Association). Founded in 1909 by the Russian emigre Wassily Kandinsky, the MNAA put on exhibitions in the city by emerging artists such as Picasso and Braque. Despite the inevitable clashes, bickering and schisms between some of the petulant egos involved, the group became a trailblazing force in European culture. Kandinsky eventually departed to found the radical modernist *Blaue*

Reiter (Blue Rider) group, which mounted its inaugural exhibition in a Munich gallery in 1911. The display has a legendary place in the history of twentieth-century art and the names of the artists whose work was displayed – with Braque, Picasso, Nolde, Klee, Schiele and Marc in the vanguard – reads like a roll call of great expressionist painters. Controversy swirled around both the *Blaue Reiter* opening and a follow-up exhibition in 1912. Some spectators were energised by what they saw whilst others were scandalised. Few were left indifferent. Then, when the exhibition left Munich and toured Europe, it literally changed the way many people looked at the world.

One might have thought that the excitement of the Munich art scene in 1913 would have been heaven for a struggling young artist from Vienna. But it was not so for Hitler. He remained wholly detached from the avant-garde and went about his business doing what he had always done; painting accurate but uninspired scenes of local landmarks such as the Frauenkirche church, the Feldherrnhalle memorial in Odeonsplatz, the Medaeval Alte Hof and the famous beer hall, the Hofbräuhaus. He later claimed that 'study led me to this metropolis of German art ... One does not know Germany if one does not know Munich (and) ... one does not know German art if one does not know Munich.' Evidently, Hitler had to eat and his orthodox work would have sold more quickly to visitors than experimental form. But, even in his copious down-time, there is no evidence that Hitler was touched by the cultural earthquake going on around him or that he bothered to visit the exhibitions of works by others on his doorstep. Later, in the 1930s, the Nazis did take considerable interest in expressionism, but not to learn from it, let alone venerate the creativity. Modern art and those who made it were condemned. In 1937 the Nazis mounted a 'Degenerate Art Exhibition' in a Munich gallery and this became one of the most infamous exhibitions of the century (see chapter 4).

Not all of Munich's intelligentsia was on the political left or even in the intellectual avant-garde at this time. One of the most influential intellectuals of the twentieth century, Oswald Spengler, lived at Agnesstrasse 54 in Munich for much of the time between 1913 until his death in 1936. His seminal work *Decline of the West*, published in 1919, was a best-seller and had a profound influence on the development of Nazi ideology. Spengler later came to hate Nazis – and they him – although by that time much damage was done. Spengler's pseudo-scientific studies of race, decadent civilisations and the purity of elites provided spurious intellectual cover for the Nazi machine.

Schwabing: 'Munich's Montmartre'

Hitler's apparent lack of contact with other artists of Munich was even more puzzling given his physical proximity to the buzz of activity. Schleissheimerstrasse was on the fringe of Schwabing, Munich's bohemian quarter, and the area might have been dubbed 'swinging' by later generations. It was not so much a district as a 'scene' or 'a mass collection of oddballs' in the words of one local. A favourite 'oddball' haunt was the **Café Stefanie**, at the corner of **Amalienstrasse** and **Theresienstrasse**, which was sadly destroyed during the Second World War.[4] The Café was mockingly nicknamed *Grossenwahn* (megalomania) because of the arty, intellectual crowd that regularly gathered there. With their egos fueled by cheap beer and schnapps, the bohemians opined long into the night about how they alone would make the world a more perfect place before staggering into the night to sleep off the drink and nurse their hangovers the following morning.

The house journal of this trendy 'in-crowd' was one of Germany's best known satirical magazines, the leftist *Simplicissimus*, which had its editorial office in Munich. Writing about the traditional German elite, it was feisty enough to provoke a furious Kaiser; cartoonists were fined and at one point the editor fled to Switzerland to escape prosecution. Later, the Nazis did what the Kaiser had failed to do and publication of the magazine ceased abruptly when Hitler came to power in 1933.

One famous resident of the area, the Jewish anarchist writer Erich Mühsam, dubbed Schwabing 'Munich's Montmartre' (the quintessentially bohemian district in Paris). Well known for his biting satire and cabaret routines, Mühsam described his fellow Schwabing dwellers as 'painters, sculptors, writers, models, loafers, religious founders, philosophers, revolutionaries, reformers, sexual moralists, psychoanalysts, musicians, architects, craftswomen, run-away girls of good family, eternal students, the industrious, the idle, those with a lust for life and those who were world weary, those who wore their hair unkempt and those who parted it neatly.'

Mühsam observant wit did not go down well with the authoritarian right in Munich. He was heavily involved in the Bavarian revolutionary government in 1919 and imprisoned when it collapsed (see below). Released under the general amnesty for political prisoners of 1924 – which also liberated Hitler (see chapter 3) – he returned to become a leading light in the Munich arts community for the next decade. He was arrested again in 1933, but this time there was no reprieve. Mühsam was one of the first people picked up by the Nazis when Hitler came to power; he was held in the Oranienburg concentration camp, where he was battered to death by SS Guards in 1934.

Temperamentally incapable of integrating himself with the pre-war arts scene, Hitler's attempts to mix with a more conventional artistic set after the war were scarcely more successful. Munich diarist Fritz Reck recalled an early encounter with the future Führer when, shortly after the end of the First World War, Hitler turned up at a chic house-party thrown by the composer and one-time director of the Bavarian state opera company, Clemens von Franckenstein (sic) in Munich. Normally an unprepossessing, insignificant figure, on this occasion Hitler commanded attention through his dress: gaiters, a wide-brimmed floppy hat and riding crop (although there is no evidence that he could ride), 'which he cracked to on his boots to impress the other guests whilst a pet collie dog trotted along.'

For a while the host apparently indulged Hitler while maintaining his distance with a series of subtle put-downs, which the other guests understood perfectly but which Hitler did not. Lacking the social skills needed to integrate with the group, Hitler reacted in the only way he knew how: he launched into speech. 'He talked on and on, endlessly. He preached. He went on at us like a division chaplain in the Army. We did not in the least contradict him or venture to differ in any way but he began to bellow at us. The servants thought we were being attacked and rushed in to defend us.' Polite society was, on this occasion as so often in the future, dumbfounded by what had happened and did not know how to respond. When Hitler left the house Reck recalled that the vacated space was filled by embarrassment, 'When he had gone, we sat silently confused and not at all amused. There was a feeling of dismay, as when on a train you suddenly find you are sharing a compartment with a psychotic. We sat for a long time and no one spoke.'

Hitler and the First World War

By 1914 Hitler might well have drifted into almost complete obscurity. He had neither enrolled to study design nor broken into the artistic milieu of Munich. Worse still, the Austro-Hungarian authorities were now on his trail. As an Austrian citizen, Hitler was obliged to undertake military service for the Emperor. Officials from the military wanted to know where he was and why he was avoiding conscription. They eventually tracked him down in February 1914 and demanded that he attend an interview in Salzburg, but the examination turned out to be a failure. Years of near-destitution had taken their toll on his health and physique. Hitler was rejected as being too weak to be of any use in the Emperor's army. Later, the whole affair became immensely embarrassing for the future Führer as he tried to project an image of himself as the epitome of strength and force. After the annexation of Austria in 1938, the Gestapo desperately hunted – but failed to find – Hitler's medical records from the examination, which only came to light after the war.

In the summer of 1914, however, Hitler's cycle of slow decline was suddenly broken. In later years he would boast that his emergence from the penury of Munich was a result of his own determination and 'indomitable will'. In reality, pure happenchance played a far bigger role. In June 1914 the podgy Austrian Archduke Franz Ferdinand and his wife embarked on an imperial visit to Sarajevo, an outpost of the Austro-Hungarian Empire. While there, they were shot dead by a Serbian nationalist and the shockwave triggered the First World War. In the febrile summer of 1914, many embraced the coming of war as a necessary step to reset Europe. Novelist and Munich resident Thomas Mann, for example, wrote gleefully, 'War! It meant a cleansing, a liberation ... and an extraordinary sense of hope.' Another who celebrated the oncoming conflict was Hitler. One photograph shows him in the jubilant throng in the central city square, the Odeonsplatz, on 2 August 1914.[5] There are few photographs of Hitler beaming with joy but this is one. Dressed in his Sunday-best clothes, like others in the crowd, his face radiates a peculiar fervour for the coming of war. In the light of what followed, the enthusiasm for hostilities at the time now seems utterly baffling.

Despite being an Austrian national, Hitler wrote to King Ludwig of Bavaria asking to enlist in the Bavarian army. By some bureaucratic bungling or oversight, which has never been properly explained, the request was granted, and a few days later the Austrian Hitler joined the Bavarian Infantry. Along with other volunteers, he gathered at a school building at **4 Elizabethplatz**.[6] After a few weeks rudimentary training in the schoolyard, Hitler and his regiment were dispatched to Flanders where they were quickly thrown into action. The horrors of war soon took their toll and the Bavarians suffered the most appalling losses; some seventy per cent of troops were killed or wounded within weeks. Hitler was given the rank of corporal and his task was to carry messages between different sectors of the front. It was a dangerous duty and the casualty rate amongst the 'runners' was high. Hitler was decorated with the Iron Cross for his service an award of which he made much in the years to come.

Whereas most combatants recalled the war as an indescribable trauma, Hitler looked back on the period as 'the greatest and most unforgettable time of my earthly existence'. It was in the army, and with the war, that he felt a sense of purpose which had hitherto escaped him. For many of his generation the First World War left scars so deep that they could never again contemplate fighting, but Hitler drew the opposite conclusion. He decided that life was an eternal struggle in which adversaries must be overcome at whatever cost.

Even in the midst of war Hitler wrote to a friend, 'I think so often of Munich,' which he hoped would, like the rest of Germany, be 'purer and cleansed of alien influence ... and internationalism broken' by the war. However, he began to avoid visiting the city, even on leave. The mounting losses in terms of both blood and treasure led to an increasing pessimism in Munich and, as the euphoria of 1914 evaporated, a blame-game for the eventual rout of 1918 began. Tensions across Germany mounted. The southern Bavarians in particular increasingly blamed the militaristic Prussian northerners for the German causalities and defeat. Hitler did not himself witness the end of the war. Blinded by a gas attack in the last weeks of the conflict, he was convalescing in a hospital in northern Germany when the news came through. The defeat left him hysterical with grief; by his own account he pounded his pillow and wept for the first time since his mother died. He was also very angry and swore revenge on the politicians in Berlin whom he blamed for the national humiliation.

Post-Conflict Trauma and Chaos in Munich

Hitler returned to Munich on 21 November 1918. Like many other veterans, he was not immediately discharged from military service but remained in the army and continued to live in the regimental barracks in **Lothstrasse 29**.[7] Now in his thirtieth year, the army filled a void and solved the immediate problem of what to do with his life. It gave him both a sense of purpose and, even more importantly, food and some meagre wages.

In common with many other Germans, he was in a state of shock. Bavaria and Munich had been traumatised by four long years of war and the sudden, dramatic and unexpected defeat. In addition to war casualties, a virulent strain of influenza – Spanish flu – was about to kill many more people and add to the desolation. But worse was to come and the apparent stability of the pre-war Munich was lost forever. As Hitler biographer, Professor Ian Kershaw, comments, 'It would be hard to exaggerate the impact on the political consciousness in Bavaria of events between November 1918 and May 1919.' The city to which Hitler returned was a cauldron of political activity and what happened next had profound consequences.

The king, Ludwig III, rapidly abdicated and fled Munich. The House of Wittelsbach, which had ruled Bavaria for seven centuries, was no more and a central pillar of state simply disappeared with the monarch. The now vacant throne and the turmoil of defeat left a power vacuum that was filled by the creation of a radical Bavarian republic. Kurt Eisner, a somewhat unkempt, leftist intellectual agitator, became president, but he lacked the basic political skills that would have been necessary even under the most benign circumstances. And there was nothing benign about the politics of post-war Munich.

Eisner's shambolic administration was partly inspired by the recent Bolshevik revolution in Russia. By historical coincidence, the leader of the young Soviet Republic, Vladimir Ilyich Ulyanov, had lived in Munich before the war. Exiled and on the run from the Tsarist police, the bearded émigré, with his thick Russian accent, tried to pass himself off under the pseudonym 'Herr Meyer' and lived on Munich's **Kaiserstrasse 46**. It was here that he buried himself away and wrote one of the of the most influential revolutionary tomes of the twentieth century. The pamphlet was called 'What is to be Done?' and he published it under yet another pseudonym Vladimir Lenin.[8]

But Eisner was no Lenin. His government stumbled on for the next few weeks, scarcely able to deal with any of the looming economic, social or political crises. And then, in February 1919, Eisner was assassinated by an aristocratic, anti-Semitic student at Munich University who had recently been discharged from the army. Ironically, the Jewish Eisner was on his way to parliament to tend his resignation when he was shot.

A companion recalled how, as he left for the parliament, 'His friends begged him to go via the back entrance of the Bayerischer Hof hotel rather than across the street ... but Eisner adamantly refused to listen. I once more reminded him of the climate of hatred whipped up against him by the press and the countless threatening letters he had received over the previous few days. But all to no avail. Eisner insisted on taking his usual route across the street to the state parliament: "You cannot evade assassination forever, and, after all, they can only shoot me dead once."' The two continued on their way, deep in conversation about the unfolding political crisis, when 'suddenly two shots rang out one after the other behind us. Eisner staggered briefly, and tried to say something but he couldn't get the words out. Then he silently crumpled to the floor.' There is now a figure marked out on the pavement, in the style of a police crime scene, at the spot where he was assassinated, and a small memorial nearby.[9]

Eisner's administration had scarcely lasted one hundred days and his death triggered a period of almost complete chaos in Munich. A disparate group of radicals now declared the foundation of a Bavarian Republic in April 1919, which attempted to break away from the rest of Germany and establish a kind of Soviet-style republic based on a network of workers' councils. Concepts such as work, hierarchy or the existing rule of law were abolished overnight by revolutionary decree. They were, insisted the new regime, the illusory trappings of a clapped-out bourgeoisie order. The nature of the republic was perhaps embodied by the new 'foreign minister', a certain Dr Franz Lipp, a former journalist who had been treated for mental illness but not, apparently, restored to full health. Lipp sent cables to Lenin and to 'comrade' Pope in the Vatican, complaining that the previous administration had fled taking with them the keys to the toilets, before declaring war on Switzerland. The new administration then issued a decree that all bars and cafés should shut at six o'clock in the evening. This was not popular with the workers. The culture minister was chased through the streets of Munich by an angry mob and the order rapidly rescinded.

The Bavarian revolution did not last more than a couple of weeks and was put down with great brutality. The German army and the Free Corps swung into action to round up the ring-leaders, most of whom were shot. There is a memorial plaque to some of the victims of the Free Corps in the beer-garden of the **Hofbräukeller** which reads: 'Following the military defeat of the Soviet Republic these workers and craftsmen were denounced and without legal judicial proceedings were taken by the Freikorps ... on 5 May 1919 to the garden of the Hofbräukeller keller and murdered.'[10]

The republican fervour on the one hand, and the brutality with which it was repressed on the other, left deep and lasting scars in Munich, as it did in other parts of Germany. Violence entered the political bloodstream and Bavarian politics became infused with a toxic mix of prejudice, suspicion and falsehood. Zealous nationalism and an obsessive anti-Marxist agenda were mixed with an increasing hatred of other groups. Prussian militarism was held to have been responsible for starting the First World War, while shady Jews were alleged to have undermined the war effort and profited from the sacrifice. Ultra-right *Völkisch* groups flourished and even many leftist groups shared a nationalist tinge. All these could be contained – just – so long as people had jobs, food and hope. But the bitterness and hatred resurfaced in a terrible form when they did not (see chapter 4).

Exactly what Hitler thought about these tumultuous happenings – or even precisely what he did during them – is far from clear. He lived in close proximity to the events and was a member of the armed forces so might have been deeply involved. But it seems he was not. He remained a peripheral observer. Just as before the war he had failed to get involved in Munich's thriving arts scene, he now kept his distance from the political chaos which engulfed the city. Curiously, his lengthy, waffling autobiography *Mein Kampf* passes over this most turbulent period of Munich's history in just a few vague paragraphs.

A Meeting in the Sterneckerbräu Keller

Hitler's most significant early engagement with the post-war politics of Munich was as an army informer, or snout. Unsurprisingly, the military authorities were doing all they could to keep abreast of the melee of people, parties and meetings swirling around the city and intelligence was vital. It was in this capacity that, on the evening of the 12 September 1919, Hitler walked into the shabby, smoked-filled '*Leiber* room' of the Sterneckerbräu beer keller on a central Munich street called **Tal**.[11] There he found a smallish group of people – 'chiefly from the lower classes' according to his recollections in *Mein Kampf* – gathered for a meeting of the German Workers party, or DAP. If any building could be awarded the dubious title as the birthplace of Nazism this is probably it. Today the ground floor is an electrical store and the rooms above are the offices and consulting rooms of professionals. In the early part of the twentieth century, however, the building was called the Sterneckerbräu beer hall, and it was here that Hitler made his way through the smoke and the chatter to a small backroom in the keller. Hitler was ordered to attend a meeting of DAP to find out more about the group and keep an eye on what they were doing. The political situation in Munich was highly unstable at this point and the authorities had a full-time job in tracking the different groups and parties that were vying for influence in the city. With just a handful of members, the DAP was just one of many fringe groups which, as Hitler recalled, 'sprang out of the ground only to vanish silently after a time.'

This party might have been no different. The DAP had been founded just a few months before, in January 1919, by a locksmith and sports journalist who blamed Marxists and Jews for Germany's woes. Hitler filed his report on the meeting and that, at least as far as his commanding officer was concerned, might have been the end of the evening's work. Hitler, however, had been quietly impressed by one of the pamphlets distributed by the party and decided to attend the next meeting. He had been toying with the idea of throwing his hat in the bear pit of Munich's politics and found his own party but soon received orders to join the DAP. The group looked as though it would have a longer shelf life than many; military intelligence decided that it needed to be properly penetrated and perhaps used as a base in the future. A month later, in October 1919, Hitler made his first political speech as a member of the DAP to an audience of around a hundred people at the Hofbräukeller beer hall (see above). Soon after, he became the key leader within the DAP, which had now changed its name to the National Socialist German Workers Party (NSDAP), or Nazi for short.

Hitler liked to boast subsequently – at his trial, in *Mein Kampf* and in endless speeches – that from a meeting of a few people in the back room of pub in September 1919 he had built a movement of millions. It was yet another theatrical exaggeration. In fact, as many as fifty people were at the first meeting and by 1923 party membership stood at some 55,000. This was admittedly a rapid increase – some 2,000 new members a week – but came at time when politics was at the forefront of many people's minds, and they were hardly the figures of a truly mass movement.

In February 1920 Hitler unveiled the twenty-five-point party programme at the Hofbräuhaus, one of the many meetings which the party would hold at Munich's famous old beer hall. This gathering passed off without incident although many of the others turned into riotous brawls between the Nazis and their opponents. The first four points of the manifesto launched that night demanded 'the unification of all Germans in the Greater Germany ... The abrogation of the Versailles Treaty ... land and territory for our surplus population,' and insisted that 'only a member of the race can be a citizen. A member of the race can only be one who is of German blood ... Consequently, no Jew can be a member of the race.' The stipulations continued, unaltered, in what would become a chillingly familiar mantra for the next twenty-five years. There were occasional challenges to the programme and suggestions that it should be amended, but Hitler personally stonewalled them all. The principles were, he insisted, 'immutable'.

'Tristan in the Thierschstrasse'

A few months later, in the spring of 1920, Hitler was discharged from the army. He left his barracks and rented a small back bedroom at **Thierschstrasse 41**.[12] Described as 'dismal' by one of the few visitors who ever set foot in the cramped room, it had little furniture and just a pair of moth-eaten rugs on the linoleum floor. One occasional guest was Ernst Hanfstaengl, who dubbed Hitler the 'Tristan of Thierschstrasse', an ironic reference to the Wagnerian hero. He recalled that the small room was 'modest in the extreme', and that Hitler lived here like 'a down-at-heel clerk' and frequently wandered around in carpet slippers with no collar on his shirt and no braces to keep his trousers in place. His room was stacked with books, including much military history, semi-pornographic arts magazines, biographies and Edgar Wallace thrillers. His landlady, Frau Reichert, described Hitler as 'an ideal tenant' who never caused any problems and always paid his rent on time. 'He is such a nice man,' she said, although she did have one slight reservation. 'He does have the most extraordinary moods. Sometimes weeks go by when he seems to be sulking and does not say a word to us. He looks through us as though we were not there.'

Hitler remained in Thierschstrasse for years, although Haenfstangl suspected that it may have been 'an act' on Hitler's part to identify with 'the workers and the have-nots'. Hitler subsequently rented a second room to use as an office (today the room is used for storage). Later in the decade he certainly spent much time at his chalet in Berchtesgaden (see chapter 9) and was a regular guest at the plush Hanfstaengl home in **Gentzstrasse 1**.[13] Hanfstaengl became an enthusiastic Nazi after hearing Hitler speak in a Munich beer hall. Well-connected (he met Franklin Delano Roosevelt while he was a student at Harvard), Haenfstangl both financed Hitler and gave him something of the home life which he otherwise lacked. As a reward, Haenfstangl was subsequently appointed head of international press for the Nazis, but fell out badly with both Göring and Goebbels. In 1937 he fled Germany and worked with US intelligence during the Second World War.

As with his life before 1914, there are many missing details about Hitler's life while he lived at Thierschstrasse. Without any fixed routines or close friends, he lived in something of a twilight world. Some historians have taken up the tempting challenge of filling in the gaps and concluded that part of the reason behind Hitler's furtive behavior was homosexuality. There is disputed circumstantial evidence to support the supposition that he had liaisons with other men, and the head of security in Munich, General von Lossow, claimed to have a file of reports compiled by informers. All were young and each had been approached in one of the many small restaurants or taverns in Munich. Most claimed the person who befriended them talked at length about politics before taking them back to his apartment. Eighteen-year-old Michael, for example, claimed to have been picked up by Hitler near the Burgerbräukeller in Rosenheimer Strasse, and 'having been unemployed for months and because my mother and brothers were also suffering from hunger I accompanied the gentleman home. In the morning I left.' Another youth reported that 'in a café near the university I, Franz … made the acquaintance of a gentleman who spoke in an Austrian dialect … he invited me to stay the night with him and I accepted … his name is Adolf Hitler; he wore a gabardine overcoat and one of his distinctive features was a lock of hair that kept flopping over his forehead.'

A deep and bitter antagonism developed between Hitler and Lossow following the attempted *putsch* of 1923 (see Chapter 3). Through intermediaries, Lossow apparently let Hitler know that he possessed the file and that he would be prepared to reveal the contents in the event of any serious injury to him or his men. While the credibility of some accounts were questionable the threat – and the file – may have saved Lossow's life. When other Bavarian leaders were murdered in the 'Night of the Long Knives' a decade later, Lossow survived untouched (see Chapter 5).

Whatever the truth, Hitler's sexual orientation was part of a deeper enigma. He was intensely secret about his background, family and personal life. He compartmentalised his acquaintances with hermetic precision so that people in different groups never met and nobody had a clear picture of exactly how he lived. His official autobiographical version in *Mein Kampf* sketched out his early years, including those in Munich, but it begs many questions and later in life he refused to be drawn on details or elaborate further. The public image – carefully crafted by him and key propagandists – was the private man. Perhaps there was nothing behind the mask, no hinterland, just a terrifying void that sucked in others too. The normal range of human emotions such as love, affection, gaiety, joy, laughter, compassion, empathy, etc. are almost wholly absent in the personal accounts of Hitler. As biographer Ian Kershaw comments, he had 'few intellectual gifts or social attributes … no more than an empty vessel outside his political life, unapproachable and impenetrable even for those in his close company, incapable it seems of genuine friendship.' While he had a sharp, cunning mind and undoubted oratorical skill, there remains 'the emptiness of the private person. He was, as has frequently been said, tantamount to an "un-person".' Some psycho-history has argued that this emotional black hole and isolated lifestyle, apparent even from the earliest days in Munich, meant that he was 'a suicide waiting to happen'.

Early in 1920 the fledgling DAP party set up an office of sorts in a backroom of the Sterneckerbräu keller. Office furniture was sparse: two cupboards, a table, some chairs borrowed from the bar, a light and a telephone. Hitler was the organiser. The following year the party began to use a room at **Corneliusstrasse 12**, which they continued to occupy until 1925.[14] Many of the party meetings took place in the cafés or beer kellers of Munich and Hitler held a regular Monday evening gathering in the Café Neumayr, just south of St Peter's church on **Petersplatz**.[15] In this old-world, wood-panelled, irregular-shaped room with built in benches, Hitler would talk amongst party faithful and try out new lines for his speeches (today the café is a pizza restaurant).

Ex-servicemen and the young were key target groups for recruitment. Analysis suggests that a large bulk of the members were under thirty and well-versed in the use of use of force. Many were engaged in providing 'security' for Nazi meetings and intimidating opponents. The use of thuggery was widespread. In the frequently brutal world of early Weimar politics the Nazis both contributed, and responded, to the violence with gusto. They were the embodiment of Goebbels' cynical dictum, 'Those who control the streets control the masses, and he who controls the masses conquers the state.'

The Nazi battles with socialists and communists are legendary. Less well understood is that, especially in the early days, Hitler's priority was to dominate any potential competitors on the nationalist right too. Hitler himself was sentenced to a month in prison for his part in smashing up the meeting of a rival Bavarian nationalist party in the autumn of 1921 at the **Löwenbräukeller** beer hall.[16] Unabashed, Hitler commented famously. 'It's alright – we got what we wanted. [Their leader] did not speak.' Then, as later, the silencing of opponents by whatever means was essential to the Nazi's success. If the Löwenbräukeller was an important landmark in the rise of the Nazis it was also a staging post in their fall. In November 1943 Hitler addressed senior members of the Nazi party in the beer hall at the height of the battle of Stalingrad. But by now the swagger had disappeared. This speech was sombre in tone and the reverse in Russia marked the beginning of the end for the Nazi regime.

Hitler served his short sentence in Munich's main Stadelheim prison in 1921. When they came to power, the Nazis used the same building to hold their opponents, but were far less lenient (see Chapter 6). More political street fighting ensued during 1921, and after one infamous brawl at the Hofbräuhaus beer hall in November the Nazi heavies adopted a new identity: henceforth they became known as the *Sturm Abteilung*, or SA for short. Kitted out in army surplus uniforms, they became popularly known as the 'Brown Shirts' and continued to threaten those who did not think like them for over a decade until Hitler finally decided that they had outlived their purpose. In the end the SA leaders, too, were detained in the Stadelheim prison where they were murdered (see Chapter 5).

'Heavens! He's Got a Gob on Him'

When explaining the rise of Hitler, thuggery and oratory walk hand in hand. While the Nazis set about silencing opponents by force, the party's most important weapon was the rhetorical power of its leader. At one early meeting Hitler launched into a diatribe against Bavarian nationalism which left other members spellbound. 'Heavens! He's got a gob on him – we could use him,' commented the party's then leader, and Hitler soon became the star turn at meetings. From the beer halls of Munich he began to develop forms of oratory and presentation that broke new ground in political communication. In his guttural, rasping regional accent, his manipulation of the power of the spoken word was a skill that he worked on throughout his political career. It is estimated that Hitler made over five thousand speeches in his lifetime, yet even if the figure is correct, only a fraction of the German population would ever have had any direct contact with him. As time went on, the propaganda image became even more important and reached its zenith at Nuremberg (see Chapter 10).

Alongside the use of brute force, Hitler relied more on presentation and the spoken word than any other leader of the modern age. In *Mein Kampf* he argued, 'The power which as always started the greatest religious and political avalanches in history has been, from time immemorial, none but the magic power of the word, and that alone.' He claimed that 'only a storm of hot passion can turn the destinies of peoples.'

In fact, the passion was tightly controlled and rehearsed down to the tiniest oratorical flourish. Everything about a speech interested Hitler. The draft text was worked over and over until it was word perfect. Gestures were rehearsed for hours in front of a mirror to ensure that each movement of his body language reinforced the words coming from his mouth. Even the acoustics and lighting of a venue where he was to speak would be checked out carefully beforehand. During the performance – it is hard to think of another word – Hitler might sweat up to five pounds in weight and his aides lined up bottles of mineral water for him to rehydrate.

One of Hitler's great rhetorical tricks, perfected in the Munich beer halls, was not to speak. He used the power of silence to generate tension. Then his speeches frequently began in low, hesitant phrases, not all of which were even finished. Gradually, the flow of words would come in cadences, rising and falling and the tempo quickening until he hit the climax. Not a few observers concluded that for Hitler the speeches were a substitute for sexual gratification.

One of Hitler's acolytes, Albert Speer, later recalled that when he spoke it was 'urgency and hypnotic persuasiveness. The mood he cast was much deeper than the speech itself.' Every speaker requires an audience with receptive minds, however. In the turbulence of post-war Bavaria, Hitler found those minds. In November 1921 the US Consul General reported back to Washington that the Nazis were the most active force in Bavaria and that the ability of Hitler to sway an audience was 'uncanny'. But rowdy meetings in Bavarian beer kellers were of little interest to Washington at that point and Munich might as well have been on the steppes of Mongolia.

Others were less impressed and saw through the techniques to a content that promised the impossible and varied little. Hitler's adversary in Munich, General Lossow, claimed, 'I noticed that his long talks almost always contained the same points: one part of his remarks is obvious to every German and another part of them ... departed from a sense of reality and proportion for what is possible and achievable.' Normal dialogue, said Lossow, was problematic. Either Hitler was talking or he was distracted, unable to concentrate for any length of time on what anyone else said, let alone accommodate a viewpoint that differed from his own. In short, he was a poor listener and almost wholly unable to deal with challenges to his preset world views.

Hitler's conversation could also be tiresome. Like a bar-room bore, he had the capacity to drone on and on for hours while those around him sometimes struggled to stay awake. His conversation could be agile when he chose but the seemingly insatiable capacity to talk, often on well-worn themes, frequently led to monotonous monologue which tested all including the most devoted followers. Just days before the end of the Third Reich in 1945, even the ever-toadying Goebbels' patience wore thin. One of the final entries in his diary recorded a diatribe in the bunker in which 'he [Hitler] tells me yet again the whole story of the Luftwaffe's development, which I know since he has frequently explained it to me already.' Yet by that time Hitler was capable only of ranting at those immediately around him and 'hypnotic persuasiveness' was exposed as a cruel illusion. The initial charisma had required a context which no longer existed. It was telling that after 1944, when the war began to turn against him, Hitler fell silent and seldom spoke or broadcast in public again. The apparent magic of his speech departed long before the man.

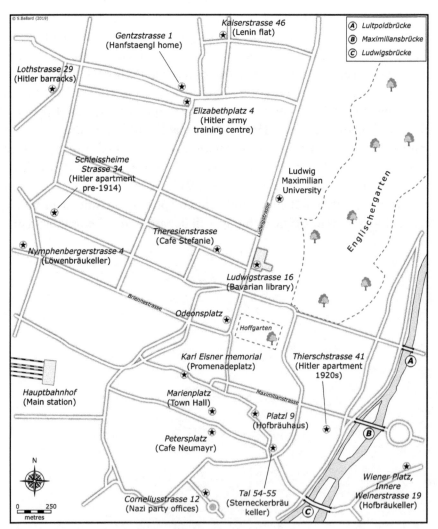

© S.Ballard (2019)

Kaiserstrasse 46
(Lenin flat)

Gentzstrasse 1
(Hanfstaengl home)

Lothstrasse 29
(Hitler barracks)

A Luitpoldbrücke
B Maximiliansbrücke
C Ludwigsbrücke

Elizabethplatz 4
(Hitler army
training centre)

Schleissheime
Strasse 34
(Hitler apartment
pre-1914)

Ludwig
Maximilian
University

Englischergarten

Theresienstrasse
(Cafe Stefanie)

Ludwigstrasse

Nymphenbergerstrasse 4
(Löwenbräukeller)

Briennestrasse

Ludwigstrasse 16
(Bavarian library)

Odeonsplatz

Hoffgarten

Karl Eisner memorial
(Promenadeplatz)

Thierschstrasse 41
(Hitler apartment
1920s)

A

Hauptbahnhof
(Main station)

Marienplatz
(Town Hall)

Maximilianstrasse

Platzl 9
(Hofbräuhaus)

B

Petersplatz
(Cafe Neumayr)

N

0   250
metres

Corneliusstrasse 12
(Nazi party offices)

Tal 54-55
(Sterneckerbräu
keller)

C

Wiener Platz,
Innere
Weinerstrasse 19
(Hofbräukeller)

Map I: Hitler, Munich and World War I

Chapter Three

The Munich *Putsch* 1923: From Bürgerbräu Keller to Landsberg Prison

The **Odeonsplatz** lies at the heart of central Munich. The impressive square is dominated by a huge canopied arcade called the Feldherrnhalle, constructed in 1844 as a giant war memorial to commemorate the derring-do of the Bavarian army.[1] After 1933, however, the Odeonsplatz became home to a Nazi shrine which venerated some of their dead. All who passed were expected to give the Nazi salute; a likelihood reinforced by the watchful eye of jack-booted SS guards who kept vigil over the memorial day and night. Some avoided the spot, and paying homage to the Hitler regime, by dodging down a narrow back street behind the Odeonsplatz called **Viscardigasse**.[2]

Its more popular name, however, became 'shirkers alley' and today a jagged line of polished, bronze-coloured cobble stones marks the route taken by the brave passive resisters.

The story of the stones and why they are there takes us back to Hitler's first violent attempt to seize power in Munich, in 1923. The events are known as the Beer Hall *putsch* (a forced overthrow of government, or coup d'état), and they marked a 'before' and 'after' in Hitler's career. Prior to 1923 Hitler was a familiar face around the beer halls of Munich, known as a local rabble-rouser and leader of a formidable political force, but little recognised outside Bavaria. After 1923 his name became more prominent and it was the *putsch* that gave Hitler a national – and international – profile.

1923: Germany's 'Annus Horribilis'

By 1923 five years had passed since the end of the First World War, but Germany continued to lurch from one crisis to another. Defeat and the humiliation at Versailles were a national psycho-trauma which had led to a collapse of morale and political stability. Monarchy, a key part of the German body politic for centuries, had been swept away. To the horror of the conservative right, the Kaiser was ousted and replaced by the Weimar Republic. Instability and political violence were part of everyday life in the early years of the new order. Attempted revolutions from the left had been crushed with great force by regular army units and by the Free Corps, whose precise role in state security was ill-defined and whose relationship with the government ambiguous (see Chapter 1).

Political assassinations were frequent. The former finance minister who had signed the Armistice to bring war to an end, for example, was gunned down by a far-right hit squad in 1921 while on a country walk. The serving foreign minister was murdered in the centre of Berlin a year later. It seemed that no leader was safe from domestic terrorism. However, the lenient sentences passed on right-wing assassins (when they were caught) did little to deter others, while the law bore down heavily on left-wing trouble makers.

For millions of ordinary Germans, the most lethal threat was abject poverty. Diseases like TB went untreated while a generation of children was growing up malnourished and with conditions such as rickets. One eyewitness recorded that 'never in my life have I seen such swarms of starving people wandering about.' By the autumn of 1923 the country was on the verge of complete economic, political and social breakdown: it was Germany's '*annus horribilis*'. Communists, anarchists, nationalists, conservatives, monarchists and regional separatists spawned scores of factions, which all struggled with one another to gain the upper hand.

Other countries had found radical solutions to end the political bedlam created by the First World War. A year previously, in October 1922, Benito Mussolini had put an end to similar chaos in Italy by establishing a fascist dictatorship following his 'March on Rome'. In September 1923 General Miguel Primo de Rivera had halted turmoil in Spain by launching a successful *Golpe de Estado* to take over the country, suspend democracy and establish a military dictatorship. As the communists gained a foothold in other parts of Germany, many across the German right, especially in Bavaria, wondered if some kind of military backed government might not be the best option for them, too.

The fundamental challenges faced by the Weimar Republic were economic. Germany was ruined by four years of war. Some two million men were dead and, apart from the human tragedy, much of the labour force was literally crippled as another five million men returned home wounded. There was a huge financial cost, too. On top of the massive debts racked up for its own war effort, Germany also faced a huge bill – called reparations – from their opponents. During 1922 the debilitated German economy was unable to continue the reparations payments, whereupon French and Belgian troops simply occupied the Ruhr valley in the west of the country. The Ruhr was one of Germany's most prosperous and important industrial areas; the French/Belgian occupation was yet another blow to national pride and also meant the loss of an important source of revenue to the cash-strapped national treasury. A low-level resistance movement sprang up in the Ruhr but was brutally repressed by French troops who shot some one hundred Germans. The loss of production led to a steep increase in unemployment, which rose from 2% to 25%. This further hobbled Germany's ability to pay reparations and the Weimar government resorted to printing money. The surge in the paper money supply solved the short-term problem of debt repayment but carried another consequence as lethal as it was predictable: rampant hyper-inflation.

As the government lost control of the economy, prices began to rise alarmingly. By October of 1923 some six million Marks were needed to buy what had cost just one Mark before war. The value of money lasted but a few hours. Older people saw their entire worldly wealth, accumulated over a lifetime, evaporate within a matter of days. Writer Sebastian Haffner described how, as a fifteen year-old, he witnessed the impact of a cost of living spiraling out of control, 'A pound of potatoes which yesterday had cost fifty thousand marks now cost one hundred thousand. The salary of sixty-five marks brought home the previous Friday was no longer sufficient to buy a packet of cigarettes on Tuesday.' Many of the most vulnerable could not survive. Haffner observed 'an elderly lady seated on a park bench looking strangely blank and stiff. A little crowd gathered round her. "Dead," said someone, "Of starvation," said another. It did not surprise me particularly. At home we often went hungry.'

In Munich many decided that the time might have come to cut loose from the sinking ship of the Weimar Republic. Germany comprised seventeen states but it was dominated by Prussia. The big northern state accounted for some sixty-five per cent of the total population and was home to the capital, Berlin. As the crisis deepened, a scarcely dormant Bavarian resentment with Berlin, Prussia and the ailing Weimar government's leftist president, Friedrich Ebert, grew. Right-wing nationalists who governed Bavaria began to toy openly with the possibility of secession, or what might now be dubbed 'Bavexit', from the rest of Germany. Many Bavarians had been born into an independent Bavaria and the state had only been incorporated into Otto von Bismarck's unified Germany, in 1871. By the autumn of 1923 the deepening economic and social crises – now critical – looked as though they might develop into a constitutional crisis too. Bavarian independence would transform this constitutional crisis into an existential crisis both for the Weimar Republic and a united Germany.

One who shared the conservatives' contempt for the Weimar administration was the local Munich rabble rouser, Adolf Hitler. But unlike right-wing Bavarian nationalists, he did not seek a breakaway Bavarian republic. Hitler wanted to overthrow the government in Berlin, oust the Weimar government of 'November traitors' and establish a new National Socialist state. On the evening of 7 November 1923, Alex Frey, an old comrade from the Bavarian infantry, ran into Hitler on the street and recalled that 'he was alone, prowling along in the manner of a predator before it leaps, imagining its prey. He didn't see his surroundings.' Exactly why Hitler was so preoccupied soon became clear. With the situation deteriorating by the day, the only question in Hitler's mind was not 'if' his young Nazi party should make a move on Berlin, but 'when'.

'The National Revolution has Begun'

With the national economic and political crisis spinning out of Isar control, leaders of the Bavarian state convened a public meeting on the evening of 8 November 1923. Bavaria's premier, State Commissioner Gustav Ritter von Kahr, wanted to address the people of Munich about the chaos that was engulfing Germany. The venue was **Bürgerbräukeller**, a beer hall in Rosenheimerstrasse, close to the river.[3] Holding the assembly in one of the city's beer halls was not surprising; some of the more spacious kellers were frequently used for large public gatherings and in Bavaria beer and politics went hand in hand. Moreover, the Bürgerbräukeller was one of the city's more reputable watering holes; one guide described it as 'an eminently respectable beer hall ... with a better class of clientele.' That night, however, it became the scene of an extraordinary series of events which would have long-lasting repercussions. The building itself was demolished in 1979. Today the Bürgerbräukeller site is occupied by a hotel and an agency which protects intellectual property rights called GEMA. On the pavement at the entrance to the GEMA building is a plaque which marks the spot where Georg Elser later attempted to assassinate Hitler. (see Chapter 6).

Despite circulating just fifty invitations and one small newspaper advertisement, the meeting was packed. Some 3,000 people crowded into the main hall which was soon thick with smoke and the yeasty aroma of Bavarian *pils*. At one end the brassy, rhythmic thud of an Oompah band distracted the expectant crowd, few of whom paid much attention to Adolf Hitler, who stood alone, watching and waiting by a pillar at the side of the hall.

When Premier Kahr finally arrived – late – he was accompanied by the senior military commander in Bavaria, General Otto von Lossow. The pair were obliged to shove their way through the crowd with the help of a police guard to the front stage. After a short formal introduction, Kahr began to speak about the threat posed by Marxism to Germany, Bavaria and good order generally. A provincial lawyer by trade, Kahr was no natural orator and had difficulty holding the crowd's attention. The low murmurs of a distracted audience threatened to prematurely end his address, but Kahr ploughed on with his speech, apparently oblivious to its limited impact; until shots rang out.

While Kahr had been speaking inside the hall, scores of armed Nazis pulled up in trucks outside the Bürgerbräukeller. Dressed in old army uniforms with swastika armbands, the men barged past the police guard on the door and forced their way down the aisle towards the stage. Their leader, Hermann Göring, barked orders for everyone to remain in their seats. Kahr looked up from his speech, bewildered, as most people were. What was going on?

Hitler was about to explain. Pushing his way through the tumult and standing on a chair he bawled 'the National Revolution has broken out' at the top of his voice, but his next words were lost in the growing din. Pulling out his Browning automatic pistol, Hitler fired shots into the ceiling and the crowd fell silent. He had not arrived to kill Kahr, he shouted, but to lead a coup. The police and army were onside (or so he claimed) to overthrow the governments in Berlin. Then the triumvirate of the most powerful men in Bavaria – State Commissioner Kahr, local army chief, General von Lossow, and local police chief, Hans von Seisser – were marched out of the main hall at gunpoint to a side room. Hitler promised the crowd that they would 'return in 10 minutes' while armed Nazi heavies sealed all the exits.

In the small side room Hitler insisted that the three join him in a march on Berlin to overthrow the government just as Mussolini had done with his successful 'March on Rome' to take over the Italian government a few months before. The Bavarian leaders were presented with a dramatic ultimatum: either they comply with Hitler's demand or he would shoot them. 'I have four bullets in my pistol,' he told them, 'three for my collaborators if they desert me, and the last one for me.' Kahr, Lossow and Seisser were all Bavarian conservatives with little sympathy for the shenanigans of Weimar leaders in Berlin but they were horrified at the armed insurrection that was now taking place. They were being invited to join in what was, at the very least, an act of high treason. And if events spiraled out of control it was a move that might well trigger a civil war across the whole country.

Not surprisingly, the three balked at the decision they were being asked to take. Clearly at risk of their lives if they answered with a flat 'no', the Bavarian leaders stalled for time. What exactly, they asked, was the Nazi plan? In reality, Hitler himself did not know. The Nazis pledged to overthrow the government in Berlin but had no clear strategy to bring this about. The timing of the *putsch* was dictated by simple opportunism. Hitler knew that any challenge to the Weimar government in Berlin could only succeed with the connivance of the Bavarian administration and, crucially, the state's security forces. The meeting at the Burgerbräukeller guaranteed that key Bavarian leaders would be together in one place at one time. What Hitler lacked was a coherent, well-thought-out plan to achieve his aim. Not for the first or last time in his life, he was improvising while gambling for very high stakes.

At this point Hitler sent for the one man who he hoped could swing support behind his plan to storm Berlin, General Erich Ludendorff. A legendary commander in the First World War, the general was a national hero. Still only fifty-eight years old, Ludendorff had spent the post-war years brooding over German defeat, his own role in the catastrophe, and meddling in politics. His primary purpose, like many in the High Command, was to deflect blame for the calamity from the military commanders to the civilian politicians. Ludendorff was a leading proponent of the theory that the German army had been 'stabbed-in-the-back' by leftist ministers who had first surrendered on the battlefield in November 1918 and then at Versailles in 1919. Like Hitler, he was prone to erratic mood swings, possibly the psychological consequences of the war and its aftermath.

Ludendorff was at home when the call came through to meet at the Bürgerbräukeller. As snow fell, the General was taken by car to the beer hall and was swiftly ushered into the side room where Hitler and the three Bavarian leaders were waiting for him. Exactly how much Ludendorff knew about the plot prior to the night of 8 November was a moot point at the subsequent trial (see below) and has been debated by historians ever since. He claimed to have been kept in the dark and that he only decided 'on the spur of the moment' to join the *putsch*. He was, however, a key figure in Bavarian politics and it was his unique authority that persuaded Kahr, Lossow and Seisser that that the *putsch* might be a serious proposition.

The party eventually returned to the main hall where Hitler proclaimed the formation of a new Bavarian government dedicated to the overthrow of the 'November Criminals' in Berlin. The announcement was met with rapturous applause and lusty choruses of the new national anthem with its refrain 'Deutschland Über Alles'. But not all joined in. According to the report of a police informer in the hall, one wit was heard to comment that the only person missing from the extraordinary scene was a psychiatrist. And the euphoria would not last. Within hours, Hitler would discover that the commitment of the Bavarian leaders to join the *putsch* was no more solid than the froth on a glass of Bavarian *pils*.

A Call to Arms at Löwenbräukeller

Across the city at the iconic Löwenbräukeller beer hall, another group of Nazi and nationalist *Kampfbund* heavies had gathered for an evening of songs and speeches. Their leader was Captain Ernst Röhm, a fanatically nationalist, brutish and much-scarred veteran of the First World War.

Röhm was a ubiquitous and deeply unpleasant figure in the murky world of far-right *volkisch* politics where he had extensive contacts and, crucially, access to illegal weaponry. Officially, the Versailles treaty put a strict limit on the availability of arms in Germany after 1918. Many arms caches had been closeted away from the eyes of any prying inspections, however, and as a serving officer, Röhm was key to their distribution among the paramilitary veterans' groups. When a coded message was phoned through to the **Löwenbräukeller**, Röhm called the comrades to order. To an ecstatic reception he told them that the 'national revolution' had begun and that they should prepare to take Berlin.[4] Hundreds of men then piled out into the chilly night and set off in closed ranks for the Bürgerbräukeller. En route the column halted at the eighteenth-century Franciscan Abbey church of St Anna in central Munich, but not, evidently, to pray; hundreds of rifles had been hidden in the crypt by monks worried about the possibility of a Marxist uprising, and many more weapons were concealed in the cellars of a nearby fencing club. All these were now distributed amongst the men.

At this point, the column was intercepted by a motorcycle messenger from the Bürgerbräukeller. There had been a change of plan. Röhm and his group were now ordered to occupy – by force if necessary – the Bavarian War Ministry in **Ludwigstrasse**, just off the Odeonplatz.[5] In the event, force was not necessary. The building was lightly guarded by a small detachment of troops who were in no mood for a fight. When assured that General Lossow himself had given the order, the commander hastily surrendered the building without more ado. Röhm then set up fortifications – machine guns and barbed wire – outside the building and a 'war room' inside to plan the attack on Berlin. Hitler now had the apparent cooperation of Bavaria's political leaders and controlled the military HQ in Munich. The next step needed to ensure the success of the *putsch* was to seize all transport and communications links with the city. But at this point plans for the uprising, such as they were, began to unravel.

Ludendorff ordered a detachment of 1,000 army cadets from the infantry school to occupy government buildings on Maxmilianstrasse. However, a garrison of armed police firmly resisted the young soldiers who, after a bloodless stand-off, simply melted back to their base. Another squad of paramilitaries was dispatched to take control of the main

Hauptbahnhof central railway station, but they too were foiled, this time by the local security chief. Hitler left the Burgerbräukeller to resolve the problem at the railway station but failed. Angry and troubled, he returned to the Burgerbräukeller where he was further perplexed to discover another unwelcome twist in the saga of the night. In his absence, Kahr, Lossow and Seisser had all disappeared.

Ludendorff had allowed the three leaders to return home to get some rest after what was, by any measure, a stressful evening. They, in turn, promised to meet the general later at the War Ministry in Maxamilianstrasse to firm up plans for the march on Berlin. In fact, Kahr did not return home but went to his third-floor office (room 125) at **14 Maximilianstrasse**.[6] Pacing his office, he had time to consult and reflect on the gravity of his position. Who could say what the consequences of the *putsch* might be for Germany? It was an act of treason. The prospect of success was limited and if the plan failed he might find himself on trial and in prison; or worse. Not surprisingly, Kahr now got cold feet. Meanwhile, General Lossow's ambiguous instructions that troops should prepare to mobilize for a march on Berlin were met with incredulity by other senior officers. On this occasion the Bavarian military refused to obey orders.

Hitler and Ludendorff waited at the Bavarian War Ministry building in Ludwigstrasse for Kahr, Lossow and Seisser to join them. But the three Bavarian leaders were nowhere to be found and, like a pair of spurned lovers, Hitler and Ludendorff began to fret. Phone calls to their offices went unanswered and messengers returned shaking their heads. They waited throughout the night until, as dawn broke, it became clear that Lossow had dissembled the previous evening. Whatever he had said then, he now had no intention of overthrowing the Weimar Republic by force; quite the reverse. Reichswehr (army) units loyal to the Weimar government were flooding into Munich from other parts of Bavaria. The paramilitary *putsch* forces would soon be completely outnumbered by government troops and an assault to retake the War Ministry was expected within hours. Hitler and Ludendorff realized that they had been hoodwinked and that the game was up: the *putsch* would never get off the ground in Munich, let alone lead to a triumphal march on Berlin. The two abandoned the War Ministry and returned to the Bürgerbräukeller to reassess and replan.

Collapse of the *Putsch* – a 'Defeated Army'

On the morning of 9 November it was clear that, far from taking key strategic points across Munich, the forces supporting the *putsch* held just two centres: the Burgerbräukeller and the War Ministry. In a desperate last gamble, Ludendorff and Hitler decided to march from the Burgerbräukeller through the city, though quite what they hoped to achieve was not clear. Whip up an irresistible revolutionary fervour? Drum up popular support for the Putsch? Convince the Bavarian leaders to join them? Who could say. Meanwhile, to sustain the faltering momentum, Hermann Göring took seven councilors hostage from the old Rathaus (town hall) on the charming, medieval heart of old Munich, the **Marienplatz**.[7] He threatened to shoot them if the state security services did not join the Putsch.

At around noon on 9 November a column of 2,000 people, led by Ludendorff and Hitler, left Bürgerbräukeller. At his subsequent trial, Hitler claimed that 'the enthusiasm was indescribable. I had to tell myself ... the *volk* want a reckoning with the November criminals.' Not everyone saw the column quite like that, however. There were banners at the head of the march but they were a motley crew. Some were in uniform, others not. Hundreds of men had spent the entire night in the beer hall, and it showed. According to one participant they looked like 'a defeated army which had not actually fought anyone.' The column marched down to the river Isar and over the **Ludwigsbrücke bridge**.[8] A small contingent of police threatened to halt the march, but after some scuffles were soon overcome, miraculously without death or serious injury.

The column then passed through the Isartor gate and into the broad street called Tal. This brought them into the Marienplatz, outside the town hall. No route had been planned but many expected the march to stop there while speeches were made and popular support gauged. Or perhaps they would double back in a circuit and return to the Bürgerbräukeller. In the event, neither of those things happened. Suddenly, and apparently without warning or consulting others, Ludendorff began to stride down Wienstrasse and then Perusasstrasse towards the Odeonsplatz and the War Ministry. Perhaps Ludendorff intended to relieve Röhm, who was by now besieged by government forces, although exactly what was going through the veteran General's mind remains a mystery. Nevertheless, where Ludendorff led others would follow, and so they did.

Carnage in the Odeonsplatz

As the marchers filed down the narrow Residenzstrasse a crackling tension filled the air, which did not auger well. A tank stood in Odeonsplatz with its barrel pointing up the street towards the marchers. A thick cordon of troops, mobilized from their barracks in **Türkenstrasse 17**, stood resolute in the square outside the War Ministry.[9] Yet more soldiers were on the esplanade of the Feldherrnhalle overlooking **Residenzstrasse**, while others watched on, weapons in hand, from the balconies of the Residenz building on the other side of the narrow street.[10] When Ludendorff's column moved forward there was a sharp click of rifle bolts being primed and the barking of orders. The stage was set for a massacre waiting to happen. Ludendorff strode on, unable to believe that any German soldier would ever open fire on him or men that he led. But they did.

Who pulled the first trigger was never established, but within seconds a volley of shots rang out from all sides. Hitler, at the head of the column, linked arms with the man next to him, who was killed immediately in the hail of rifle fire. The bullet that killed him missed Hitler by just 30cm and the weight of the dead man pulled Hitler to the ground so abruptly that he dislocated his shoulder. Further back there was panic and mayhem as volley after volley rang out and others fell too.

When the firing ceased and silence descended on the narrow, cobbled street, the tally of the carnage was evident. Twenty people lay dead; four policemen (one married just months before) and sixteen marchers. Another hundred or so were wounded, some – like Hermann Göring who was shot through the groin and thigh – seriously. Many fled the scene as fast, and as far, as they could. There would, they knew, be an inevitable consequence of the debacle as the authorities sought retribution and punishment of those responsible.

Hitler Arrested

By mid-afternoon on the 9 November it was clear that the *putsch* was over and the Weimar Republic saved if, indeed, it had ever really been threatened: the 'March on Berlin' had never even made it as far as the Odeonsplatz in Munich. Nevertheless, the tension generated by the events of the previous twenty-four hours subsided only slowly. Gangs of paramilitary nationalist thugs roamed the city making random attacks on any Jews or opponents they could find. The security services now took no chances of more bloodshed and declared a curfew. That night the bars and beer halls of Munich were silent. The city was in lockdown.

Inevitably, the myth-making started immediately as those responsible sought to defend their reputations and, if need be, liberty. It was said that Ludendorff had marched boldly through the hail of bullets to remonstrate with the police; others saw him dive for cover just like everyone else. How Hitler managed to escape from the melee unscathed was a miracle. He and his supporters quickly fabricated a story which hit the Munich rumour mill and reached the ears of the ever-caustic Munich diarist Fritz Reck, who wrote, 'According to this version – *his* version – Hitler concocted a fantastic story about a crying child he had tried to rescue from the whizzing bullets.' No other eyewitness ever saw the child and quite what it might have been doing there under the circumstances of a stand-off between a Nazi mob and the Bavarian security services was never explained. 'Undoubtedly, the purpose of the story was to cover his ignominious flight with a sentimental tear-jerker,' sniffed Reck.

In reality, Hitler had fled the scene. Amidst swirling rumors as to his whereabouts he was put up in a 'safe house' by his loyal side-kick, 'Putzi' Hanfstaengl. Apart from evading the police search, Hitler's most pressing problem was his painful, swollen and dislocated shoulder. This was eventually reset by a sympathetic physician and then, with the aid of Helen Bechstein, wife of the wealthy piano manufacturer and keen Nazi, a plan was hatched to spirit Hitler out of Germany back to his native Austria. But it came too late. Within days, Hitler's hiding place in the Hanfstaengl's attic was identified and the bedraggled would-be revolutionary was captured and led away by the police.

Following his detention, Hitler was held in custody at Landsberg am Lech, some 60km west of Munich, to await trial. Landsberg, a charming medieval town on the bubbling river Lech within fine views of the Alps, had a newly built prison on its outskirts. Hitler was a high security risk – there was a chance that the Nazis would attempt to spring him from jail

– and the normal prison security was bolstered by detachments from the Bavarian army. Custody was restrictive but far from arduous. The modern cells (his was number five on the second floor) were light and airy; possibly more so than the poky room he rented at Thierschstrasse (see Chapter 2). Prisoners held on political charges and for dueling were treated leniently and allowed many privileges, including alcohol, tobacco and visitors.

But Hitler wanted none of it. His shoulder still gave him severe pain, but much worse was the mental anguish of the failed *putsch*. Far from leading a glorious entry into Berlin, he was now confined to a single cell. Dreams of heading a new Germany were shattered. At the very least he now faced the very real prospect of being thrown out of the country altogether. As an Austrian national, whatever sentence was handed down after trial for the botched *putsch* could include being returned to Austria with a long ban on returning to Germany. Listless and forlorn, Hitler went on hunger strike and rapidly lost weight. Days were punctuated by visits from those Nazi comrades who could still show their face without being arrested but their visits seldom did more than trigger the prisoner into a rant about how he wanted to commit suicide. Death did indeed seem a real prospect for a possible capital offence.

The Hitler Trial – 'a judicial farce'

The court convened in Munich on 26 February 1924 and so began one of the most sensational trials in modern history. But what should have been an exercise in blind justice rapidly came to resemble a badly staged melodrama mixed with surreal tinges from the trial of *Alice in Wonderland*. When the hearing commenced, the national hero, Ludendorff, was the centre of attention. By the end it was all about Hitler. The hearing gave him the platform he yearned for and the kind of exposure that he had hitherto only dreamed about. Allowed to speak for hour after hour, almost without interruption, an attentive domestic and international press corps took down his script and carried his words to a huge audience. Ludendorff by contrast was a poor public speaker – one journalist described his defence statement as 'ineloquently written and ineloquently read' – who made little impact. As the weeks passed the hearing became known in some quarters as 'the Hitler trial'. It was an extraordinary transformation from failed revolutionary to household name.

The hearing took place on the second floor of **Blutenburgstrasse 3**, in what had been the canteen of a military academy (the area was much damaged in the Second World War). The school had been temporarily suspended as a precautionary measure by the authorities, who were alarmed to discover that many of the army cadets had joined the *Putschists*.[11] The building was one of the few locations close to the city centre with a space large enough to accommodate the accused, the lawyers, the public and hordes of journalists who turned out to cover the proceedings. A thick police cordon was mustered to protect the building from possible further attacks by paramilitary nationalist groups. During the recesses, Hitler was held in room 160 on the second floor and each evening he and the other defendants were taken to **Blutenburgstrasse 18**, where they were held in cells overnight.[12]

From the outset there were anomalies in procedure and none of them bode well for the interests of justice. Firstly, the ten defendants were charged only with High Treason – effectively trying to overthrow the Republic by force. This alone was a serious charge, but twenty people had actually died notably the four heroic policemen who had been killed in the line of duty while suppressing the *putsch*. Surely someone was responsible for the murders and/or manslaughter? And if not the ringleaders Ludendorff and Hitler, then who? These questions were never asked let alone answered and the scope of the trial was limited only to the lesser charge of High Treason.

There were also doubts about the location of the trial. According to statutes, a charge of High Treason should have been heard by the centre Federal (national) court based in the city of Leipzig, in the centre of Germany. But the southern German government in Bavaria had simply never recognized the Leipzig court and insisted that the *land* retain the right to judge its own High Treason cases. In the winter of 1923 the weak, fragile, crisis-ridden national government in Berlin was in no position to resist Bavarian demands: apart from hyper-inflation, the country was in the midst of total political meltdown with yet another general election campaign underway. The last thing Berlin needed was a clash with Bavaria which might trigger yet more trouble in Munich.

As a consequence, Ludendorff, Hitler and the other defendants faced the most benign trial possible, on the softest of charges and before the most sympathetic court in Germany. One reporter covering the proceedings described them as 'a judicial farce'. Even the prosecutor seemed sympathetic to Hitler and, when listening to his closing speech, some journalists covering the trial wondered which side he was representing. Justice Georg Neithardt, one of the most reactionary judges on the bench, presided over the hearing. His quixotic rulings during the trial puzzled jurists and public alike; but they invariably gave succour to the defendants. Judge Neithardt failed, for example, to reveal that Hitler was still on probation at the time of the trial with a three-month suspended sentence hanging over him for his part in breaking up the meeting of a rival at the Löwenbräukeller (see above). Neithardt must have been aware of Hitler's record since he was the judge who had heard the case and handed down the sentence.

Ironically, it was the prisoner who now had a captive audience and Hitler was in his element. He used the court to grandstand and the indulgent Neithardt made few attempts to stop him. As a result, the defendant's long-winded diatribes, which had little or nothing to do with the facts of the case, went uninterrupted. Rants about his war record, socialism, communism, Marxism, the French, the Weimar leaders, the conduct of the war and, of course, Jews went on for hours. Occasionally, the mob of Nazi sympathisers in the public gallery became so rowdy that Neithardt's gavel was required to restore order, but time and again the judge revealed his own prejudices. Witnesses for the prosecution were jeered or heckled from the gallery while thunderous applause rang out for the defence. Against this highly charged backdrop, Hitler flipped the trial and an investigation of the *putsch* gave way to a forensic examination of the shortcomings of the government in Berlin. As the proceedings went on, some wondered who was really on trial: the *Putschists* or the leaders of the Weimar Republic?

The Plot Thickens: Who Knew What and When?

The trial delved into the messy questions of exactly who was responsible for the attempted *putsch*: who *knew* what and when in the planning stage? And more to the point, who *did* what and when did they do it in the execution of the plan? Lawyers for the defendants attempted to implicate the entire Bavarian government as represented by the triumvirate of Kahr, Lessow and Seisser. If they could demonstrate that the *putsch* attempt had been endorsed even tacitly by Bavarian leaders, the charge of High Treason would lose much of its sting. The issue would no longer be one of armed paramilitary groups launching a freelance assault on the Republic but of united Bavarian resistance to the catastrophic failings of the Weimar government in Berlin.

Hitler alleged the plot to challenge Berlin had been hatched in a series of meetings which included politicians from the highest levels of the Bavarian government. But what had been agreed? It was no secret that leaders in Munich were disgruntled with the Weimar government in Berlin but they denied sanctioning an armed uprising in Bavaria and distanced themselves from Hitler, claiming that he had deceived them. Just days before the *putsch* attempt, Hitler apparently promised the Bavarian government that he would never take any violent action against the local security services and said, 'Do not think that I am so stupid. I will make no *putsch*, I promise you that'. As so often, he had broken his word.

Yet many suspected that the Bavarian leaders – Kahr, Lessow and Seisser – had toyed with the idea of some kind of revolt against the Weimar government but then had second thoughts. Whatever their precise intention at the time, they clearly attempted to save their own political skins at the trial and claimed that their backing for the *putsch* was the result of coercion; an entire beer hall full of people, after all, had witnessed them being taken hostage. Nevertheless, the whiff of suspicion about the involvement of the Bavarian government in the affair remained. In Berlin, the German foreign minister, Gustav Stresemann, confided to the British ambassador that he was startled by the 'revelations' coming from the trial in Munich. Stresemann realised that the republic was under threat from the political right – how could he not have known – but not the extent to which the plans for a takeover had been advanced.

When further evidence about the possible implication of the Bavarian government threatened to emerge, Judge Neithardt swiftly cleared the press and public galleries and held sessions in private. His rulings were made on grounds of state security, which suggested not only the possible complicity of the Bavarian administration in the *putsch* but something even more serious. The *Putschists* had access to a large number of weapons. Yet, under the Treaty of Versailles, the number of arms in Germany was carefully controlled and monitored by international weapons inspectors:

or so it was assumed. Could it be that the Bavarians were not only challenging the Weimar Republic but also playing fast and loose with international law? If so, the French in particular would be most concerned to learn about the number of clandestine arms caches and nationalist paramilitaries in a country where they were supposed to be under lock and key. How had so many weapons landed in the hands of the paramilitaries? There were also questions for the *Reichswehr* (German army), which now seemed to have more men in uniform than were actually permitted by the Versailles agreement. Not for the last time, the issue of arms control and weapons inspections threatened to destabilise international order.

The *putsch* in Munich threatened the agreement hammered home at Versailles. However much they disliked the Weimar Republic, cooler heads shuddered at the thought of what would have happened if the *putsch* had succeeded. One immediate consequence could have been another European war. The rash action of the *Putchists* might easily have triggered a partial invasion by the French in the west and Czechs and Poles in the East with the consequence that, Germany could have been invaded on two fronts.

Ludendorff, the supposed leader of the attempted coup, did not come out of the trial well. He cut a somewhat pathetic figure in court, from which his reputation did not recover. He wanted, he said, to put 'moral coercion' on Berlin but not physical force. But it was unclear what that meant. Did he want to overthrow the Weimar Republic? No. Did he have any foreknowledge of the *putsch*? No. Did he know that the Bavarian leaders were being held in the Burgerbräukeller? No. Indeed, the weary general hardly seemed to know why he had ever gone to the Burgerbräukeller at all on 8 November.

While others dissembled and flannelled about their role in the affair, Hitler seized his moment and contrasted their ambiguity with his own clarity. 'I cannot plead guilty,' he argued, 'but I do confess the act. There is no such thing as high treason against the traitors of 1918 ... But if I really should have committed high treason then I am surprised not to see those gentlemen [Bavarian leaders] here at my side, those who willed together with us the same action, discussed and prepared things down to the smallest detail ... I do not consider myself as a man who committed high treason but as a German who wanted the best for his people.'

The *Putsch* and After

The *putsch* was an organisational shambles and strategic fiasco. The planning was characterised by poor communication, a lack of coordination, and second-rate improvisation. Far from being a serious, well-oiled assault on the German state, the Nazis looked more like hapless squaddies from Fred Karno's army. Even more tellingly, the aim was never clear and key questions had no answer. What did the *Putschists* want to replace the government in Berlin? Would a Hohenzollern monarchy be restored and, if so, would a future Kaiser rule over all Germany? Or would Bavarian independence be restored? It was never clear because the conspirators could not agree amongst themselves, nor did they have the conversation.

There were, however, several unexpected consequences that flowed from the *putsch* and these had ominous ramifications for Germany. Firstly, the affair gave Hitler the kind of national profile which he had only been able to dream about before. Imprisonment then turned him into a martyr amongst his followers and enhanced his status still further within the *volkisch* movement. In reality, prison life was not arduous and he was quickly released. Far from being a punishment, jail merely boosted his career.

Secondly, President Friedrich Ebert invoked Article 48 of the Weimar constitution to deal with the *putsch*. This gave him emergency powers to deal with situations in which 'the public safety and order in the German Reich … were seriously disturbed or endangered.' The president then effectively handed power to the Army. Article 48 was intended to be used as a backstop during national emergencies. But it became something of a legislative steroid and used increasingly whenever the state looked wobbly. Ebert used Article 48 on scores of occasions and so set a precedent which would have disastrous effects in the longer term. Subsequent chancellors had little compunction in using Article 48 emergency powers to override the constitution which was then diminished in authority with every stroke of their pens. By 1933 the Weimar constitution was so weakened that Hitler had no difficulty killing it off altogether.

Finally, in 1924 the League of Nations called in a banker called Charles Dawes to help Germany deal with hyperinflation trauma. The Dawes plan, as it became known, helped consolidate a new currency, the Reichsmark, and rescheduled German debts. This meant that the reparations could be spread over a much longer time period (under the Dawes plan Germany would have had until 1988 to pay off the war debt). From the end of 1923 the German economy became more stable and there were clear signs of economic growth. A new Chancellor, Gustav Stresemann, was elected and political stability seemed more assured than at any time since before the war. For the next five years the risk of another debilitating economic crisis diminished and the Weimar Republic grew a little stronger. Although Stresemann's administration lasted for just a few months, he became the enduring figure of German politics in the 1920s. Coalitions came and went but Stresemann remained German foreign minister, a stable point of reference. He successfully renegotiated the most onerous terms of the Versailles Treaty: reparation payments were reduced, the payment period extended and some disputed territory was returned to Germany. Stresemann also opened the doors to direct investment from the USA and a plentiful supply of finance capital began to flow into Germany. But much of this was what economists call 'hot money'; short-term loans at high interest rates. Hot money can leave a country as fast as it enters. And this is exactly what happened. As a global recession began to bite after the Wall Street Crash of 1929, liquid cash drained out of the German economy, with disastrous consequences, helping bring the Nazis to power (See Chapter 4).

The Enduring Myth

When the Nazis came to power in 1933 the *putsch* occupied a central place in their mythology. The banner at the head of the march, apparently saturated with victims' blood, became known as the 'blood banner'. It was kept with reverence in the Nazi's Munich HQ and paraded like the Holy Grail at major events. The date of 9 November then passed into the Nazi calendar as a day of supreme importance. Hitler described it as a 'Holy day for the German nation and for all time.' An annual procession was organised from the Bürgerbräukeller, following the *Putschists'* route until it arrived at the Feldherrnhalle (see the cover of this book), which was lit by flaming, smoking funeral urns while the column marched solemnly to the beat of muffled drums. Loudspeakers, hidden from view, repeated the names of the dead and played funereal music to sustain an ambience of eerie mysticism. The highlight of the spectacle was the repetition of the martyrs' names, with the crowd roaring 'present' after each one. Newsreel footage from 1938 shows Hitler shaking hands with the relatives of the dead and patting the cheek of a sobbing young girl who evidently wishes that her father or brother really was 'present'. The Reich radio broadcast exclaims that 'the comrades shot by communists and reactionaries, march in spirit with us.' In subsequent years, the *Alte Kampfer*, or veterans, gathered with Hitler to recall the events. It was at one of these festivals that Hitler was almost assassinated. (see Chapter 6).

Today, there is still a memorial which recalls the *putsch* in the Odeonsplatz. In the mid-1990s a commemorative plaque was placed in the pavement in front of the Feldherrnhalle and this contains the names of the four Bavarian policemen who died in the fight against the Nazis. The inscription reads: '*Den Mitgliedern der Bayerischen Landespolizei, die beim Einsatz gegen die Nationalsozialistischen Putschisten am 9.11.1923 Ihr Leben ließen*'; 'To the members of the Bavarian Police, who gave their lives opposing the National Socialist coup on 9 November 1923'.

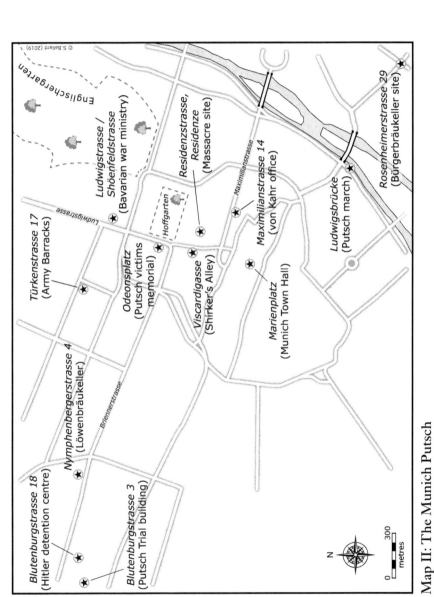

Map II: The Munich Putsch

Labels on map:
- Blutenburgstrasse 18 (Hitler detention centre)
- Blutenburgstrasse 3 (Putsch Trial building)
- Türkenstrasse 17 (Army Barracks)
- Nymphenbergerstrasse 4 (Löwenbräukeller)
- Ludwigstrasse / Shöenfeldstrasse (Bavarian war ministry)
- Englischergarten
- Odeonsplatz (Putsch victims memorial)
- Hoffgarten
- Residenzstrasse, Residenze (Massacre site)
- Viscardigasse (Shirker's Alley)
- Maximilianstrasse 14 (von Kahr office)
- Marienplatz (Munich Town Hall)
- Ludwigsbrücke (Putsch march)
- Rosenheimerstrasse 29 (Bürgerbräukeller site)
- Ludwigstrasse
- Briennerstrasse
- Maximilianstrasse

© S.Ballard (2019)

N

0   300
metres

Chapter Four

From Failed *Putsch* to Absolute Power: The 1920s and 30s

O n 30 January 1933 the befuddled, corpulent, semi-senile war hero, Field Marshall von Hindenburg, resplendent in full dress uniform and bedecked with medals, appointed the former corporal, Adolf Hitler, as chancellor of Germany. It was an extraordinary image, and an astonishing turnaround. Less than a decade before, Hitler had been jailed for attempting to overthrow the German state; and just days before, von Hindenburg had scoffed, 'That man for chancellor? I'll make him a postmaster and he can lick stamps with my head on them'. Yet Hitler was now about to become the most powerful politician in Germany. The Nazis were euphoric; 'The national revolution has begun!' shrieked Goebbels. For many others, inside and outside Germany, it was the beginning of a nightmare. Hitler's path to power in 1933 led through Munich and the city remained his power base thereafter. This chapter looks at where and how that happened.

The Wilderness Years: 1924–29

Following the failed *putsch*, Hitler was jailed and spent much of 1924 in Landsberg prison, just to the south of Munich (see Chapter 3). He was treated with great leniency by the sympathetic prison governor and guards while serving his sentence. The blow of confinement was softened by a regular flow of visitors, good food and access to a veritable library of books. He read widely – he called the experience his 'university paid for by the state' – and wrote *Mein Kampf*. In this long, rambling, diatribe, Hitler presented his Manichean view of the world: a struggle of the survival of the fittest in which there could be no mercy, middle ground or compromise. The book, which was published in Munich in

1925, became an obligatory text in Nazi Germany, making both Hitler and the publisher wealthy men. The offices of the publishing house which produced *Mein Kampf* were in **Thireschstrasse 11**.[1]

While in prison, Hitler left the Nazi organization in the hands of an acolyte called Alfred Rosenberg. A hard-line, flat-footed ideologue who was subsequently executed at Nuremberg, Rosenberg had neither the leadership skills nor political dexterity to manage the organisation effectively (see chapter 10). These deficiencies were precisely what Hitler was looking for in a caretaker leader and the party HQ at **Corneliusstrasse 12** did little more than tick over while he was in prison.[2] The HQ moved briefly to Thierschstrasse 15, but both these buildings were destroyed during the bombing of the city during the Second World War.

By late 1924 the turbulence of the previous year had cooled enough for the authorities to issue a blanket amnesty for political prisoners. Hitler was released without completing his sentence shortly before Christmas 1924. He quickly took back control of the NSDAP from the plodding Rosenberg and set himself two main tasks: the first was to inject fresh life into the party which had lost momentum and drifted in his absence; the second was to consolidate all the differing strands of the fragmented ultra-right *Völkisch* movement within the Nazi party and ensure that he, Hitler, was the undisputed leader.

In February 1925, the Nazi party was relaunched at a mass meeting in the **Bürgerbräukeller**, scene of the failed *putsch* just months before (see Chapter 3). Some 3,000 people packed into the beer hall while thousands more were held at bay by the police outside.[3] The centrepiece was a two-hour speech by Hitler ,who was now hailed as the natural leader of the ultra-right. At the end of the oration, other Nazi and *volkisch* leaders crowded onto the stage around Hitler in an ostentatious show of deference to their newly released leader – contemporary descriptions read like a scene from *The Godfather*. There were suggestions that the centre of a new, united ultra-right movement should be relocated to another part of Germany, but Hitler refused, saying, 'I can't leave Munich. I'm at home here. I mean something here. There are many here who are devoted to me, to me alone. That's important.'

Although now freed from prison, Hitler's inflammatory demagogy threatened to destroy the still-fragile stability of the Weimar Republic and he was quickly banned from public speaking in Bavaria. When most other German states followed suit the gagging order became a serious blow to the nascent Nazi party. Their leader, now a national figure who could sway crowds with his firebrand speeches, was obliged to remain silent.

Yesterday's Man

Something far more serious was also happening to stifle the Nazi's appeal, however. The German economy began to show signs of recovery. It looked as though the worst of the financial crisis had passed and that confidence was now seeping back slowly into the system after the tragedy of the First World War and the trauma of hyperinflation. Old sores from the Versailles Treaty were still highly sensitive – in particular the payment of reparations – but a patchy recovery was underway and many Germans were becoming better off. The country overtook the UK as a leading exporter and Germany notched up a healthy trade surplus, a tradition that continues today. The welfare state (initiated by Bismarck), comparatively robust Trade Unions and progressive policies helped underpin the recovery. In this context, Hitler's scapegoating of the 'November criminals' of 1918 and exhortations to topple the Weimar Republic were messages which began to sound increasingly tired and irrelevant. As the decade wore on and living standards increased, the appeal of the Nazis declined. Support for the party plummeted in the polls and in 1927–28 the speaking bans on him were lifted in state after state. Why continue gagging a man who most people no longer bothered listening to anyway? Adolf Hitler appeared to be yesterday's man.

The General Election in the spring of 1928 confirmed the Nazi slump: the party won just 2.8 per cent of the vote. They now held just twelve seats out of the nearly 500 deputies in the Reichstag, with Göring and Goebbels as the anchors of the parliamentary group. (The current German election rules have a threshold by which a party needs to gain more than five per cent of the vote; under this system the Nazis would have been taken out of the equation altogether). Even in Munich, where the party had attracted a third of voters in 1924, the Nazi vote support dropped into single figures.

Although they were lean years for the Nazis in electoral terms, it was nevertheless a busy period for the party organisation. In 1925 they moved into new offices at **50 Schellingstrasse**, in the heart of bohemian

Schwabing. They would remain there for the rest of the decade.[4] The Nazi offices were at the back of a courtyard that was shared with the party's in-house photographer, Heinrich Hoffmann. A portrait photographer, Hoffmann was part of Hitler's inner circle and was responsible for introducing the leader to his pretty young assistant, Eva Braun (see below). The only trace of the Nazis' occupancy of the building today is the motif of an eagle, half chiselled away, which stands over the entrance. The new offices were conveniently close to those of the party newspaper, the *Völkischer Beobachter*, which was edited and printed just a few doors away, at **39 Schellingstrasse**.[5] At first the *Völkischer Beobachter* was little more than an in-house party news-sheet but early in 1923 adopted a newspaper format and soon became an essential weapon in the armory of Nazi propaganda on the streets.

Schellingstrasse runs through the popular bohemian quarter of Schwabing, where Hitler had lived when he first came to the city (see Chapter 2). Several of the bars and restaurants frequented by Nazi leaders remain. One of Hitler's favourites was the **Schelling Salon**, at 56 Schellingstrasse.[6] This old-world café-diner has had an eclectic clientele over the years: other notable habitués were the Russian revolutionary, Vladmir Lenin, and the ground-breaking Norwegian playwright, Henrik Ibsen, who had both lived in Schwabing. According to legend, Hitler stopped going to the Schelling Salon when the owner had the temerity to ask him to pay off his 'slate'.

Another much-frequented restaurant was the Osteria Bavaria (today called the Osteria Italiana), at **62 Schellingstrasse**.[7] Hitler acolyte Albert Speer recalled the eatery as 'a small artists' restaurant,' and that, 'as a frustrated artist Hitler obviously liked the atmosphere.' Hitler's companions varied and a favourite mealtime topic was not politics but architecture as the leader wolfed down plates of ravioli while holding forth on his plans for rebuilding cities such as Munich and Berlin. Others observed Hitler as a solitary diner in the restaurant. Munich diarist Fritz Reck recalled a chance encounter in the diner with Hitler in the autumn of 1932. By then the Nazis were the most dynamic force in Germany and Hitler was at the centre of the national conversation. Yet the man who would be chancellor within a few weeks cut a solitary figure. 'Hitler entered and crossed the restaurant at the table next to ours – alone, by the way and without his usual bodyguard,' the diarist recorded. Reck and his companion were surprised to see Hitler, who then became uncomfortable when observed. 'His face took the expression of a minor bureaucrat who has entered into a place which he would not normally enter, but now that he is there demands for his good money that he "be served and treated every bit as well as the fine gentleman over there".' Given the political instability and violence on the streets of Munich at that time, Reck had driven into the city and prudently carried a loaded revolver. He later reflected, 'In the almost deserted restaurant, I could easily have shot him. If I had an inkling of the role this piece of filth was to play and the years of suffering he was to make us endure, I would have done it without a second thought. But I took him for a character out of a comic strip and did not shoot.' When their time came, the Nazis had no such compunction in dealing with Reck. The diarist was subsequently interned in a concentration camp where he was put to death.

Hitler continued to eat frequently at the Osteria Bavaria and in later years people would sometimes gather in the street outside waiting to get a glimpse of him as he left. One of those was Unity Valkyrie Mitford. Unity was one of the notorious Mitford sisters, daughters of an eccentric British aristocrat, related to Winston Churchill's wife and connected to the German composer Richard Wagner (thus her middle name). Unity was also a fervent Nazi sympathizer. She enjoyed several and multiple sexual relationships with members of the SS but the real object of her desire was Hitler. Mitford effectively stalked the Führer for months and waited for hours at places where she thought he might be. He finally took notice of her apparently ubiquitous presence and invited her to his table in the Osteria Bavaria. After that 'most wonderful and beautiful day of my life' she lunched with him on several occasions at the restaurant.

On the day war was declared, in September 1939, the distraught Mitford was unable to reconcile her obsession with Hitler with loyalty to country. She went to the **Englischer Garten** in central Munich, a large, undulating park that had been laid out in the eighteenth century according to the principles of the great English landscape gardener, 'Capability' Brown. It was perhaps an appropriate setting for what she did next. Using a pearl-handled revolver gifted to her by Hitler, Mitford attempted suicide by shooting herself in the head.[8] But she bungled the attempt. With the bullet lodged in her skull she was rushed to hospital, where Hitler came to visit and arranged to pay for her treatment.

Mitford was eventually sent back to England where she died some years later, the bullet still in her brain.

Schwabing was badly damaged in the war and the physical scars of the conflict are still very visible on the **walls of the university library** at the bottom of Schellingstrasse.[9] The first RAF raids on Munich probably took place in the autumn of 1940. Bomber Command war diaries record raids on unspecified German cities, which very likely included Munich given its importance to the Nazis. Certainly Nazi propaganda claimed this. On the 14 November 1940 the Luftwaffe launched an unprecedented attack on Coventry that lasted for ten hours, left the city in ruins and took the bombing of a civilian population to new levels of terror. The raid was, the Nazis claimed, in retaliation for the RAF attack on Munich. The net result of the attack on Coventry, however, was to turn world opinion – especially in the USA – against the Nazi barbarity. By the end of the war, around a third of Munich was laid waste by Allied bombing.

While the Nazis were based in Schellingstrasse, Hitler established his own, uncontested power as leader of the party. The Nazis, in turn, consolidated their dominance over the other factions of the nationalist right. Some in the party wanted a broader based leadership dedicated to pursuing Nazi ideas but Hitler demanded total fealty from all party members in order to lead as he saw fit – the Führer principle – without any constraints whatsoever. The salute 'Heil Hitler' became obligatory after 1926, for example, as Hitler insisted that he alone embodied the Nazi ideal. One faction within the party – led by the brothers Otto and Gregor Strasser – also wanted greater emphasis on the 'socialist' element of National Socialism. Hitler angrily denounced what he described as closet 'Marxists' and stamped on the critics: Otto was forced into exile while Gregor remained but was subsequently murdered during the Night of the Long Knives (see Chapter 5).

It was from the offices in Schellingstrasse that Hitler directed the development of the Nazi organisation on the ground. The NSDAP became much more than a political party in the conventional sense. It was not the only party to have its own militia, but the scale of the brown-shirted Nazi SA corps dwarfed that of other groups. The Nazis also created a regional and sectoral network which spread across Germany. Apart from building a local base, the party reached out to different groups such as farmers, health workers, civil servants, teachers, industrial workers, women and young people (the Hitler Youth). These developments were crucial in laying the foundations for future activity. When there was a sudden change in the political mood at the end of the decade the Nazis had a unique and unparalleled organisation on the ground. No other political party had established a similar network capable of mobilizing the different strands of their support.

The 'Chauffereska' and Café Society

Whilst Nazism became a clichéd synonym for ruthless efficiency, Hitler himself had an erratic work ethic and frequently left the day-to-day organisation to others. Even Ernst Hanfstaengl, at whose Munich home Hitler often stayed, found his guest an enigma. 'The affairs of the party seemed surrounded by conspiracy and intrigue. Hitler himself lived a shadowy existence and it was very difficult to keep track of his movements. He had the Bohemian habits of a man who had grown up with no real roots. He was hopelessly unpunctual and incapable of keeping to any kind of schedule.'

Hitler turned up at party offices in late morning or early afternoon (if at all) and appointments with him were virtually meaningless; people might wait for hours to meet him without any success. 'He never stopped talking all day, committed nothing to paper and was the despair of his staff,' observed Hanfstaengl. Even other leading members of the party complained that it was difficult to schedule a meeting with Hitler. Days or even weeks might pass before they could discuss important business with him. Although frequently seen at public events and meetings, he was adept at avoiding any conversations or attempts to draw him out. Before the speech he was closeted away making final changes and preparing himself. After the meeting he would sweep out, surrounded by an adoring throng.

However, he could be found holding court over coffee and cake on many afternoons in one of Munich's cafés, often in the company of his closest aides. He was a frequent visitor to the **Café Heck**, which overlooks the **Hofgarten**.[10] A more upmarket venue of choice for afternoon tea or meals was Munich's plushest hotel, the **Vier Jahreszeiten (Four Seasons)**.[11] Although often seen with people, Hitler had few, if any, friends as such. He surrounded himself with a cabal of trusted bodyguards, assistants and chauffeurs who formed his most intimate social network. The tight-knit group was often known as the 'Chauffereska' and they were not universally popular, even amongst others in the movement. The ever-sensitive and jealous Goebbels dismissed them as 'philistines' and could not understand what Hitler saw in his unsophisticated companions. 'How can a person like Hitler endure them for more than 5 minutes?' he mused anxiously in his diary. But he did. Their names have not gone down in history along with those of the better-known Nazis but they were important to Hitler. Whilst he frequently kept other Nazi leaders and professionals at arms-length, Hitler often felt more at ease with a small group of Munich henchmen, thugs, and drivers who organised his day-to-day life with total discretion. With them he could relax because they were in no way his equal and were wholly subservient to him.

Ulrich Graf, his bodyguard, trailed Hitler everywhere, as did his fierce pet Alsatian called 'Wolf'. Another of the Chauffereska who remained closest to Hitler throughout his life was the Munich-born Julius Schaub, his general factotum. According to one observer, Schaub 'followed Hitler like a shadow' and organised most of his domestic arrangements. Schaub was also imprisoned for his part in the *putsch* and remained with Hitler to the end, in 1945, at which point he fled the flames of Berlin and escaped to Bavaria. Once there, he went to Hitler's houses in Munich and Berchtesgaden to perform one final act for his master; he emptied the safes of documents, which he then set ablaze on the terrace of the Berghof where the Führer and his acolytes had once planned the 'thousand year Reich' (see Chapter 9). Schaub refused to divulge what he had destroyed to the day he died, saying only that there would have been 'disastrous consequences' had the contents become public. Quite what secrets went up in flames cannot be known, but may well have had to do with one particular scandal in Hitler's shady private life. Many suspected that, had the full story been known at the time, it would have put an end to his career.

Printzregenplatz: Scandal, Statecraft and Appeasement

In 1929 Hitler moved into a spacious, nine-room luxury apartment on the first floor of **Prinzregenplatz 16** in the smart Bogenhausen district of Munich.[12] It remained his private address until his death in 1945 and is today a municipal police station. Built in 1914, the interior was redesigned by Paul Ludwig Troost, the architect responsible for many of the emblematic Nazi buildings in the city. The hefty rent of over 4,000 Reichsmarks was paid by wealthy Nazi donors and was a long way from the three Marks he had been paying Frau Popp when he first arrived in the city. During the 1930s the flat was the scene of events both personal and political which marked milestones in the history of the Third Reich. The personal concerned Hitler's opaque private life while the political was the very public foreign policy known as 'appeasement'.

Almost immediately after he moved into the apartment, Hitler was hit by scandal of the kind that has wrecked many a political career, and it was swiftly covered up. Hitler insisted that he could never marry as he was 'married to the German people and their fate'. In reality he had never shown any interest in a settled domestic life, but he did share the apartment in Prinzregenplatz with his niece, Angela 'Geli' Raubal, with whom he appears to have had some sort of affair. Quite what the relationship consisted of baffled even those closest to him. The tryst between the forty-one-year-old uncle and the pretty niece, nineteen years his junior, was certainly unusual and struck many as downright bizarre. Raubal's existence as a lover or companion was only tacitly acknowledged, even among the inner circle of the Nazi leadership. It was certainly more than avuncular on Hitler's part and some suggested that Raubal was the object of some perverse sex games. Otto Strasser, by now banished from the Nazi party fearing for his life and so perhaps not the most reliable source, put it about that Hitler achieved sexual satisfaction with Raubal through coprophilia. Others said that Geli was the only woman that Hitler ever really loved but, if true, the emotion was expressed not with affection but as an increasingly obsessive jealousy.

On the afternoon of 18 September 1931 the feisty teenager had a furious row with her controlling uncle. What caused the dispute will never be known: perhaps the vivacious Geli wanted to go to the Oktoberfest celebrations that were in full swing across the city. Perhaps it was the longing to resume the music lessons, which Hitler disapproved of. Or perhaps it was her interest in men younger and fitter than her uncle that provoked his wrath. Whatever the cause, it was to be their final quarrel.

When Hitler's housekeeper, Frau Winter, attempted to wake Geli the following morning the door would not open. In a panic she called the Nazi headquarters, the Brown House, and was put through to Hitler's deputy, Rudolf Hess. Alarmed, Hess sped to the flat with Gregor Strasser and the two men battered down the door of Raubal's bedroom. The young woman lay dead on the bed with a bullet wound in her chest. Hitler's personal 6.35-caliber Walther revolver was on the bed beside her. It was impossible to keep a lid on the scandal and the ever-gossipy chronicler Fritz Reck heard, 'There are people who claim that the girl had been having an affair with a Jew and shot herself out of guilt and fear.'

The most likely cause of death was suicide but the rumours swirled around Munich and, as Reck recorded, 'there are hints of other things'. According to some of these, Raubal was the victim of a murder that was covered up by Nazi sympathisers amongst the police and public authorities. Some people close to the couple maintained that Raubal was pregnant. Apparently Martin Bormann arranged for the corpse to be spirited away in a sealed casket to Vienna, where Geli was given a proper Catholic funeral, which only added to the speculation. So did the priest who officiated at the burial. He reportedly scoffed at the story that the girl had taken her own life and claimed that he would never have read Mass in the case of suicide; a sin beyond redemption according to Catholic theology. 'They pretended that she committed suicide,' he said, 'I should never have allowed a suicide to be buried in consecrated ground. From the fact that I gave her a Christian burial you can draw your own conclusions which I cannot communicate to you.'

Getting Raubal's corpse out of Munich was one problem. Separating Hitler from the scandal of her untimely death was another. Hitler claimed to have been in Nuremberg, over 100 miles from Munich, on the night of the 18 September. But his story was blown by Karl Zehntner, landlord of the **Bratwurst Glöckl**, in the city centre.[13] Zehntner observed that Hitler had spent the evening with Geli in a private room on the first floor above the bar and swore that the couple did not leave until after midnight. It was testimony which subsequently may have become a death sentence. In 1934 Zehntner, an associate of Ernst Rohm, and some his staff were murdered during the Night of the Long Knives (see Chapter 5). In any event, the Nazis took no chances that the scandal would be revived.

Hitler was consoled by another strange relationship following Ruabal's death. Once again, the girl involved was less than half his age. And once again, it would end in savage, premature death. In October 1929 Hitler made a routine call on the new studio of his personal photographer Heinrich Hofmann, just off the **Odeonsplatz**.[14] There his eye was taken by a pretty seventeen-year-old assistant called Eva Braun, a local girl who had been born just a few streets away at **Isabellastrasse 45**.[15] After Ruabal's death Hitler began to see more of Braun, who lived with her parents in a first-floor flat at **Hohenzollernstrasse**.[16] By 1932 she was a regular follower on the election campaign trail; Hofmann took her along as an assistant at Hitler's request. She began to spend more time around the Führer, but her presence was always in the background, to the point where she was scarcely recognised at all by those who were not 'in the know'.

Quite what there was to know was anyone's guess. In 1935 Braun moved out of her parents' home, apparently to live with her sister. In reality, the move gave her the freedom to spend more time with Hitler, either when he was in Munich or at his country house in Berchtegaden, where she was very much at home, even when he was not (see Chapter 8). She had her own apartment adjacent to Hitler's bedroom and, without taking much interest in politics, was part of the 'inner circle'. What succour Hitler drew from his relationship with Eva remains a mystery, but she was obsessed with him and remained so right up until her death. In the first week of March 1945 Braun left Munich and flew to Berlin. There, with the Allied forces closing in on all sides, she joined Hitler in the Bunker of the Reichschancelry. During the night of the 28–29 April she and Hitler were married in a ghoulish ceremony. She then committed suicide by swallowing cyanide before he too took his own life.

1929–33: the Challenge of 'Hell Personified'

In the early months of 1929 Nazism appeared to be drifting into complete political irrelevance and the dustbin of history. But then two events occurred in quick succession which transformed the party's fortunes. The German economic recovery had been anchored by the country's ablest and most trusted statesman, Gustav Stresemann, but on 3 October 1929 he suffered a sudden and lethal stroke. How Stresemann might have handled what was about to happen next is one of the great 'what ifs' of history.

Within weeks of Stresemann's death, at the end of October 1929, the New York stock exchange registered extraordinary falls. The fire sale of stocks and bonds was the overture to a massive slump in the US economy which would also have catastrophic effects in Europe. Although the fledgling Weimar Republic had grown stronger during the second half of the 1920s, it was in no position to withstand an external shock of this magnitude, and the weaknesses of the German economy were cruelly exposed in the subsequent global recession. Export markets collapsed; businesses defaulted on their loan repayments and folded; unemployment soared. The German government relied heavily on short-term loans and these dried up in the credit crunch. Around a third of the German economy was based on agriculture and small farmers were badly hit by spiralling interest rates and foreclosures. The consequences of the Wall Street crash were dire everywhere. In Germany they would be cataclysmic. Between 1929 and 1932 industrial output halved. Unemployment rose to over six million, leaving one in three German workers without a job. As tax revenues and social security contributions slumped welfare benefits were cut. The meagre unemployment payment was all that stood between some twenty million Germans and starvation and another million people had nothing at all.

It was just a matter of time before the effects of the crumbling economy were felt in the political system. And sure enough, by 1930 the Weimar Republic began to buckle under the immense strain. According to biographer Joachim Fest, Hitler predicted what would happen next 'with almost clairvoyant accuracy'. In February 1930 he forecast that 'the victory of our movement will take place ... at the most in two and a half to three years.' It was an uncannily perceptive comment, helped by a series of missteps, blunders and bungles by the political establishment. As the then-law student, Sebastian Haffner commented, it was at this point 'that the real mystery of the Hitler phenomenon began to show itself: the strange befuddlement and numbness of his opponents who could not cope with his behaviour and found themselves transfixed by the gaze of the basilisk, unable to see that it was hell personified that challenged them.'

Paralysed, the government called a general election in the autumn of 1930. Nazi leaders were euphoric and the party machine began to whir with demonic energy. Propaganda spewed out from Goebbels' office. Teams of well-trained Nazi speakers set up thousands of local meetings to ram home their message – some 34,000 in the last month of the campaign alone – while Hitler addressed twenty mass rallies in strategic cities. No other political formation came close to mounting a campaign anything like it and the results stunned Germany. The Nazis won over eighteen per cent of the popular vote (up from 2.7 per cent) and leapt from twelve to one hundred and seven seats in the Reichstag. What had been a splinter group in the parliament was now the second largest party. International observers too felt the shockwave and some even welcomed the result; the *Daily Mail*, for example, applauded the outcome as heralding 'the rebirth of Germany as a nation'.

Swept along by the momentum, Nazi party membership swelled and larger offices were needed. Funds were raised by a levy of two Reichmarks from every member and with loans arranged through the industrialist Fritz Thyssen. The money was then used to acquire a large nineteenth-century mansion called the Palais Barlow which stood between the Karolinenplatz and Königsplatz in central Munich. The building was converted into offices for Nazi leaders and administrators, and from 1931 was known as the Brown House, a reference to the brown-shirted Nazi legions of the SA. The building was part administrative office and partly a shrine with the slogan 'Germany, Awake' over the main entrance. A prominent feature of the interior was a portrait of Hitler with the caption 'Nothing happens in this movement except what I wish', and in another room – like a chapel – was kept the 'blood flag', the banner stained with the blood of the 'martyrs' of the failed beer hall *putsch*. The **Brown House** building was destroyed by an RAF air raid in early1945 and Munich's excellent **Documentation/Exhibition centre** of the Third Reich now stands on the plot.[17]

'Future Generations Will Damn You'

Between 1930 and 1932 the new chancellor, Heinrich Brüning, implemented a tough austerity policy to balance the government's books: spending was slashed and taxes increased and Brüning was dubbed 'the hunger chancellor'. Even the most talented politician would have had a hard task selling the austerity package to a weary population, and Brüning was not such a politician. He spoke quietly and eschewed the limelight: when crowds turned out to greet him on a visit to Munich he pulled down the blinds of his railway compartment. Given the unpopularity of his austerity measures, Brüning was seldom able to garner a majority in the Reichstag and increasingly fell back on the use of emergency powers granted under Article 48 of the Weimar constitution. These allowed Brüning, as his predecessors had done, to effectively override the Parliament and avoid short-term legislative deadlock. In the long-term, the freewheeling use of Article 48 powers consolidated a precedent which would have terrible consequences.

By the summer of 1932 Brüning's popularity was at rock bottom and he was replaced as chancellor by the equally conservative, but scarcely more appealing, Franz von Papen. In July 1932 von Papen called fresh elections in an attempt to bolster his mandate, but the manoeuvre backfired. Support for the Nazis leapt again to a thirty-seven per cent share of the vote and the party more than doubled its number of deputies to 230. Support for the communist party (KPD) rose too and they gained eighty-nine seats. The Stalinist KPD, however, refused to work with others in a broad-based alliance to stop Hitler, condemning the Social Democrats as 'social fascists' and little different from the Nazis. Meanwhile, the squeeze on support for the centrist parties was evident: more than half the deputies in the Reichstag now represented parties committed to the overthrow of liberal democracy. Combined with the increasing political violence on the streets of major cities, the result sounded the death knell of the Weimar Republic.

Germany was now at fever pitch and political violence was endemic. Thuggery, torture and tit-for-tat street assassinations on left and right supplanted normal democratic discourse; one eyewitness described the period as a 'continuous Bartholomew's day massacre', in reference to the sixteenth-century slaughter of Catholics by Protestants. Recent number-crunching electoral analysis suggests that the old religious fault lines in Germany really did play a part in bringing the Nazis to power: predominantly Protestant areas were markedly more likely to support the Nazis than Catholic regions such as Bavaria. Instability was exacerbated by the seemingly endless round of elections in 1932 – two for the presidency, two general elections and regional polls – all of which added to the turmoil. In the bewildering flurry of elections the Nazi vote actually began to fall away towards the end of 1932, but by then it was too late. Clumsy political shenanigans and feuding amongst the more orthodox politicians gifted Hitler the chancellorship. Unable to agree amongst themselves about who should be chancellor, but united by their fear of communism, the bickering right-wing political factions made a fatal blunder. They settled on Hitler as chancellor and head of a 'Government of National Concentration'. Established politicians held the mistaken belief that they would be able to manipulate the Nazi leader and, in what must rank as one of the most foolish miscalculations of modern history, von Papen told associates 'we have hired Hitler'. Hitler, meanwhile, could scarcely believe his luck. When, on 30 January 1933, he was appointed to high office by President Hindenburg, Hitler ascribed his ascent to a 'miracle' and an 'act of God'. His erstwhile companion in the Munich *Putsch* of 1923, Field Marshall Erich von Ludendorff, saw it in very different terms. With eerie prescience, Ludendorff immediately sent the aged president a telegram, denouncing Hitler as a dangerous demagogue and predicting that, 'this sinister individual will lead our country into an abyss and our nation to unprecedented catastrophe. Future generations will curse you in your grave for this action.'

1933–38: Munich, Capital of the Movement

Having gained power in January 1933, Hitler moved with lightning speed to eliminate opposition and concentrate power in his person (see also Chapter 5). The fate of opponents was about to become clear in one of Munich's central squares, the **Königsplatz**, which had originally been laid out in the time of King Ludwig I of Bavaria.[18] In May 1933 Nazi students descended on the square with armfuls of books from Munich's universities as part of the 'national revolution' to cleanse academic institutions. Novels such as Erich Maria Remarque's *All quiet on the Western Front* and Thomas Mann's *Death in Venice* were tossed onto the flames, along with the heavier works of thinkers from Karl Marx to Sigmund Freud, in an orgy of book burning. Even the works of the deaf and blind activist Helen Keller were held to be a threat and destroyed. The conflagration shocked the civilised world both inside and outside the country. Goebbels declared the age of 'Jewish intellectualism is dead' and backed the students' right to 'clean up the debris of the past'. Chillingly, Heinrich Heine, one of Germany's most influential nineteenth-century authors and himself a Jew, had already predicted as far back as 1822 what would happen next. 'Where they burn books,' said Heine, 'so too they will end up burning people.' The Nazi passion for cultural cleansing did not stop with the printed word, however. The new masters of the Third Reich declared war on artistic forms which did not conform to Nazi ideals and Munich remained at the centre of the battle (see below).

Hitler described Munich as 'the capital of the Movement' and a full-scale Nazification of the city began almost as soon as he took power. A whole set of new buildings began to mushroom in the area around the central Königsplatz. One side of Arcisstrasse, adjacent to the Königsplatz, was compulsorily purchased and existing buildings bulldozed. **The Führerbau** – or Hitler's official office in Munich – was constructed in their place. His personal bureau was on the first floor above the portico.[19] Today, the building is used as a music conservatoire. Towards the other end, and connected via underground passageways, was an identical building with more offices for party bureaucrats. Between them on the surface, on both corners of Arcisstrasse and Briennerstrasse, were two large mausoleums. They were called the **'Temples of Honour'** and contained the remains of the sixteen Nazis who had died during the *putsch* (see Chapter 3). Each of the temples, open to the sky, contained eight sarcophaguses, while an 'Eternal Watch' of SS sentries maintained a permanent round-the-clock vigil over the macabre scene. At the end of the war the bodies were removed, the pantheons demolished and today only the raised plinths of the temples remain in their place.[20]

The most imposing building of the scheme was the Führerbau. This building was inaugurated with a visit from Benito Mussolini in 1937 and the fascist leader returned again in the summer of 1940. Paris had just fallen to German troops and the two dictators toasted the success and discussed their next moves. More importantly still, the Führerbau was the location for one of the most crucial meetings of the twentieth century. It was here that an emergency summit was held on 29 September 1938 to solve what was known as the 'Munich crisis' (see also Chapter 9).

The Munich Crisis 1938

With Europe on the brink of war, it was here that the leaders of Germany, Italy, France and Britain met for critical talks about Hitler's ambitions for expansion and his claim on Germans who lived within the newly created Czechoslovakia the *Sudetendeutsch* (see Chapter 9). Two representatives from the Czech government were invited but not allowed to participate in the talks; they were kept waiting in another room in the building. Meanwhile, an eager press corps and expectant crowds waited for news in the Königsplatz. Eventually, the delegations arrived, entering the cavernous hall and up the grand marble staircase where they waited outside Hitler's large office on the first floor overlooking the Königsplatz.

The tiny British delegation headed by Prime Minister Neville Chamberlain was first to arrive, followed by the French Premier Daladier and his aides. In their plain civilian suits, they were soon swamped by a sea of Nazi and Fascist uniforms as the German and Italian contingents converged on the building. While the delegations stood around waiting for the conference to begin, Chamberlain tried to break the ice with Mussolini by chatting about angling. *Il Duce* stared back at him blankly and the small talk about fly-fishing fizzled out. There was a further delay when the French premier refused to start without his senior aide, Léger, who, he explained limply, 'knows everything, I know nothing'. Léger in turn, had inexplicably gone missing, apparently looking for his secretary who had with her a vital bundle of papers. Eventually, the talks got underway at around 1pm and would last a full twelve hours. It was not until the early hours of the following day that all sides agreed the 'Munich Accords' and conflict was avoided.

The hastily convened conference was one of the most important meetings of the twentieth century but there was no clearly defined aim and no agenda. Foreign attendees were swiftly disabused of clichéd ideas of Teutonic Nazi efficiency by the shambolic organisation. The senior British official present, Sir Horace Wilson, commented drily that preparations for the meeting were 'very imperfect and there appeared to be no arrangements for the taking of notes.' As a consequence, there is no proper transcript of the meeting nor is it clear who was in the room at any one time – functionaries, diplomats and advisers entered and left the room throughout the day – which merely added to the sense of confusion.

The seating arrangements were, said Wilson, 'completely impromptu'. Those who could squeeze in sat around a small table while others – including Hitler and Mussolini – sat in armchairs or on a long leather sofa. Without a designated Chair, Mussolini eventually took control as he was the only person with the necessary language skills – he had some German, French and English – to steer the conversation. Nevertheless, progress was tedious and whatever anyone said had to be translated into the languages of the others.

The group paused for lunch at 3pm and took a break for dinner at 8pm but otherwise the stuttering, elliptical discussion about the future of the *Sudetendeutsch* (Germans living in Czech territory) Czechoslovakia, and central Europe continued into the early hours. Finally, a draft agreement was reached which all parties could sign up to, but even then there was a moment of farce. Hitler was the first to try and took up the pen only to discover that the inkwell was empty and the nib dry.

'Peace in our Time'

As experts busied themselves preparing a final draft – and the final incisions into Czech territory – Chamberlain asked Hitler if he would care for a private chat. Not surprisingly, Hitler 'jumped at the idea', according to one observer, and invited Chamberlain to his Prinzregenplatz apartment the following morning. Again, there were no witnesses at the meeting – the two leaders met alone with just an interpreter present – but the meeting concluded with a short, formal declaration.

> We, the German Führer and British Prime Minister have had a further meeting today and we are agreed in recognising that the question of Anglo-German relations is of the first importance for the two countries and for Europe. We regard the agreement reached last night ... as symbolic of the desire of our two peoples never to go to war with one another again.
>
> We are resolved that the method of consultation shall be the method adopted to deal with any other questions that may concern our two countries, and we are determined to continue our efforts to remove possible sources of difference, and thus to contribute to assure the peace of Europe.

But that, too, turned out to be a promise as empty as the inkwell in the Führerbau. Chamberlain had, of course, been duped by Hitler. Within months, Europe would be plunged into war. But in September 1938 the old prime minister returned to England in triumph and was fêted as a peacemaker. When his plane arrived at Heston airport he was mobbed by enthusiastic well-wishers. Waving his piece of paper with Hitler's signature, he declared that he had returned from Germany having achieved 'peace with honour. I believe it is peace for our time.' It took less than a year for the delusion to be exposed. By the autumn of 1939 Britain was at war with Germany and the Second World War was underway.

Aryan Art, Degenerate Art

A few months after seizing power, Hitler declared that Munich would henceforth be the 'Capital of German Art'. He was anxious to foster an essential Nazi culture and nowhere was this more clearly demonstrated than in his adopted city. Like many an architect, he dreamed that altering the physical surroundings of the city could help influence ways of thought and give concrete form to a new code of ethics. Many of the grand plans would have involved bulldozing great chunks of the city. Hitler was introduced to Professor Paul Ludwig Troost, who he entrusted with much of the replanning. Hitler was in awe of Troost and, uncharacteristically, abandoned his own baroque designs for the city in deference to those of the professor. 'What a piece of good luck that I met this man!' exclaimed Hitler. Others agreed. Nazi leader Albert Speer, himself a trained architect, commented dryly that 'it is ghastly to think what Hitler's architectural taste would have been like without Troost's influence.'

Thankfully, little of the Hitler-Troost scheme for Munich ever came to fruition and just a few of their buildings remain as reminders of the city's Nazi past. One is the *Haus der Deutschen Kunst* – **The House of German Art** – which was built on the edge of the Englishergarten.[21] Hitler himself arrived to lay the foundation stone in October 1933, but a murmur went through the crowd when the silver hammer he was given to tap the stone split in two on impact with the slab. It was an inauspicious start that rattled the superstitious Führer. The bad omens returned when the architect, Troost, died a few months later leaving his widow, Gerdy, to finish the project.

Hitler took an obsessive interest in the project and spent hours poring over minute details of the design, but though better than anything he might have devised, it offered nothing new. The stilted, classical, derivative scheme is similar to that of many other buildings designed by the unimaginative Troost, such as the Führerbau and the Temples of Honour (see above). When the new gallery opened in the summer of 1937 with the first *Grosse Deutsche kunstausstellung* (German Art Exhibition), the inauguration was marked by a massive and somewhat peculiar ceremony. Thousands of marchers snaked their way through Munich in a procession called 'Two Thousand Years of German Culture', a 3km cavalcade of Nazi kitsch to celebrate their version of history. A model of the art gallery building led the column, followed by floats of Viking boats, giant Norse gods, Brunhildas, spread eagles, flaming torches and phalanxes of Aryan soldiers amongst the scores of outsized images. There was artistic license aplenty: the fantastical column projected a version of history that had never happened, enacted by people who had never lived, in places that never existed.

Others, however, found their license to think, speak, paint, draw or create firmly revoked. Hitler proceeded to open the gallery with a speech that promised an implacable 'war of destruction against the forces of cultural disintegration ... chatters, dilettantes and art forgers will be picked up and liquidated.' It was a declaration of the open hostility to many of Germany's greatest cultural figures. Max Beckmann, perhaps the most famous painter in the country, heard Hitler's speech on the radio. He and his wife quickly packed what they could and immediately fled Germany, never to return. Many others soon followed. The great German expressionist artist, Otto Dix, was sacked from his job in Berlin and retreated to Lake Konstanz in the deep south of Germany. From then on, he could only paint landscapes and ruefully reflected that this was a fate tantamount to forced emigration. Others quickly joined outstanding German artists like George Grosz and writers like Bertholt Brecht who had already fled the country. Ernst Ludwig Kirchner, one of the founders of *Die Brücke* (The Bridge) group, which had revolutionized twentieth-century art, destroyed all the paintings and equipment in his studio. Then, in 1938, he committed suicide.

The opening exhibition, like the parade, was a sanitised version of history and war. It was as though the industrial-scale slaughter and mutilated remnants of the Western Front had never happened. The dead and mutilated depicted again and again in the works of the expressionists, were simply airbrushed out of Nazi imagery. The new order was summed up by an image of Hitler as a medieval knight holding a swastika banner. Inside the new exhibition was a pantheon of Aryan racial purity, statues of women with perfect breasts and men with what looked like surgically enhanced buttocks. Many visitors found the nudity overwhelming. It was like a static naturist colony inhabited by classical athletes, all with cold, vacant stares and without a trace of warmth that makes human life worthwhile. One young art student later recalled being struck – as any seventeen-year-old might be – by 'the enormous number of nudes', which gave the museum its nick-name 'house of tarts'. The works were for sale and the largest crowds gathered around those works that had been purchased by the Führer himself. The exhibition was repeated every year, though the style and the layout remained wearily similar. And every year Hitler – always the largest buyer – continued to acquire more of the works. In July 1939 he bought over 250 pieces of art, though whether he ever had time to appreciate them is a mystery because just six weeks later his armies invaded Poland.

Today, the **Haus der Kunst** is a functioning art gallery and culture centre. Vistors are welcome to explore the gallery and enjoy a range of exhibitions which run throughout the year.

'Degenerate Art'

The very day after the House of German Art opened, in July 1937, another exhibition was opened just across the park.[22] The collection gathered together some 650 works from the 6,000 works that had been snatched from galleries and museums across Germany. The Nazis called the display *Entartete kunst* or '**Degenerate Art**' but it rapidly became one of the famous – and most popular – art exhibitions of the twentieth century. The very word 'degenerate' carried a particular weight in the early twentieth century. A branch of medical and anthropological science was engaged in measuring skulls, noses and ears in an attempt to establish common norms. Significant deviations were held to be 'degenerate'.

And so it was with art or music; jazz, too, was labelled 'degenerate' music by the Nazis.

Just over a hundred artists were singled out to be pilloried but the list actually reads like a who's who of twentieth century art. Impressionists, expressionists, cubists and dadaists were all represented; and denounced. Works by Max Beckmann, Marc Chagall, Otto Dix, Franz Marc, Piet Mondrian, Paul Klee, Wassily Kandinsky, George Grosz, Ernst Ludwig Kirchner, Oskar Kokoschka, Emile Nolde, and Max Ernst were amongst those on display.

The object was not to praise but to bury the works. It is one of the few occasions in which an exhibition has been mounted on such a scale with the sole intention of mocking and ridiculing the works and techniques on display. According to Nazi ideology, the works were shocking and threatened to undermine the moral fabric of the state, though in some cases it was difficult to understand why. Some works seemed wholly innocuous. One of the Franz Marc's paintings, for example, depicted a happy cow; it was too much for the censor who insisted that no such animal existed and so should be banned. Viewers who did not immediately get the point were assisted by appropriate commentaries tagged to individual canvasses. 'An insult to German womanhood', and 'Nature as seen by sick minds', were favourite tags. Goebbels paid actors to mix in the crowd and pour scorn on the works described as 'banal daubers'. Even those who did not know much about art were told what to think. One of the essential features of the expressionist movement was the psychological delving into innermost thoughts. But, of course, under Nazism there could be no private, inner thought or personal space. The personal was now controlled and there could be no distinction between the private and the public individual.

Only six of the artists *were* actually Jewish but the labels Bolshevik, Masonic, Jewish, etc. became interchangeable and bandied about so indiscriminately that exhibits were categorized at random. One artist above all, Emil Nolde, must have been alarmed to find more than twenty of his works in the exhibition. Nolde had been a Nazi party member since 1920. But even sixteen years of continuous affiliation were not enough to save him and he – or rather his paintings – were rounded up along with the others. Nolde's great altarpiece depicting the crucifixion was condemned as 'an insolent mockery of the divine'.

An estimated three million visitors saw the blockbuster exhibition. Bernard Schultz, later one of Germany's most important abstract painters, recalled how he and his fellow art academy students went to the exhibition, filled not by revulsion but by awe. 'We knew that we may never get the chance to see these works again before they were burned or destroyed'. On leaving Munich, the exhibition travelled for four years and attracted vast crowds. Ironically, it remains one of the most visited exhibitions in the history of art. When it was over, some works were ceremonially destroyed; but not all. The crafty organisers auctioned off several of the pieces in Switzerland for hard currency. Buyers there may not have known much more about art but they were at least free to think and spend their money as they chose.

The Nazi witch-hunt against modern art did not end in Munich, however. After German troops rolled into Paris in 1940, a detachment of the SS paid a visit to the studio of Pablo Picasso. Possibly the most famous artist of the twentieth century, Picasso was known for his bold and daring innovations and none more so than his giant canvas, *Guernica*. The huge painting portrays in startling, disjointed detail the bombing of civilians and destruction of buildings during the Spanish Civil War. The attack on the small market town in the Basque country was carried out by the Luftwaffe and was an episode which, even at the time, shocked the world in its barbarity. The original was elsewhere but one SS official picked up a postcard of the canvas, 'Did you do this,' he demanded to know of Picasso. 'No, you did,' replied the artist. The story may or may not be apocryphal, but the mutual contempt between Nazism and free thinkers was real beyond doubt.

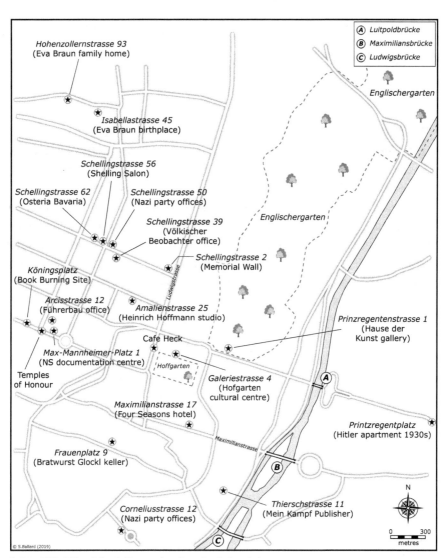

Hohenzollernstrasse 93
(Eva Braun family home)

Isabellastrasse 45
(Eva Braun birthplace)

Schellingstrasse 56
(Shelling Salon)

Schellingstrasse 62
(Osteria Bavaria)

Schellingstrasse 50
(Nazi party offices)

Schellingstrasse 39
(Völkischer
Beobachter office)

Schellingstrasse 2
(Memorial Wall)

Köningsplatz
(Book Burning Site)

Arcisstrasse 12
(Führerbau office)

Amalienstrasse 25
(Heinrich Hoffmann studio)

Cafe Heck

Max-Mannheimer-Platz 1
(NS documentation centre)

Temples
of Honour

Hoffgarten

Galeriestrasse 4
(Hofgarten
cultural centre)

Maximilianstrasse 17
(Four Seasons hotel)

Frauenplatz 9
(Bratwurst Glockl keller)

Corneliusstrasse 12
(Nazi party offices)

Thierschstrasse 11
(Mein Kampf Publisher)

Englischergarten

Englischergarten

Prinzregentenstrasse 1
(Hause der
Kunst gallery)

Printzregentplatz
(Hitler apartment 1930s)

Ludwigstrasse

Maximillianstrasse

Ⓐ Luitpoldbrücke
Ⓑ Maximiliansbrücke
Ⓒ Ludwigsbrücke

Ⓐ

Ⓑ

Ⓒ

N

0   300
metres

© S.Ballerd (2019)

Map III: The Nazi Organisation in Munich

Chapter Five

Operation *Kolibri* (Hummingbird): The Night of the Long Knives

E arly on Saturday, 30 June 1934 a detachment of SS troops barged into the rooms of the Hanslbauer Hotel on picturesque **Lake Tegernsee**, just to the south of Munich.[1] The occupants were dragged from their beds and shoved into the courtyard where they were bundled into waiting cars. With exquisite synchronisation, the process was repeated at selected addresses in towns and cities across Germany. Hammering on doors, SS heavies roused the occupants who were then detained or simply shot dead where they stood. Bewildered, almost none of the victims could comprehend what was happening to them, but over the next two days it was a scene repeated hundreds of times. Meanwhile, leading Nazis sat with Hitler in the party's Munich HQ, the Brown House, anxiously taking calls, reading messages and crossing names off lists. Much of the slaughter took place in broad daylight and guns were the weapons of choice. This most notorious of purges rapidly became known as the 'Night of the Long Knives' and was a key step in Hitler's seizure of absolute power.

Gleichschaltung and the Suicide of German Democracy

When Hitler assumed the chancellorship of Germany on 30 January 1933 he moved with lightning speed to consolidate his power. Nominally head of a coalition, the other political partners were no match for the Führer's ruthless pursuit of total control and were wholly ineffective in constraining him. They were still playing by the old rules whilst he was writing his own. On 28 February the German Reichstag was burned down in a mysterious fire. The blaze was blamed on a Dutch communist called Marinus van der Lubbe. Whether he really was the arsonist has been a matter of controversy ever since. It was widely suspected that he was fitted up by the Nazis, who had themselves started the blaze. In any event, they left nothing to chance: the hapless van de Lubbe was swiftly beheaded. Whatever the true story, the fire gave Hitler the excuse he needed. He claimed that the conflagration was part of a conspiracy aimed at overthrowing the new government and that the institutions of the German state were now under attack.

Hitler angrily demanded emergency powers from the aged President Hindenberg who granted them without demur. The Führer now had a free hand to pursue his foes with a vengeance. Now known as 'enemies of the state', opponents were quickly rounded up and within days 3,000 people were in custody. Elected politicians were detained. Newspapers and magazines closed down while journalists were arrested or fled. Fresh elections were convened at the beginning of March and gave the Nazis forty-four per cent of the popular vote. Even with the opposition reeling, they were still short of a majority, but by then ballots and democratic norms scarcely mattered. There would be no further free elections in Germany under the Third Reich and Hitler moved seamlessly from being an elected chancellor to an elected dictator.

On 22 March the concentration camp of Dachau, just outside Munich, opened its gates to receive the first batch of political prisoners (see Chapter 8). The following day, 23 March, the newly elected deputies met in the Kroll Opera House across the square from the now burned-out shell of the Reichstag in Berlin. Hitler presented the assembly with demands for yet more power in a measure which, without irony, was called 'The Law for Alleviating the Distress of People and Reich'. Article 1 stated baldly that: 'Laws for the Reich can be enacted by the Reich cabinet as well as in accordance with the procedure provided by the Constitution of the Reich.'

In other words, all the usual legislative scrutiny could henceforth be bypassed so that Hitler could now railroad through any measure he pleased. Approval for new laws was inevitable. Many opposition deputies were absent – detained or in hiding – while SA thugs prowled menacingly around the corridors of the building to intimidate any waverers. The vote was a foregone conclusion: the measure was passed with 441 deputies in favour and an extraordinarily courageous eighty-four deputies against. They were led by the leader of the Social Democrats, Otto Wels, who made a valiant and passionate speech against the measure, ending with the prophetic words, 'You can take our lives and our freedom, but you cannot take our honour. We are defenseless but not honourless.' But it was to no avail. It was the last time anyone spoke out against Hitler in the legislature. The Reichstag effectively signed its own death warrant and put an end to German democracy. The real distress of the people, however, was about to begin.

A flurry of measures followed but all with a single purpose ; to muzzle dissent. The policy was called *gleichschaltung*, the synthesis or harmonisation of all aspects of society to align with Nazi principles. In April 1933 a new state security service was set up to play a key role in enforcing the policy. It was called the *Geheime Staatspolizei* though it was better known by the short form, the Gestapo. By the summer of 1933 Martin Bormann and Rudolf Hess were appointed as leading officials in the Reich. With the Reichstag now effectively neutered, the two Nazi officials assumed unprecedented executive powers, and they generated unparalleled fear.

Regional autonomy, judicial independence, civil service neutrality and education were among the sectors brought under direct Nazi control. Free trade unions were another target. On 1 May 1933 Hitler addressed 100,000 workers at a traditional May Day rally. His speech dwelt on the important role of the German worker in the new state and dignity of the working class. The following day Trade Union offices were raided, their bank accounts seized, their leaders arrested and the right to strike and free collective bargaining abolished. Worker representation now depended on the Nazi regime and, overnight, many became vassals of the state. Trade unions were replaced by a Nazi workers' association called the DAF, headed by the eccentric, alcoholic Robert Ley: from now on the DAF would ensure that workers complied with Reich policies rather than represent the interests of labour within the economy.

Ernst Röhm and the Enemy Within

As Hitler's grip on power tightened, it was not the independent institutions outside the Nazi party that he now feared most but a group within it: the *Sturm Abteilung* (SA). Members of the SA, commonly known as the Brownshirts after the colour of their uniform, were a formidable fighting force in opposition. They had been formed in 1921 as a unit to both protect Nazi meetings and smash up those of opponents. In the rough and tumble world of Weimar politics the Nazis were not the only party to have such a group, but the SA were the most disciplined and the most violent. Now in government, tens of thousands more recruits had signed up to become Brownshirts and there were around three million men in their ranks. Towards the end of 1933, however, Hitler began to fret about the SA and, in particular, about the group's leader, Ernst Röhm.

Röhm had been a key personality on the German nationalist right and an immensely powerful figure in his own right. He was one of the earliest members of the NSDAP and it was his clandestine links to the army, funding and weapons that allowed the Nazi party to flourish. Like Hitler, he had been tried and imprisoned for the central role he had played in the *putsch* of November 1923. He had broken with Hitler in the mid-1920s and left Germany to work as a military adviser in Latin America, but returned to the Nazi fold at the end of the decade. The relationship between the two was so close that, almost uniquely in the party ranks, Röhm used the familiar '*du*' form of speech when addressing the Führer. Hitler, in turn, had good reason to be grateful: Röhm had his own extensive network of trusties and confidents on the far right which he used to further the Nazi cause. He was also a natural leader of the increasingly powerful SA and even the jealous Goebbels was forced to confide in his diary that 'Chief of Staff Röhm has accomplished the miracle of moulding lose, scattered groups into a tight-knit, tear-proof organisation.' But whilst Röhm accepted the Führer's leadership of the party, he was keen to maintain a degree of independence not available to any other Nazi leader. Even if not an equal, Röhm certainly did not consider himself to be just another acolyte.

Röhm also had his own thoughts about what the Nazi government should do now that it was in power ideas that diverged from those of Hitler. Röhm had been close to Gregor and Otto Strasser; the two brothers were Bavarians and veteran Nazi ideologues who placed a firmer emphasis on the left wing 'socialist' element of National Socialism. Disagreements between the anti-capitalist Strasser brothers and Hitler came to a head in the early 1930s. Otto was expelled from the party and fled the country. Gregor, who had studied pharmacology at the Ludwig Maximilian University in Munich, returned to his life as a chemist but would soon regret that he had not followed his brother.

Röhm's familiarity and independence of mind became an increasing source of concern to Hitler. Much more than that, however, was the SA muscle that Röhm might deploy in pursuit of these ideas. The hundreds of thousands of uniformed heavies of the SA had been essential in strong-arming the Nazis into power. But did the Führer still need the SA now that he had full control of the apparatus of the state? What Hitler sought was unquestioning loyalty and acknowledgment of his role as leader. With Röhm and the SA he could not be sure. Many SA paramilitaries were drawn from the unemployed and working class. Some were even ex-communists who had veered from one extreme to the other in the chaos of the 1920s. As Nazi strength rose, some activists switched sides and merged into the ranks of the SA until there were more communists than Nazis in the SA; or so the joke ran. Many in the SA, it was said, were brown on the outside, red on the inside, and their expectations of a direct reward from National Socialism were high.

A 'Second Revolution'

A clash between Hitler and Röhm was inevitable and went to the very essence of their different views about the nature of Nazism. When Hitler became chancellor in January 1933 he bargained that, with enough cunning, guile and ruthlessness, he could take absolute control of the German state. This required winning over the German elite and in particular the army chiefs. The Brownshirts wanted a 'second revolution' and continued to behave as though they were still in rowdy opposition. According to their view, the national socialist state could only be established once the traditional German elite was overthrown. A key element in the old order which needed to be toppled was the powerful *Reichswehr* (the army). The military high command were a prime target for Röhm, who argued that the 'grey cliffs [the colour of German army uniforms] must be swept away by the brown tide,' with the *Reichswehr* eventually subsumed into the SA. With three million men in SA uniform and the *Reichswehr* limited to just 100,000 by the Versailles treaty, army chiefs were alarmed and appalled by the prospect.

By the summer of 1934 the simmering tensions between Röhm and some other Nazi leaders about the direction of the government could no longer be concealed; when the new Nazi Interior Minister, Wilhelm

Frick, proposed a clampdown on unruly SA members, for example, Röhm threatened Frick with a public whipping. Meanwhile, those Nazis fearful of the SA fanned well-founded rumours of sexual promiscuity in the all-male ranks. The über-masculine SA was underpinned by a strong homoerotic culture personified by Röhm himself who flaunted his homosexuality.

The growing disagreements focused Hitler's mind on how he intended to wield power in the future. Voltaire once quipped that 'while most states have an army the Prussian army has a state,' and Hitler was determined to harness this dominant, north-German militarist culture. He decided that he needed the army and the German establishment more than he needed the SA and that the time had come to jettison his erstwhile comrades who had cleared his path to the chancellery. In the spring of 1934 Hitler met with the German military high command for clandestine talks aboard the battleship *Deutschland* and a secret deal was struck. The military chiefs agreed that Hitler could succeed the ailing President Hindenburg and so combine the powers of the chancellery and presidency as head of the Nazi state. For his part, Hitler agreed to bring Röhm and the SA to heel.

Tackling the powerful Röhm and his mass ranks of loyal followers would not be an easy task. Without careful planning, any move against the SA leadership might rapidly backfire: Hitler could find himself on the losing end of the fight and then ousted from power. To assist with the task of dismantling the SA, Hitler turned to Heinrich Himmler. Born in Munich in 1900, Himmler had studied agriculture at the University of Munich Technical College and had earned a living by chicken farming. He was a man of unprepossessing appearance; some thought he had the countenance of a provincial schoolteacher. Yet the blue-grey eyes which gazed out from behind rimless spectacles belonged to one of the most terrifying members of the Nazi entourage. A Nazi veteran who had played a prominent role in the *putsch* of 1923, he joined the newly formed Hitler bodyguard, the *Schutzstaffel* (SS). The black-uniformed SS were originally an elite sub-unit of just three men inside the SA, but as they became more important Himmler's standing in the party grew too. In 1930 Himmler was elected as a member of Reichstag and subsequently became the leader or *Reichsführer* of the SS. In 1931 Himmler hired a new twenty-seven-year-old assistant called Reinhard Heydrich who moved to Munich in the summer of that year. Heydrich was appointed head of the new security service, later called the *Sicherheitsdienst* (SD), which began to gather intelligence on other political parties and any opposition to Hitler within the Nazi movement.

Night of the Long Knives

In the early summer of 1934, under Himmler's watchful eye, Heydrich began to draw up lists of names in the strictest secrecy. Those identified were deemed to be not so much enemies of the people as 'enemies of the party'. The codename used by Heydrich was 'Operation *Kolibri*' – the German word for Hummingbird – and under this guise sealed instructions were sent out to SS units all over Germany. Those names on the lists were about to be liquidated.

At the end of June 1934 Ernst Röhm and several other SA chiefs checked in to the Hanslbauer Hotel in the spa town of Bad Wiessee, on the banks of Lake Tegernsee, just 50km south of Munich. The Building was recently demolished. The plans for demolition overcame varied arguments by some objectors who wanted to preserve the hotel as a historic monument. Warm weather and the surrounding Alps make the Tegernsee a popular destination for those looking for a short break from the city. On 28 June Hitler put a call through to the hotel. He told Röhm to gather all the SA leaders there as the Führer would be joining them in a couple of days to discuss various important topics. Röhm suspected nothing and even set about organising a banquet with a non-meat option for the vegetarian Hitler. But as the quiet waters of the lake lapped gently against the hotel jetty, the stage was set for a bloodbath.

In the early hours of Saturday, 30 June, the Führer's plane touched down at the Oberweissenfeld Airfield just outside Munich (the athletes' village for the 1972 Olympics now stands on the old airfield site). Several black Mercedes were waiting on the tarmac to collect Hitler and his party. As dawn broke, the cars sped on to the Hotel Hanslbauer where, at around 7am, the SA leaders were roused from their beds by the hammering on their doors. Röhm was startled to see Hitler at his bedroom door. He had expected to see the Führer later in the day but not now, not like this. Pistol in hand, Hitler told his erstwhile comrade that he was under arrest. Others were pulled out of their beds. Several SA men were, like Röhm, homosexual and some were in bed with each other. According to local Munich gossip, not all the SA leaders surrendered themselves easily. The Munich-based diarist Fritz Reck recorded, 'I understand that Hitler himself took on the job of killing some of his enemies in the course of his Apache-style raid on Bad Wiessee, and that one of his intended victims fought back. Bellowing with rage, brandishing his pistol, he chased his Führer downstairs to the basement, where Hitler finally found refuge behind an iron-sheathed door.'

It seems unlikely that deaths occurred in the hotel, but plenty of people were arrested. The convoy of cars then hurried back from the Hotel Hanslbauer with the detainees along the winding lakeside road towards Munich. With Röhm safely in custody, the SA was effectively powerless. It was now time to go for other opponents. From the party HQ, the Brown House in Briennerstrasse, Goebbels hit the phones, uttering the codeword 'Kolibri' to units around Germany: the 'Night of the Long Knives' was underway.

Across the country SS units swung into action in what became one of the most notorious purges in history. SA leaders arriving at Munich railway station for the 'important meeting' with the Führer were immediately arrested and discovered that they now had a new destination. Instead of making their way south to the Hanselbauer hotel, they were taken for a short ride across town to the Stadelheim Prison, where they were swiftly executed by a waiting firing squad (see also Chapter 6). Many others, who had no idea what was happening let alone why they were being held, were bewildered even at the point of execution. Those who asked why were met with silence or insults, which they found even harder to fathom.

The confusion of the victims was understandable, not least when the killing spread far beyond the ranks of the SA. People who had expressed doubts about the Nazis, or who knew too much, or who were simply the object of personal jealousies amongst the party leaders, were also on the death lists. The Strasser brothers, once prominent figures within the Nazi movement and who had quarreled with Hitler, were immediate targets, even though they had left the party. Otto Strasser fled and escaped by the skin of his teeth to Austria before the Gestapo barged into his house. Gregor Strasser was not so lucky. Arrested, he was shot through the bars of his cell, slithering about in his own blood while trying to avoid the hail of bullets. Some time later, Gregor's remains were handed to his widow in an urn bearing the number sixteen by way of identification. All that remained of another journalist victim were his bloodstained glasses which were returned to his widow without any further explanation (see Chapter 6).

General von Schleicher, Hitler's predecessor as chancellor, was at home when a gang of SS men appeared and barged their way into his study. When he confirmed his name they shot him dead. Then, when his wife Elizabeth ran into the room to find out what the commotion was about, they shot her dead too. Schleicher had attempted to thwart Hitler's rise to the chancellorship, a 'crime' that the Führer could not forgive. General von Bredow, a close friend and ally of von Schleicher, was also shot dead at his own front door as he arrived home.

Another of Hitler's predecessors in the chancellery, Franz von Papen, was also on the hit list. Von Papen was vice-chancellor and nominally Hitler's deputy in the coalition cabinet that was supposed to be governing the country. Mistakenly believing that there was still space for dissenting voices in Nazi Germany, von Papen had recently spoken out publicly against some aspects of the regime in an address to students and staff at Marburg University. He called for a return to old values and used terms like 'common weal' and 'solidarity' in ways which did not chime with the Nazi ideology. That von Papen survived the weekend was a minor miracle and largely because he was a personal friend of the decrepit President Hindenburg. Three of his advisers, who had helped with his Marburg speech, were not so lucky: all were murdered.

Amongst the prominent political victims was the seventy-two-year-old former conservative Bavarian leader, Gustav von Kahr. In 1923 Hitler had hijacked von Kahr's meeting at the Bürgerbräukeller in Munich to trigger a *putsch* (see Chapter 3). But the two had crossed swords at the subsequent trial and Hitler neither forgot nor forgave Kahr's 'treachery'. According to the gossip picked up by the diarist Fritz Reck, the old man was 'not shot; he was trampled to death by the SS in the courtyard of the Hotel Marienbad [in Munich]'. In fact, he may have been detained in his own apartment but he was certainly tortured while being transported to Dachau and his badly beaten body was found in a swamp by the camp a few days later (see Chapter 8).

Other victims of the purge included journalists, lawyers, leftist trade union officials, non-Nazi youth leaders; almost anyone in any position of authority or influence who had not fallen in behind the regime. Fortunately for Germany, one politician who survived – just – was the former Mayor of Cologne, Konrad Adenauer. A neighbour of von Schleicher's, the fifty-eight-year-old was doing some light gardening and heard the shots when the Gestapo appeared at his house. Detained and interrogated for two days, Adenauer managed to convince his captors that he was not 'nationally unreliable' and eventually released. But he took no further chances and, realizing that he was still in danger, went into hiding for a period of weeks. His fate was also Germany's. After the Second World War Adenauer became chancellor and successfully steered the country back to prosperity and respectability in the 1950s.

Others were eliminated, not because of what they had thought or said but simply because of what they knew. Knowledge could be a dangerous commodity in the new Germany, and their deaths apparently fell into the category of 'unfinished business'. One such example was that of Father Bernhard Stempfle, an anti-Semitic catholic priest and journalist who had assisted Hitler in writing *Mein Kampf*. But Stempfle was not just a Nazi fellow traveller; he had been a close confident of Hitler's and had helped cover up the scandal of the death of Hitler's niece, Geli Raubal (see Chapter 4). Perhaps it was his intimate knowledge of these events that led to his death. In any event, his bullet-riddled corpse, with neck broken, was found dumped in a Munich suburb. On the evening before her death, Raubal apparently had a tense dinner in a private room with Hitler the night before she died. The only people who witnessed any of the conversation were the head waiter and the owner of the tavern. They too were murdered during the weekend.

Amidst the widespread slaughter there were, inevitably, errors. Fritz Reck recorded, 'The case of Willi Schmidt, the music critic for a Munich newspaper, who was killed in the Putsch through oversight you might say, an unfortunate confusion of identity. It seems that the Nazis, looking for *their* Schmidt in the telephone book, killed a whole column of Schmidts before they got to the one they wanted. This is known as being "better safe than sorry".' The assassins had confused the unfortunate music connoisseur, Dr Wilhelm Eduard Schmidt, with a friend of the Strasser brothers. Schmidt's body was so badly beaten that, when the mistake was realised, it was returned to his distraught and perplexed widow in a sealed coffin. This was followed a few days later by an apology for the 'regrettable error'.

Ironically, one of the last to die was Ernst Röhm, who was detained in the Stadelheim prison. It seems that even Hitler vacillated before finally ordering the execution of his old comrade. Guards entered cell number 70, where Röhm was held, and left a loaded revolver to give him the honourable 'officer's option' of committing suicide. Röhm would have none of it and apparently insisted that 'if the Führer wants me dead let him do it himself.' In fact, it was the head of the Dachau concentration camp who returned to shoot Röhm at point-blank range. According to the gossip picked up by Fritz Reck, 'Röhm died bravely, as a soldier should, after registering a complaint about the quality of the coffee served in prison. The version disseminated by Goebbels and his underlings, that he hid under the bed, is one more lie … the kind of vicious, cowardly slander of a man no longer alive to answer it, in which they specialise.'

Back in Munich, Hitler sat in the Brown House taking calls from around the country and ticking names off his list. Exactly how many names he ticked off, or the original number of names on the roll, will never be known. Some estimates put the figure at around 1,000 victims in all, but the Nazis were keen to erase the precise record. On Monday, 2 July Himmler and Göring ordered the security services to destroy all documentary evidence relating to 'the action of the last two days'. After the carnage of the weekend, this was an order that no one would question and it was obeyed to the letter by terrified officials.

Even with much evidence destroyed, the Nazi regime was still left with plenty of explaining to do. As they had with the Reichstag fire, the Nazis claimed that a conspiracy was being hatched. On 3 July an official edict declared that the action of the previous seventy-two hours had been taken 'to thwart attempts at … high treason', and were 'essential for the national defence'. This time the Nazis claimed that Röhm had been on the point of organising a *putsch* with General von Schleicher to over-throw the state. The regime had been forced to act to ensure the internal security and well-being of the citizens; or so ran the official line.

Was there, as Hitler claimed, a plot? There was a singular lack of evidence and even at the time sceptics offered a more accurate insight into the bloody events. Many rightly concluded that Hitler wanted to eliminate the SA as part of a deal with the French and/or the *Wehrmacht* and that he had also taken the opportunity to settle some old scores and take out a gruesome insurance policy against future opposition. As historian Paul Maracin commented, 'In this one incredibly sanguinary swoop, Hitler eliminated all meaningful opposition within Germany … Who would now dare to stand in his way? The implacable Röhm had been effaced. In addition to the hundreds who perished in the purgation many dissidents were placed in concentration camps. Some were later released. Others were not. Hitler was now master of Germany, Commander in Chief of the Armed Forces. To defy him was to court death.'

At a cabinet meeting on Tuesday, 3 July the extra-judicial killings were rapidly legalised into 'executions'. Röhm himself was described as 'debauched' although his overt homosexuality was well-known to the Nazi leadership. It was, after all, Hitler himself who had gone to great lengths to stifle the rumours and scandal surrounding the SA, not least because of the questions that it raised about his own opaque private life. As the leftist British *New Statesman* magazine commented in a caustic editorial, Hitler had 'known for years the true character of the scum who had helped him to power.' And quite why Röhm should have chosen to launch an overthrow of the state from his holiday hotel miles from anywhere was a question never answered. At the same meeting the shaken von Papen offered his resignation from the vice-chancellorship. Only Hindenburg's refusal to accept kept him in office but he was now a marginalised, neutered figure. The *New Statesman* predicted that 'he may count himself lucky if he keeps his freedom in a decent obscurity.' Like von Papen, the families and friends of the deceased were cowed into silence by sheer terror and mourned their loved ones in private. Only a few spoke out. Fraü Schmidt was one. Grieving, angry, courageous and well-connected, she would not be silenced. She harried party officials relentlessly and scandal was raised in the highest echelons of the party. Himmler made clumsy threats while Hess tactlessly suggested that Schmidt be commemorated as a 'martyr to the cause'. Eventually the widow had no choice but to accept a rare public apology from the Nazi regime and a lifelong pension as recompense for her loss.

Goebbels managed to put most of the supine press on lockdown and there was little official media coverage. Nevertheless, a purge on this scale could scarcely go unnoticed, even in the new Germany. Some days after the massacre, Hermann Göring, who had played a pivotal role in the organisation of the butchery, was invited to dinner at the residence of the British ambassador, Sir Eric Phipps. Göring arrived late and apologised, with the excuse that he had been delayed after a day's hunting. 'For animals, I hope' replied Phipps icily.

It was clear that the purge had broken all rules of civilised behaviour and hit international headlines. Details were, of course, scant and fact-checking almost impossible but attempts were made, especially in the foreign press. The British *New Statesman* magazine, for example, ran a long editorial on 'Hitler's Purge'. Whereas the Nazi press trumpeted that it had been greeted with unprecedented enthusiasm, the *New Statesman* was sceptical, 'That,' it sniffed, 'must be regarded as – to put it mildly – a rhetorical exaggeration. The great majority of Germans had, and still have, but a hazy notion of the massacre at the weekend and what lay behind it. Their own press is rigorously censored and foreign papers which are more informative have been at a premium ... it is reported indeed as we write that their sale has been completely barred in Munich.'

The high command of the *Riechswehr* was naturally delighted. Hitler had removed his private army and the threat to their military pre-eminence was now passed. Having eliminated opposition on right and left, Hitler also had reason to be satisfied. He was now firmly in control of the Nazi movement, and the German army, so often a thorn in the side of civilian politicians in the past, was muted and compliant. Some commentators predicted that the chancellor would now be in hock to the military, but they were mistaken. The German Army, the Foreign Office and military intelligence did hatch conspiracies against Hitler in 1938, and again in 1939, but for various reasons these never got off the ground. Following the catastrophic defeat of the German Army at Stalingrad in 1943, the pressure on the high command became even more acute. It was evident that only they could possibly prevent Hitler from leading Germany into an abyss. Various high-ranking officers and Prussian aristocrats formed clandestine networks, the most famous of which spawned the Operation Valkyrie plot to blow up Hitler in 1944. But by then it was too late.

In the last days of the war, late in March 1945, Goebbels reflected in his diary that the Night of the Long Knives had been a historic mistake, but not for any humanitarian reasons. With the allied armies closing in on Berlin and the Reich literally collapsing all around them, Goebbels recorded a conversation with Hitler. Typically, they cast around for others to blame for the calamity and in this exchange settled on the German Army and Röhm. Goebbels now blamed defeat on bourgeois elements in the officer class who had failed to embrace the spirit of National Socialism and so give a vigorous lead. 'I point out to the Führer at length,' recorded Goebbels, 'that in 1934 we unfortunately failed to reform the *Wehrmacht* when we had an opportunity of doing so. What Röhm wanted was, of course, right in itself but in practice could not be carried through by a homosexual and an anarchist. Had Röhm been an upright and solid personality, in all probability some hundred generals rather than some hundred SA leaders would have been shot on 30 June.'

Shortly after Goebbels wrote this, he and Hitler committed suicide. Just weeks later, Himmler took his own life too. Heydrich, the other author of the Night of the Long Knives, was already dead, assassinated by Czech partisans in 1942. After the war, the West German government – now led by survivor Konrad Adanauer – tried to exercise justice on behalf of some of the hundreds of people killed in the purge. Amongst those brought to trial in Munich in 1957 was one of Hitler's closest henchmen, Sepp Dietrich, who had butchered various victims. Having only just been released from jail following a conviction for murdering captured US soldiers in Belgium, he was now put on trial again for the crimes he committed in 1934. Dietrich was found guilty of manslaughter and given another eighteen-month sentence. Unlike his victims, however, Dietrich then went on to enjoy almost a decade of liberty before he died of a heart attack in 1966.

Chapter Six

Sophie Scholl, Georg Elser and the Nazi Resisters

'One people, one Reich, one Führer' – a nation united behind Hitler – was the gist of Nazi propaganda repeated ad infinitum to Germany and to the rest of the world. But beneath the veneer the true picture was less clear. A substantial chunk of the German people supported the Nazis in the early 1930s and the party's message was carefully calibrated to appeal to certain groups suffering from the economic recession. Hitler offered hope to some but he never won over the majority of voters in free elections. Then, after 1933, there were no further ballots. Without elections, it was increasingly difficult to distinguish between genuine levels of support for the regime and the puffed-up images of Nazi propaganda. The use of brute force, however, was a constant and essential to Hitler's survival. An entirely new state apparatus was created to coerce critics and sustain the new regime. A network of informers reported back on the views of friends, neighbours and family. A new, parallel arm of the judiciary with sweeping powers called Peoples' Courts was created in 1934 to try 'political crimes'. And forces like the Gestapo and SD became watchwords for arbitrary authoritarian brutality.

Opponents ranged from Catholic conservative monarchists to radical leftist republicans, but this diversity and a lack of structure limited their effectiveness. In the words of historian Joachim Fest, 'German resistance to the Third Reich never existed in the sense of a unified group or movement sharing a common set of ideals. In fact, the term resistance, which was not coined until after the war, encompasses numerous groups that acted separately and often held differing views.' As a consequence, there was no serious, cohesive internal threat to the Hitler regime. But there were individuals who fought back with great courage and this chapter looks at some of those who defied the Nazi behemoth in Munich.

Georg Elser and the Thirteen Minutes

On 8 November 1939 a massive explosion rocked Munich's **Bürgerbräukeller** beer hall, shattering windows and bringing down a large section of the ceiling.[1] The Second World War had been underway since September but the flying glass and falling masonry were not the result of an RAF raid; those would not hit Munich for a good while yet. This blast was the result of a bomb planted inside the keller by a carpenter called Georg Elser. Single-handedly, this lone assassin had very nearly managed to kill Hitler and other senior Nazis. There were several plots to kill the Führer during the Third Reich but Elser's was one of the best planned, most meticulously executed and came closest to success; had Elser succeeded in killing Hitler in 1939 it must surely rank as one of the greatest 'what ifs' in history. (The Bürgerbäukeller was demolished in 1979 and a new building of the GEMA organisation now stands on the site. On the pavement at the entrance is a plaque which marks the exact spot where Georg Elser attempted to assassinate Hitler).

The Bürgerbräukeller was packed that evening with the *Alte Kampfer*, the old fighters or veteran Nazis who had participated in the *putsch* of 8 November 1923, which began in the same hall (see Chapter 2). They knew that it was a fixed event in the Nazi calendar which the Führer attended without fail. And so did Georg Elser, a thirty-six-year-old carpenter from the small town of Königsbronn, deep in the Swabian countryside to the north west of Munich. He lived in various places around Lake Konstanz but was something of a loner and always self-contained. The Nazis refused to believe that this unprepossessing, rather frail looking man could possibly have planned to blow up the Führer of his own volition. One Gestapo report marked him down as 'a talented craftsman but in his private life he was eccentric.' That at least was an assessment which many who knew him would have judged as fair. He was a convinced anti-Nazi and dabbled with the Communist Party, but his politics were also rooted in Protestantism. A church attender in his youth, Elser believed in a higher morality and the imperative to do good. What nobler a cause could there conceivably be than killing Hitler and the Nazi high command?

Elser visited the Bürgerbräukeller during 1938 to size up his task and prepare the explosion. Over the following months he observed, sketched and began to plan. As an expert carpenter and cabinet maker, Elser had the know-how and patience to complete his task. He made meticulous drawings of one of the beer hall's big internal support pillars, good to the nearest millimetre. In the spring of 1939 he took a job in a quarry, the perfect place from which to accumulate all the parts and materials that he needed to make his bomb. Security at the works was breathtakingly lax (the quarry owner was subsequently jailed for his negligence) and Elser was cautious; over time he acquired the components he needed and was careful not to leave any kind of trail or arouse suspicion.

In the summer of 1939 Elser took a job in Munich and began to assemble the pieces at a small workshop at **59 Türkenstrasse**.[2] In the evenings he regularly ate the cheap meals served up at the Bürgerbräukeller before returning to his room at **94 Türkenstrasse**, where he lodged with the Lehmann family.[3] But unlike many of the other drinker-diners, he did not always head for home at closing time. On more than thirty occasions Elser closeted himself away until the staff left and the building was locked for the night. Then, like one of the phantom nocturnal workers in a fairytale by the brothers Grimm, he began to set about his task. Dismantling the wooden panels, he hollowed out a space in the pillar large enough to accommodate an explosive device. And, of course, by morning the panels were back in place so that nobody noticed what he was doing. When the building was unlocked again at dawn the following day, he slipped out of a back door and merged quietly into the street with others making their way to work. No one ever looked twice at his workman's bag full of the masonry and plaster that he had just removed.

In the first week of September Elser installed his explosive device in the pillar and on the night of 4–5 November he attached the timer in a padded case to muffle the sound. When this was set he slid out again and walked to the Isarplatz where he drank coffee at a kiosk to celebrate his work. A couple of days later, ever meticulous about his work, Elser returned to check the timers were working properly. Once satisfied, he made his way to the town of Konstanz, about two hours south of Munich on the German-Swiss border. Elser had worked in the area and knew it well. He assumed the frontier between the two countries would be open and relatively easy to cross, as it had been on his last visit. But this was a costly error and now both his planning and his luck began to run out. The border was closed off. No doubt exhausted and euphoric in equal measure, Elser began to behave somewhat oddly, prowling along the border fence looking for a way through. When challenged, he could not offer any coherent explanation about why he wanted to cross to Switzerland and he was detained. At that point the border guards had no idea who Elser was or the enormity of what he had just done.

On 8 November the Führer arrived at the packed Burgerbräukeller to keep his date with the *putsch* veterans. Fuelled by plenty of beer and sausage, they were in high spirits ready to enjoy their annual fest with Hitler in their midst. Normally, Hitler would have entertained them with a speech lasting a couple of hours, but on this occasion he was preoccupied. The Second World War, just weeks old, was developing apace and crucial decisions about the invasion of France weighed on his mind. He needed to return to Berlin as soon as possible, but the weather was so poor that it was not deemed safe to travel by plane. The controller of railways promised to have Hitler back in the capital by the next day but only if he departed in good time from Munich. The Führer's private train would have to leave at 21.31pm. As a consequence, Hitler cut short his speech and hurriedly departed from the Bürgerbräukeller earlier than planned. Just thirteen minutes later Elser's bomb exploded, bringing down the roof of the hall around the speaker's rostrum. Eight people were killed. All the windows of the keller were blown out and a shaken Nazi chief, Julius Streicher, reported that 'tables and chairs have been reduced to thousands and thousands of splinters and right where my chair was is now an iron beam weighing hundreds of pounds.'

News of the explosion reached Hitler as he made his way to Berlin. The party stopped at Nuremberg where Goebbels wanted to send some messages via telegraph from the station. He returned to the train ashen faced. Hitler and his party were dumbfounded but when the shock wore off their mood turned to fury. Himmler ordered the creation of a 'Burgerbrau Special Commission', which was duly established at the Gestapo HQ, located in the former royal Wittelsbacher palace at the corner of Briennerstrasse and Turkenstrasse. The original building was destroyed by allied bombing and today the site is occupied by a bank called the *Bayerische Landesbank*, at **20 Briennerstrasse**. There is an information display about the old Palais and the **Gestapo HQ** on the ground floor.[4] Opposite is a small square which is called *Platz der Opfer des Nationalsozialismus* (square of the victims of National Socialism).

A sculpture in the centre of the square represents a prison cell with an eternal flame burning inside.[5]

The official investigation into the explosion was hampered by endless bickering as the different branches of state security quarreled amongst themselves and competed rather than cooperated to hunt down the Führer's would-be killer. Nevertheless, every square metre of rubble was trawled for clues. The investigators quickly established that the bomb had been placed in the wood panelling which encased one the load-bearing support pillars. The more vexing question was who had put it there? The mystery unravelled only slowly until the pieces led to the strange carpenter detained in Konstanz. And then the revenge was swift. On the morning of 13 November the Nazis swept into Elser's home town and rounded up anyone who had a connection with Georg eliminate his parents, siblings, and their neighbours. Up to a thousand people were detained to help the Gestapo with their enquiries, including the innkeeper of the Bürgerbräukeller who was held for three months.

The Nazis could not believe that Elser acted alone. They concluded that he must have been a puppet of British intelligence or even of Georg Strasser, the dissident Nazi exiled in Switzerland. Elser was subjected to long periods of interrogation by the Gestapo, interspersed with beatings which were so violent that even family members did not recognise him. Himmler in particular was personally humiliated. He had been granted almost unlimited control over security in the Nazi state, yet for all the phone-tapping, the spying, the informing and the surveillance a one-man operation had come within minutes of taking out an entire swathe of Nazi high command, including the Führer himself. Hitler's survival was due more to the weather than Himmler. Shamed, the Nazi security chief flew at Elser and one eyewitness (a Nazi official who subsequently joined the Bavarian resistance) recalled, 'Elser was bound up and Himmler was kicking him hard with this boots and cursing him wildly. Then he had a Gestapo man ... drag him into the washroom of the Gestapo chief and beat him ... so he cried out in pain.' And so he was taken back and forth. 'But Elser, who was groaning and bleeding profusely from his mouth and nose, made no confession; he would probably not have been physically able even if he had wanted to.'

A detailed record of the interrogation was kept by the Gestapo, but much of the transcript was destroyed in the war. One of the fragments

Schleissheimerstrasse 34, the address where Hitler lived when he first arrived in Munich. (*Photo: Greg Williams*)

The Hofbräuhaus, one of Munich's historic Beer Kellers and used by Hitler throughout his life in Munich. (*Photo: Wiki Creative Commons Licence/Kiban*)

The entrance to the school in Elizabethplatz, where Hitler spent some weeks training with the Bavarian Infantry in 1914 before leaving for the Western Front. (*Photo: Greg Williams*)

Buildings from the old barracks in Lothstrasse, where Hitler lived at the end of the First World War. (*Photo: Greg Williams*)

The Sterneckerbräu Beer Keller building. (*Photo: unknown*)

Thierschstrasse 41, where Hitler lived during the 1920s. (*Photo: unkown*)

The Löwenbräukeller Beer Hall. (*Photo: Greg Williams*)

The polished cobbles which mark 'Shirkers' Alley'. (*Photo: Greg Williams*)

The Shelling Salon in Shellingstrasse, much frequented by Nazi leaders. (*Photo: Greg Williams/ CC-BY-SA 3.0*)

An expectant crowd waiting at the Bürgerbraükeller for the start of a Nazi meeting. (*Photo: Bundesarchiv, Bild 146-1978-004-12A/Hoffmann, Heinrich/ CC-BY-SA 3.0*)

Nazi militia occupy the Marienplatz in central Munich during the failed *putsch*. (*Photo: Bundesarchiv Bild 119-1486 CC/3.0*)

The impact of the Second World War is still clearly visible on this wall at the bottom of Schellingstrasse. (*Photo: Greg Williams*)

The *putsch* trial: Ludendorf, Hitler and Röhm outside the court. (*Photo: Bundesarchiv, Bild 102-00344A / Heinrich Hoffmann/CC-BY-SA 3.0*)

One of the 'Temples of Honour' which stood in Arcisstrasse; today only the foundations remain. (*Photo: Bundesarchiv, Bild 183-S22310/CC-BY-SA 3.0*)

The main staircase of the Führerbau. (*Photo: Greg Williams*)

The annual Nazi parade to commemorate the *putsch* passing over the Lüdwigsbrüche bridge. (*Photo: Yad Vashem Photo Archive, Jerusalem*)

The collapsed roof of the Bürgerbräukeller. (*Photo: Bundesarchiv, Bild 183-E12329/ CC-BY-SA 3.0*)

(*Right*) The plaque for Elser, at the spot where he planted his bomb. (*Photo: Greg Williams*)

(*Below*) Bronze copies of the White Rose student leaflets set into the pavement outside the main entrance to the Ludwig Maximilian University. (*Photo: Greg Williams*)

The Atrium of the of the Ludwig Maximilian University. (*Photo: Greg Williams*)

Munich's Old Town Hall. (*Photo: Greg Williams*)

Munich's old Synagogue. (*Photo: Wiki license creative commons*)

The gates at Dachau. (*Photo: National Archives Records of the Office of War Information (OWI) 208-AA-206K-11, Public domain*)

Young and old survivors of Dachau cheer the arrival of US troops in April 1945. (*Photo: US National Archives and Records Administration, College Park and United States Holocaust Memorial Museum*)

An entrance to Berghof, Hitler's Mountain Retreat (in background, right). (*Photo: Bundesarchiv, Bild 183-1999-0412-502/CC-BY-SA 3.0*)

The Eagle's Nest. (*Photo: unknown*)

Court Room 600 at Nuremberg. (*Photo: David Mathieson*)

The Nuremberg parade grounds today. (*Photo: David Mathieson*)

Nazi defendants in the dock at Nuremberg. (*Photo: US National Archives and Records Administration, Public Domain*)

which survived showed that during his long interrogation Elser cited the 'dissatisfaction of the workers that I had observed since 1933' as a motive for his attack. 'In my opinion conditions for the workers have only got worse ... wages kept decreasing and deductions [tax and social insurance] kept increasing.' Elser also complained that by the late 1930s it was no longer possible to change jobs at will. As a natural itinerant, this was something that he had frequently done and was to him an essential freedom. 'I began to contemplate,' he continued, 'how one could improve the condition of the working class and avoid war.' As Elser's biographer, Helmut Haasis, notes, other workers also grumbled about their conditions under the Third Reich and Elser was 'not an isolated loner'. The Schwabian carpenter was a mouthpiece for disillusionment shared by others and unique only in his courageous act rather than in his thoughts (see below).

What happened next to Elser is something of a puzzle. Even when the Gestapo had finished with him, and extracted every last piece of useful information, he was not then tried or immediately executed. Instead, Elser was kept under close confinement, though apparently with unusual privileges for a prisoner of his singular category, and he survived until just before the end of the war. He was finally executed in Dachau, on Himmler's orders, in the spring of 1945. His survival for some six years after attempting to assassinate the Führer gave rise to a number of conspiracy theories. Some held that Elser had been working with the Nazis to demonstrate Hitler's divine providence in defying death, but no evidence has ever been produced to substantiate the claim. Others said that he was being kept alive for a show trial after the war had been won.

But there was neither victory nor trial and in death Elser's image drifted into a kind of shadowy obscurity, much as he had lived his life. Later in the war, in the summer of 1944, a group of brave army officers, led by the aristocratic Count von Stauffenberg, also attempted to blow up Hitler. Like Elser, they failed, but were better remembered. Without the panache or connections of the noble von Stauffenberg, the shabby working-class loner Georg Elser was largely overlooked for decades. When the Bürgerbräukeller was demolished at the end of the 1970s a small plaque was placed on the spot of the pillar where Elser planted his bomb. Finally, **a small *platz* was named in Elser's honour**, close to his former lodgings in Munich, and a stamp issued in 2003 to commemorate the 100th anniversary of his birth.[6] More recently still, his life has been the subject of two German films; neither, however, has had the success of Hollywood's *Operation Valkyrie* – which starred Tom Cruise – about the von Stauffenberg plot.

Sophie Scholl and the White Rose

On 9 May 1942 a lively, sassy young student arrived in Munich from the nearby city of Ulm. Although the war weighed heavily on everyone's mind, she was looking forward to taking up her place to study biology and philosophy at the Ludwig-Maximilian University in the centre of the city. The LMU, as it is commonly known, was – and still is – one of Europe's most prestigious academic institutions, and like so many others, this student was fulfilling a dream. Her name was Sophie Scholl and it was her twenty-first birthday. In less than a year, however, Sophie would be dead, killed not in uniform or as a civilian victim of aerial bombing, but because of her active resistance to the Nazi tyranny. Today, the main square of the university is named in honour of Sophie Scholl and her brother, Hans. Set into the pavement immediately in front of the main entrance to the LMU are bronze copies of the leaflets which led to their deaths, and inside the impressive entrance hall, the Atrium, is a **permanent exhibition** about the Scholl siblings and their group called the **White Rose**.[7]

Early in February 1943, just a few days after the defeat of Stalingrad, the Public Prosecutor filed a report about 'subversive activities' in Munich at the city's Supreme Court. It alleged that the previous night 'at least 20 places in the city of Munich' had been covered in graffiti with the words 'Freedom' and 'Down with Hitler', and swastikas had been crossed out using a metal stencil and coal tar paint. Most of the daubing was on the walls of the university and on advertising pillars in surrounding streets such as Ludwigstrasse, Amalienstrasse, Salvatorstrasse and Altheimer Eck. In addition, some 1,300 anti-Nazi leaflets were scattered around the local area. The report concluded icily 'The perpetrators are unknown'.

In fact, the perpetrators were a bunch of students and their identities were soon exposed. Sophie Scholl, along with her brother Hans, managed to distribute around 10,000 anti-Nazi leaflets before they were tracked down and executed. Together with other students Willi Graf, Alexander

Schmorell, Christoph Probst and Professor Kurt Huber, they were at the centre of an underground anti-Nazi resistance group which called itself the White Rose. Quite why they chose the name has never been fully established but it has entered into history as a watchword for resistance to totalitarian brutality.

There was little in the group's background or biographies to indicate that they would become rebels prepared to risk their lives in order to oppose the regime. Along with almost an entire generation they were subjected to the incessant blare of the Hitler cult and dragooned into the Third Reich. But the speeches, parades and banners gradually lost their appeal. Individually, each of the teenagers developed a scepticism about the propaganda which, for some, was being hardened by the direct experience of war. By happenchance, they found that their paths converged as students enrolled at university in Munich. It was the summer of 1942. The mood was beginning to change and even Goebbels' best efforts could not stifle an uneasy feeling that the war was not unfolding as promised.

The group formed – a glance, a knowing look, a critical word – over lunch or seminars until expressions of frustration crystalised into tentative proposals for action. Secrecy was paramount and the group remained limited to a handful of students and one LMU professor called **Kurt Huber**. One of the main squares of the university is today named in his honour.[8] By any conventional standard Huber was a wholly undistinguished and unremarkable member of the university body. Swiss born in 1893, he studied psychology and music; he was something of an authority on folk tunes and one of his many disagreements with Nazism was its absurd insistence that only the major scale should be used in music for the true Teutonic ear. His right leg was lame and he walked with a limp. He had difficulty controlling other limbs and his hands trembled incessantly. His classes were delivered with difficulty because of a speech impediment. Not surprisingly, in an esteemed institution like the LMU, his shambling figure was not marked out for any kind of promotion and, while his job was steady, he never rose beyond the rank of assistant professor. Curiously, in the light of subsequent events, Huber was actually a member of the NSDAP. Nazi affiliation was almost obligatory; around eighty per cent of the teaching profession were enrolled into the party and in Huber's case it was his wife who, apparently without telling him, signed him up so that he could enjoy the enhanced salary paid to Nazi members. Yet while Huber may have been formally enrolled into the ranks for the NSDAP, he was very definitely not a Nazi by conviction.

Huber's well-attended lectures contained oblique critical references to Nazi ideology and these signals were soon picked up by the students of the White Rose group. With extreme caution the students and their mentor circled each other, testing the bond of mutual confidence until Huber joined the group. Once in, Huber committed time and energy to working with the students. A full-throated, open opposition to Nazism was obviously out of the question and so the group began to produce leaflets which could be distributed clandestinely. It was Huber who wrote the final White Rose leaflet, which they were never able to circulate because, by then, the members of the group were all dead or in hiding. One copy, however, was smuggled to England, where thousands more copies were printed. These were returned to Germany by the RAF, which dropped them over German cities on their way home from bombing missions.

The Conspirators

Along with Sophie, the effective leader of the group was her brother, Hans Scholl. He was born just weeks before the end of the First World War, in Württemberg, southern Germany. In 1933 he joined the Hitler Youth movement and initially enjoyed the '*bündish* culture' of outdoor camps and hikes, but as he matured Hans became disenchanted with the Third Reich. It was the experience of war, however, which really turned Scholl against the Nazi regime. He enrolled as a medical student at LMU but was soon sent to support the invasion of France, an experience that opened his eyes to the true nature of warfare. Later, in 1942, Scholl was ordered to the eastern front and what he saw there only strengthened his resolve. The war crimes committed by German troops against the local population were swift and brutal. For Scholl they were the final straw and he was more determined than ever to subvert the Nazi war effort. He returned to Munich to live with his sister at **Franz-Joseph-Strasse 13**. The building is in the courtyard behind the block of apartments on the south side of the street and has a plaque on the wall which reads:

Sophie and Hans Scholl, who led active resistance against the Third Reich under the sign of the White Rose, lived here in the back building from June 1942 until their execution on 22 February 1943.[9]

From here, Scholl began to draft the first of four anti-Nazi leaflets. He wrote them with a fellow student, Alexander Schmorell, who was born during the febrile events of 1917, in Orenburg, Russia. His Russian mother died when he was an infant, whereupon his widowed German father, a doctor, took the family to live in an upmarket Munich suburb in 1921. The young Schmorell followed his father's footsteps and entered the faculty of medicine as a student in 1940, watching in horror as events unfolded around him. He was appalled by Nazi ideology and his hatred of the Hitler regime became even more pronounced when Germany invaded the homeland of his beloved Russian mother in 1941. Tall and athletic in appearance, Schmorell had the bearing of an officer and could have become one had he so wished. But his contempt for the Third Reich extended to the trappings of the *Wehrmacht*. It was said that he could hardly bear to wear his uniform and, whenever he had the chance, reverted to 'civvies' so that 'his style ran more to turtleneck sweaters and well-cut three-button coats that, along with his habitual pipe, gave him rather the look of a young English squire.' With others, he drafted a White Rose leaflet highlighting the murder of Jews.

Christoph Probst was a native Bavarian, born in November 1919, just a year after the end of the First World War. Although he completed his obligatory military service for the Third Reich, Probst was a committed Christian with a humanist outlook on life. His family was of the cultured, bourgeois middle class: Probst's father was a friend of Emile Nolde and Paul Klee, two of the artists later persecuted by the Nazis for their 'degenerate art' (see Chapter 4). In 1939 he enrolled as a medical student in Munich, married, and quickly became a father of three children. Both at home and college Probst had a full life and promising future, but when the Scholls were arrested, the Gestapo descended on his flat and discovered the draft of a White Rose leaflet with his handwriting on it. Now linked to the group, the incriminating evidence was more than enough to have him detained too.

Wili Graf was born to staunch Catholic parents in the Saarland of northern Germany in 1918. Like many Catholics, the Graf family was deeply suspicious of Nazism from the outset. The young Wili avoided

Nazi organisations like the Hitler Youth or any social contact with classmates sympathetic to the Nazis; he deleted friends from his address book who fell under their spell. In the early 1930s he joined a Catholic youth group which the Nazis eyed with great suspicion but were afraid to dismantle because it enjoyed the protection of the ecclesiastical hierarchy. Nevertheless, in January 1938 Graf was briefly imprisoned by the authorities for his involvement with the group and became even more alienated from the Third Reich and all it stood for. Cerebral, serious and aloof, Wili Graf was something of a loner.

White Rose leaflets began to appear during the summer of 1942. The group had secretly acquired an old, crude printing press which they set up in a studio at **Leopoldstrasse 38**.[10] It was a laborious process. All the leaflets had to be produced by hand and then surreptitiously scattered as flyers or sent anonymously through the post. The first leaflet laid out their complaints and aims: 'Nothing is so unworthy of a civilized nation as allowing itself to be "governed" without opposition by an irresponsible clique that has yielded to base instinct.' It described the 'shame' which many Germans were already feeling and predicted that worse was to come. When 'the most horrible of crimes – crimes that infinitely outdistance every human measure – reach the light of day,' the leaflet prophesied that the sense of collective guilt would be magnified many times over.

'What Does My Life Matter …?'

In January 1943 Scholl and her group were emboldened by a minor fracas that took place in Munich. The local Nazi *gauleiter* (local ruler), Paul Giesler, convened a large meeting of students in the main auditorium of the **Deutsche Museum** on Museum Island in the River Isar.[11] He intended to pump up the young people with more Nazi propaganda, but the event did not go as planned. After telling the students that they should pay heed to the 'light, joyful and life-affirming teachings' of Adolf Hitler, Giesler turned to the role of gender in the new order. Women, he said, would be better off as mothers than as students and for those 'not pretty enough to catch a man, I'd be happy to lend them one of my officers.' When female students responded to the comment with angry catcalls and heckling, Giesler ordered SS guards to detain them. Male students then stepped in to defend the women and the scuffles degenerated into a melee which spilled out into the surrounding streets.

Bolstered by student unrest, the White Rose stepped up their activities, printing and distributing more leaflets. But then they over-reached themselves. On 18 February 1943 Sophie and Hans Scholl arrived early at the LMU with a suitcase stuffed with new leaflets. They left some in the lecture theatres and scattered what remained over the balcony of the huge atrium. And that is when they were spotted. Jacob Schmid, a university superintendent and fervent Nazi, saw what they were doing and locked the doors. The Scholls were trapped. Worse still, they were carrying a handwritten draft of their next leaflet and within hours the orthography had betrayed Christoph Probst. All three were detained and interrogated at the Gestapo HQ in Briennerstrasse, where Georg Elser and so many others had been tortured. This was mentioned at the beginning of this section.[6]

Sophie Scholl, Hans Scholl and Christoph Probst were taken from the Gestapo HQ to the imposing **Justizpalast** in the centre of Munich and tried by the so-called People's Court on 22 February 1943. The hearing in court room 253 lasted less than half a day and all were found guilty of high treason,[12] a capital offence. The presiding judge, Rowland Freisler, a notorious Nazi jurist, summed up, telling the three that their amateur, hand-printed leaflets and daubings had 'sabotaged the war effort … propagated defeatist ideas … vulgarly defamed the Führer … and threatened the security of the nation.' On this account, Freisler stripped them of 'honour and rights as citizens … for all time,' and sentenced them to death. Sophie Scholl seemed insolently resigned to her fate and commented, 'What does my death matter, if through us thousands of people are awakened and stirred to action?'

The three were all taken to Munich's late-nineteenth-century **Stadelheim Prison** where they were guillotined later that day.[13] Tragically, the Scholls were far from exceptional in their fate. Between 1933 and 1945 some 40,000 people were sentenced to death by military and civilian courts in Germany. More than 1,000 were executed at the Stadelheim and today there is a memorial to the victims of National Socialism in the courtyard. Other core members of the White Rose tried to flee Munich but were quickly hunted down by the Gestapo. Less than a month later, on 19 April 1943, Alexander Schmorell, Wili Graf and

Kurt Huber were also put on trial, along with a handful of students who had helped the group. Schmorell, Graf and Huber were sentenced to death while the others were given stiff prison sentences. Many of the White Rose group are buried in the large **Perlacher Forst cemetery** next to the Stadelheim prison. The Scholls and Probst are at the south-east corner of block 73 while Schmorrell is at the south-east corner of block 76. Within the cemetery there is also a mass grave of over 4,000 Nazi victims. Ironically, Judge Freisler did not live much longer than members of the White Rose: he was killed by falling masonry during an air raid on Berlin in 1945.

'Cogi Non Potest Quisquis Mori Scit'

Exactly what impact the brave students of the White Rose had is hard to gauge now. Predictably, they were denounced by Nazi students. Some must have been further terrified into mute conformity by the fate of their now-vanished classmates. Others, like the clandestine diarist Fritz Reck, were inspired. Soon after the trial he went into Munich, 'once so gay and beautiful', but now reduced to much rubble after yet another air raid, where he heard about the martyrdom of the young Scholls. There was, of course, little coverage in the Nazi-controlled press, but people gossiped. 'I got only bits and pieces of the whole story,' he wrote, 'but the significance of what I heard was such I could hardly believe it. The Scholls are the first in Germany to have had the courage to witness for the truth. The movement they left at their deaths will go on, and as is always the case with martyrdom, they have sown seeds which will raise important fruit in time to come. This young brother and sister went boldly about their work, almost as though they were defying death ... [but] in lives well lived.'

Reck went on:

> Their bearing before the tribunal, of the girl especially, was inspiring. They flung their contempt of the court, the Party, and that insane, would-be great man, Hitler, into the faces of their judges, and at the end, did something which carries the icy breath of the Eternal about it for us who survive ... The Scholls departed from this life quietly and gravely and with wonderful

dignity gave their young blood. On their gravestones let these words be carved, and let this entire people, which has lived in deepest degradation these last ten years, blush when it reads them: "*Cogi non potest quisquis mori scit*" (he who knows how to die can never be enslaved). We will all of us, someday have to make a pilgrimage to their graves, and stand before them, ashamed.

Subsequently, Reck discovered a personal contact with the White Rose that he had not anticipated. 'I found my doctor, grieving over the death by the guillotine of his stepson, who wrote the leaflets distributed by the Scholls, and was beheaded with those two youthful martyrs: with great effort, he had managed to forestall the corpses being dismembered and put into bottles of Lysol in anatomy classes.'

The White Rose was effectively silenced but other small cells continued to function, chipping away at morale and providing a glimmer of hope for those who longed for an end to the Nazi regime. According to Reck, anonymous letters continued to arrive throughout the summer of 1943 and helped curtail enthusiasm for Nazism. Sent to local bureaucrats, from a 'revolutionary executive', the letters claimed that there would be a settling of scores whenever the war came to an end. By chance, Rech managed to get hold of a copy which told the recipient that they were being watched and that: 'You will henceforth remain under the most intensive observation. If there should occur a single further instance of activity on behalf of the present regime, or if any additional reports are confirmed of harm done to political opponents, the sentence of death which has been pronounced against you for future execution will be extended to include your entire family. Execution will be by hanging on the day of overthrow of the regime.'

According to Reck, the letters had some effect and some state functionaries began to modify their behavior with an uneasy feeling that the longevity of the Third Reich may well be limited. Those who sent the letters were, of course, operating clandestinely. Hundreds of Germans are, like the White Rose, now being commemorated and honoured for their acts of resistance, from helping Jews to escape to avoiding time in the Hitler Youth. But the names of many, many more will never be known and have taken the secrets of what they did to the grave.

The Church and Father Rupert Mayer

In the summer of 1937, the priest at **St Michael's church** in the centre of Munich limped laboriously up the stairs of the pulpit.[14] Father Rupert Mayer had been badly wounded in the First World War, an injury that crippled him with one leg shorter than the other, but the congregation was prepared to wait. The beautiful rococo chapel had been a favoured place of worship since the sixteenth century with commoners and kings alike – several Bavarian monarchs lay in eternal repose in the crypt – and the building seemed frozen in time. When he began to preach, many sitting in the pews knew what to expect because Father Mayer had become famous for his clever use of the Holy Scriptures to make outspoken criticisms of the Nazi regime.

The church was one of the very few German institutions to retain any degree of independence from the state, and so was able to coordinate a level of opposition to particular policies. But this challenge too was limited, and dangerous in practice. Support for the church itself was patchy – most industrial workers in cities like Munich were not churchgoers – and was split into different denominations. Some priests were attracted to the non-material aspects of Nazism and supported the party as a block on atheistic communism. Mistakenly, they believed that whatever else the Nazi state controlled, it would leave the sanctity of religion in peace. By the time they realised what was happening it was too late, and for their own safety, apart from anything else, many priests opted to render unto Hitler that which corresponded to Hitler.

Yet, amongst the clergy there were also hundreds of heroic exceptions, persecuted pastor-critics of the Nazi regime such as Dietrich Bonhoeffer and Martin Niemöller. It was Niemöller who penned the immortal lines: 'First they came for the Socialists, and I did not speak out – because I was not a Socialist. Then they came for the Trade Unionists, and I did not speak out – because I was not a Trade Unionist. Then they came for the Jews, and I did not speak out – because I was not a Jew. Then they came for me – and there was no one left to speak for me.' Niemöller and Bonhöffer were from northern Germany, but in Munich too there were courageous individuals who dared to raise their voice, and Rupert Mayer was one.

As it turned out, that summer of 1937 would be one of the last occasions on which Mayer was allowed to speak in public because his sermons were too much for the authorities. At the beginning of June 1937 he was arrested and tried in what is now room 248 of the Justiz Palast (see above). But Mayer was a difficult case for the Nazis to deal with: decorated with an Iron Cross for his bravery in the First World War, he was a known patriot and a popular figure among the Munich faithful. There then followed a game of cat-and-mouse as the Nazis attempted to silence Mayer without actually killing him, and so turning the turbulent priest into a martyr. He was interned in Sachsenhausen concentration camp but released when it was feared he might die there. He was subsequently banished to a rural monastery and allowed to live, on condition that he made no more public utterances. In 1945 he returned to the liberated Munich as a hero and died suddenly in St Michaels while celebrating mass in November that year. In death, the Catholic Church embraced Mayer and, following several posthumous honours, he was beatified in 1987. His tomb can be found in the Bürgersaal crypt – some 200m west from St Michael's church – where it has been visited by millions of pilgrims, including the Pope.

While Mayer was the most outspoken critic of the Nazi regime in Munich, he was not wholly alone. The Archbishop of Munich during the 1920s, 30s and 40s was Michael von Faulhaber who preached in the 'Münchner Dom' (Munich Cathedral). The twin-towered cathedral is a dominant feature of the city skyline and is also commonly known as the 'Frauenkirche'.[15] A political opponent of the Hitler regime, Faulhaber was obliged to tread a fine line. Theologically he questioned the compatibility of Nazi ideology with Christianity and spoke out against some Nazi policies saying, 'Love of one's own race does not justify hatred of another.' Publicly, however, he recognised the Nazi government as legitimate and demanded that his clergy remained loyal to the state. There is a memorial stone to von Faulhaber in the Munich Frauenkirche. Incidentally, it was here in 1951 that Faulhaber ordained a young priest called Joseph Ratzinger, who later became better known as Pope Benedict XVI.

There was also resistance to Hitler in Munich from the Protestant churches. The leading dissenter was Bishop Hans Meiser. Like a latter day Luther, the bishop Meiser led a campaign around Bavaria and was firmly in the sights of the authorities. Huge congregations turned out to support him, while also declaring their allegiance to the state. In October

1934 the authorities forced entry to St Matthew's church in Munich and arrested the Bishop. Then they demolished the building.

The Death of the Free Press – 'the Poison Kitchen' and Fritz Gerlich

Press freedom formed no part of the Nazi vocabulary and the party quickly eliminated any newspapers in Munich that were hostile to Hitler. The social democratic newspaper *Münchener Post* (Munich Post) had long been a thorn prepared to puncture the bubble of Nazi propaganda. The paper had a healthy record of publishing leaked documents and inside gossip about the Nazis, some of it fed by Hitler's opponents in the party. As a consequence, Hitler reserved a special ire for the journal. He alleged that the journalists there were permanently cooking up slanders about him and called their newsroom 'the poison kitchen'.

On taking power in January1933, Hitler took his revenge on those journalists who had used their freedom to torment him and the *Münchener Post* was high on the list marked for reprisals. With immense courage *The Post* continued to publish until March 1933 when it was shut down. As one local commentator put it, 'The order of the day became "*Gleichschaltung*", "realignment," or forced conformity, savage normalization. Goebbels and other Nazi propagandists made it their crusade to get the German body politic "adjusted" to the new reign of terror.' Just to be sure that the Post would be permanently out of circulation, a detachment of the SS was dispatched to the paper's editorial offices in **Altheimer Eck 13**.[16] They were 'on a mission to trash and pillage' the offices of the newspaper. One local recorded that the SS were sent to smash up the newsroom, 'Trash and pillage they did. I saw a faded newsprint photograph of the after-action damage to the *Munich Post* – desks and chairs smashed, papers strewn into a chaos of rubble, as if an explosion had gone off inside the building.'

One of the best known anti-Nazi journalists in Munich was Fritz Gerlich, former editor of the *Münicher Neueste Nachrichten*, which had its editorial offices in **Sendlinger Strasse 8**.[17] Gerlich started out as a fervent German nationalist but was so severely myopic – he was obliged to wear thick, steel-rimmed glasses – that he was judged unfit for military service in the First World War. In 1918 he joined the All German League, one of the many right-wing groups that sprang up at the end of the First World War. As a journalist, he met and interviewed Hitler several times in the early 1920s and was so impressed by the Nazi leader that a rapport developed between the two. But then the relationship soured. The scales fell from Gerlich's eyes after the Munich *Putsch* (see Chapter 3) and he began to expose Hitler as a dangerous, vicious agitator. In 1930 Gerlich became editor of a Catholic newspaper but did not let up in his campaign against the Nazis. Headlines calling for the arrest of Nazi leaders or describing their parliamentary group as 'sub-human' simply infuriated Hitler further. On 9 March 1933 the Nazis took their revenge. A squad of brown-shirted SA, led by Hitler's personal driver and his publisher, stormed into the paper's offices, screaming 'where is that bastard Gerlich?' Once found, they smashed him around the face several times before detaining him in **Himmler's police HQ in Ettstrasse 2**.[18] Gerlich was subsequently sent to Dachau, where he was murdered during the Night of the Long Knives, although details of his death are unknown. All that his widow received was a small box containing his blood-stained spectacles without any further explanation or comment (see Chapter 5). Gerlich is one of the central characters in the well-produced and informative TV biopic *Hitler the Rise of Evil*.

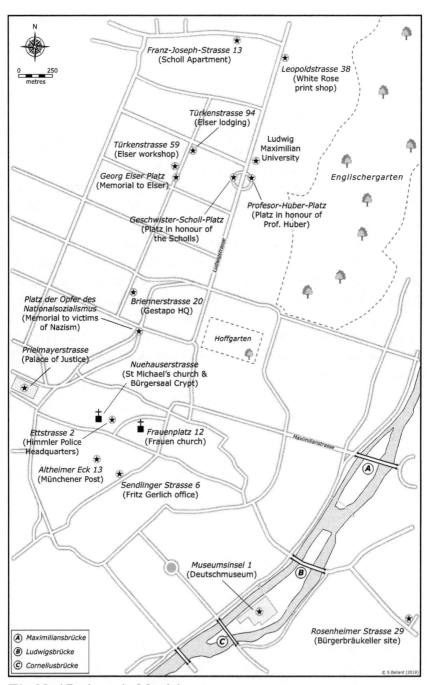

N

0   250
metres

Franz-Joseph-Strasse 13
(Scholl Apartment)

Leopoldstrasse 38
(White Rose
print shop)

Türkenstrasse 94
(Elser lodging)

Türkenstrasse 59
(Elser workshop)

Ludwig
Maximilian
University

Georg Elser Platz
(Memorial to Elser)

Englischergarten

Geschwister-Scholl-Platz
(Platz in honour of
the Scholls)

Profesor-Huber-Platz
(Platz in honour of
Prof. Huber)

Ludwigstrasse

Platz der Opfer des
Nationalsozialismus
(Memorial to victims
of Nazism)

Briennerstrasse 20
(Gestapo HQ)

Hoffgarten

Prielmayerstrasse
(Palace of Justice)

Nuehauserstrasse
(St Michael's church &
Bürgersaal Crypt)

Maximilianstrasse

Ettstrasse 2
(Himmler Police
Headquarters)

Frauenplatz 12
(Frauen church)

Altheimer Eck 13
(Münchener Post)

Sendlinger Strasse 6
(Fritz Gerlich office)

Museumsinsel 1
(Deutschmuseum)

A

B

Rosenheimer Strasse 29
(Bürgerbräukeller site)

C

Ⓐ Maximiliansbrücke
Ⓑ Ludwigsbrücke
Ⓒ Corneliusbrücke

© S.Ballard (2019)

The Nazi Resisters in Munich

Chapter Seven

Kristallnacht and the Persecution of the Jews

On 9 November 1938 senior Nazis gathered in the Gothic *Tanzaal* (ballroom) of **Munich's Old Town Hall**.[1] It was the fifteenth anniversary of the Beer Hall *putsch*, a sacred day in the Nazi calendar and that evening Hitler was due to give his customary speech to a commemorative dinner of party veterans, the *Alte Kampfer* (see Chapter 2). On this night, however, the Nazi high command was in a state of high dudgeon. A German diplomat had been assassinated in Paris, and his assailant was Jewish. Hitler abruptly cancelled his speech and went into a conclave with close confidents. Goebbels demanded 'an answer' to the assassination. 'Let the SA have a go, then,' replied Hitler. Goebbels then reappeared to address the assembled guests. The party, he told them, would not organise any reprisals for the killing of the diplomat but, he added he added ominously, should there be any 'spontaneous' acts of revenge the government would not seek to prevent them. In reality, the scope for 'spontaneous' political action of any kind beyond the control of government had long since disappeared in Nazi Germany. As international tension mounted and war loomed closer, the Nazi regime wanted to ensure the 'integrity' of the Reich. And that meant putting pressure on the Jews by whatever means to speed up their exodus (see Chapter 9). Goebbels words were the green light for what became known as *Kristallnacht* (Night of the Broken Glass). Within days, thousands of Jews were murdered or detained while their shops, homes and synagogues were torched in an orgy of destruction.

A Murder in Paris

Although *Kristallnacht* was given the go-ahead at the old town hall in Munich, the spark needed to ignite the carnage was triggered hundreds of miles away in Paris. In the summer of 1938 a diplomatic stand-off developed between Poland and Germany over the status of Jews who, although born in Germany, were from families of Polish origin. The Nazi regime in Berlin decreed that these Jews would no longer have an automatic right to remain in Germany, even if it was the land of their birth. The Polish government in Warsaw, however, responded that there would be no automatic right of return or residency in Poland. The group faced a precarious future with their rights of nationality and residency not recognised in either country: they were, in very real terms, about to become 'citizens of nowhere'. Hitler put an abrupt end to the wrangling by ordering the immediate expulsion of the 'Polish' Jews at the end of October. They were given just one night to prepare, and were allowed to leave with only the possessions that they could carry.

But forced exit from Germany did not mean automatic entry to Poland; on government instructions the Polish border guards refused to let them pass. And so for days, carrying only their miserable suitcases and without shelter from the cold or rain, thousands of forced migrants shuttled to and fro in the no-man's land either side of the border between Germany and Poland. Amongst the hapless, helpless crowd were Sendel and Riva Grynszpan, Polish Jews who had emigrated to, and been living in, Germany for more than a quarter of a century. Sendel and Riva had some of their family with them but their seventeen-year-old son, Herschel, had been sent to live with a relative in Paris where he was a student. On Thursday, 3 November Herschel received a desperate note from his family telling him of their plight and asking for money as they had none. What Herschel did next would have consequences which he cannot possibly have foreseen. On Monday, 7 November he purchased a gun, a box of bullets and made his way to the German embassy in Paris. He asked to see a diplomat, who he knew, called Ernst von Rath. Herschel shot von Rath five times at close quarters and two days later the young diplomat died from his wounds. Herschel stated that he was motivated by a desire to protest at the plight of the German Jews and avenge the treatment of his family. For the Nazi high command, von Rath's murder provided the perfect excuse to unleash a new round of torment on the country's Jews.

Anti-Semitism was a cornerstone of the Nazi ideology and the populist beer-hall rhetoric of the 1920s had already taken more concrete form in measures adopted from 1933. The objective of Nazi policy was to make life so arduous for the Jews that they would emigrate. But, understandably, the Jews of Munich, like others across Germany, resisted emigration. After all, where would they go? The prospect of being uprooted from their traditional community to start life with nothing in new and strange countries was clearly fraught with difficulties. Many Jews mistakenly hoped that Nazism was a temporary nightmare which they would best survive by keeping their heads down as far as possible and simply staying put much as their forbears had had to do in centuries past.

It was a calculation shaken to the core by *Kristallnacht*, which marked a step change from previous Nazi policy. The 10 November 1938 was the start of a spike in Nazi hostility to the Jews on German soil. Nothing quite like it had been seen since the medieval anti-Jewish pogroms that had plagued Europe centuries before, in another age and it was the most important pointer yet on the road that led to the Shoah, or Holocaust.

The 'Blood libel' and Other Myths

The persecution of Jews, which led to the horrific programme of slaughter carried out by the Nazis in the 1930s and 40s, had deep roots. The oldest reached back into the middle-ages and were religious in origin. Jews were held to be 'Christ killers' responsible for the betrayal and execution of Jesus. Elements of both the Roman Catholic and Lutheran churches concurred that Jews might pose a mortal danger and various anti-Semitic tropes were nurtured. The 'blood libel' alleged that some Jews consumed the blood of kidnapped Christian children while other Jews were portrayed as scheming usurers, intent on bleeding dry (in financial terms) honest Christian merchants. A casual, cultural anti-Semitism was incorporated with ease and present in the works of nineteenth-century artists, from Wagner to the fairytales of the Brothers Grimm. Some of this fantasy then morphed into conspiracy. Anti-Semite theories claimed that international Jewry was engaged in some sort of clandestine operation to upend Christian civilisation and so dominate a new global order at their most bizarre, conspiracy theorists claimed that corporate capitalism and Marxist communism were working in league with each other to ensure the triumph of the Jewish elite.

Tragically, these obnoxious fantasies were never confined to Germany or German-speaking peoples. Anti-Jewish pogroms were not invented by the Nazis; they had been seen across Europe for centuries, often as a more potent force in many places other than in Germany and anti-Semitism remains a malignant problem to this day. Jew hatred, however, did become an important thread in the narrative of the German nationalist *völkisch* movement and racial theory and anti-Semitic tropes became an essential part of Hitler's oratory. The old scapegoat could now be conveniently resurrected and blamed for Germany's woes after the First World War while also providing a shadowy foe against which the Nazis could define themselves. Not for the first or last time, populist politicians found it easier to blame 'foreigners' than address the root causes of national shortcomings.

The 'vicious form of an old tradition'

In the first few weeks of Nazi rule, discrimination against Jews ran at a relatively low level compared to the measures that followed. Nevertheless, warnings about where the Nazis' racism might lead were sounded with increased alarm. On 1 April 1933 – just two months after Hitler came to power – the Nazis organised the first boycott of Jewish shops and businesses. The threat to the half a million Jews living in Germany was ominous and quickly noticed across Europe. The *New Statesman* magazine in Britain, for example, warned, 'Anti-Semitism is no new thing in Germany. Massacres, burnings at the stake, desecration of synagogues and the violation of cemeteries, robberies and confiscations, compulsory herding in Ghettoes and the wearing of a badge of shame – these were for centuries characteristic of life for Jews in Germany as they were for other countries of East and central Europe … Hitler's anti-Semitism is therefore the continuation of a particularly vicious form of an old tradition.' Far from Jews mounting a conspiracy against Hitler, the magazine praised the international Jewish community for its self-restraint and commented that the Jews 'have with them in every civilized country a great body of opinion … It is the friends of Germany who feel most strongly the stain upon her honour.'

Exactly how much most Germans believed the Nazi propaganda has been intensively researched and some studies suggest that even many Nazi voters were only mildly anti-Semitic. It is almost certainly true that the vast majority of Germans did not spend their time obsessing over one per cent of the population. The important point, however, is that whatever their reservations, millions of people turned out to support a party that was viciously anti-Semitic. Perhaps they were not really listening. Perhaps they did not care. Either way, it was a reckless error that would have catastrophic consequences.

Young Albert and Munich's Jews

The Jewish presence in Munich was almost as old as the city itself and could trace its roots back to the thirteenth century. Medieval pogroms and expulsions had taken their toll but the community had been stable and integrated since the eighteenth century. The Jewish population was not large: according to the census of 1933 the Jewish community of Bavaria numbered some 42,000 people; just over half a per cent of the total population. The largest congregation of Jews – some 10,000 – were in Munich but again, in a city of 750 000, this represented a tiny fraction of the population. By any stretch of the imagination, the so-called 'Jewish Question' about which the Nazis were so fond of talking was an entirely abstract one for most people. Many Munichers or Bavarians would never have met a Jew in their lives. Others who did may never have realised it because many Jews merged seamlessly into the local community and were thoroughly integrated with their neighbours. One such family was the Einsteins, who arrived in Munich in 1880 to start an electrical business. Their young son, Albert, was enrolled at the local Catholic school. He was a diligent student who began to take an unusually sophisticated interest in mathematics and physics, though this was not always evident to his teachers. By his late-teens Albert was reflecting on relativity and in 1905 published his 'Special Theory', which revolutionised our understanding of time and space.

Because of this untroubled integration, many people responded slowly to the Nazi hatred. As the Bolsheviks in communist Russia complained about 'false consciousness' putting a break on the understanding of Marxism, so Nazis complained about workers failing to understand the need for racial purity. One local Gestapo report complained about 'the attitude of the peasants who lack any sort of racial consciousness'. When some boot-boys from the Hitler youth erected a 'Jews not wanted here' sign outside one Bavarian village, local peasants were alarmed; the buyers of their hops were frequently Jewish traders. By daybreak the following morning the sign had been mysteriously altered to read 'Jews very much wanted here'.

The Nazis tried desperately to raise consciousness in cities but their attempts similarly met with limited success. On one busy shopping Saturday in May 1935 the local Munich party bosses gave the green light for a rowdy anti-Jewish demonstration in the city centre. But when the violence spiraled out of control the event backfired. Disgruntled locals blamed not the Jews but Nazi hooligans for the disturbances and the local police chief was forced to publicly condemn the thugs in a humiliating climb-down. Housewives were another source of woe to the party in Munich. Even as late as 1936 women flocked to the annual sales to snap up discounts being offered by a Jewish department store in the city. In response, local Nazi bigwigs grumbled that the women 'had still not understood, or wanted to understand, the lines laid down by the Führer for solving the Jewish Question.'

Nevertheless, the storm clouds were gathering. In the autumn of 1938 war was averted – just – when Britain and France backed away from open conflict and decided not to defend Czechoslovakia (see Chapter 9). Nazi self-confidence soared in the wake of the capitulation but conflict seemed inevitable. As part of the preparation for war, Hitler was determined to drive all remaining Jews out of Germany. As the international situation deteriorated in 1938 the fate of the remaining German Jews became ever more perilous. By then more than 100,000 Jews had left Germany since the Nazis came to power, but some 370,000 more remained. In Munich the number of Jews still numbered just under 9,000, but only because those who had emigrated had been replaced by others who fled the vulnerable isolation of the countryside to what they hoped would be a more secure community in the city.

The Nazi state then stepped up the boycotts and the systematic discrimination against Jews began to bite. Jews with German names were forced to take additional names; Israel for men and Sara for women. Their passports were stamped with a prominent 'J'. Normal life was made impossible under these precarious conditions. According to some figures, there were nearly 1,700 Jewish-owned businesses in Munich at the start of 1938. By October there were just over 650. In June of 1938 the main Munich synagogue, one of the largest in Germany, which had stood in Herzog-Maxstrasse for more than half a century, was bulldozed to the ground. The local Jewish community was given two weeks' notice that the site needed to be cleared for a car park. The imposing tower of the building was an established local landmark but one which the Nazis were not prepared to tolerate. There is now a small memorial plaque where the synagogue once stood.[2]

Towards the end of the 1930s the Jewish population in Bavaria shrank by around half and in Munich there were just a few thousand Jews left living in the city. Nazi pressure on the community increased yet further as the regime sought to drive the remaining Jews out of Germany altogether. All they needed was a pretext. And that was provided by the assassination in Paris of the German diplomat in November 1938.

Kristallnacht in Munich

At 1.20am on 10 November, Heydrich, Chief of the SA security service, sent out a telex message – 'Subject: Demonstrations Against Jews Tonight' – from Munich to all units around the country. He warned them that, because of the von Rath murder, 'Demonstrations against Jews are to be expected in the entire Reich in the course of this night.' His instructions continued, '[these] are not to be prevented, merely supervised,' unless German lives or property were in danger. As a consequence, an entire section of the German population was exposed to extreme violence. Heydrich, a principal author of the subsequent Holocaust, initially lived in two rooms in the centre of Munich, at Türkenstrasse 23. In 1932 he and his wife moved to more spacious accommodation at Zuccalistrasse 4, near Nymphenburg palace, away from the city centre.

The first disturbances in Munich were reported just before midnight when the fire brigade noted a blaze at Augustenstrasse 113. By daybreak forty-two Jewish owned businesses had been attacked and some destroyed. The most notable was Uhlfelder, one of the city's biggest department stores. The shop was something of a local landmark. It had been in business for more than half a century, employed nearly 1,000 well-paid local workers and boasted exciting innovations like the escalator – one of the few in Munich at the time – that ran between the three floors of the store. Yet on 9 November 1938 Uhlfelder was ransacked by SA troops who pillaged much of the merchandise before torching the building. Whatever stock had not been looted was subsequently sold off at knock-down prices, the company wound up and the site given to the Löwenbräu beer company. The Jewish owner, Max Uhlfelder, and his son were rounded up with around 1,000 other Munich Jews and sent to Dachau. To add insult to injury, they were presented with the bill for clearing up the damage to their shop. Then, after agreeing to forfeit just about all their assets, the Uhlfelders were released in 1939 and eventually found sanctuary and a new life in the USA. After the war, Max Uhlfelder returned to Munich and attempted to rebuild his business, but it proved impossible. He eventually sold the land to Munich City Council and today it is the site of the **Munichner Stadtmuseum**, the city museum.[2] Fittingly, there is a permanent exhibition about National Socialism in Munich in the museum.

Equally appropriately, on the opposite site of the square is Munich's new synagogue, Jewish cultural centre and the **Jüdisches Museum München**. The museum tells of the history of the community in the city over the past 200 years.[3] In total, some 30,000 Jewish men were arrested and held in concentration camps such as Dachau (see chapter 7). Like the Uhlfelders, their release was conditional on leaving Germany but they could not expect to take any possessions of value or their wealth with them. And the Nazi regime, which had already stripped Jews of citizenship under the Nuremberg laws of 1936, now began to pile yet more pressure on those Jews who remained in Germany.

After the wanton destruction of Jewish life and property on 10 November, Hermann Göring issued a new edict, 'The Order Eliminating Jews from German Economic Life' just two days later. The object was to codify the systemic discrimination against the Jews. Henceforth, Jews who were managers or held executive positions in firms would be sacked without compensation. Jews would be excluded from public spaces such as theatres, cinemas, other places of entertainment, parks and, more seriously, state schools and universities. Even street benches became a means of distinguishing Jews and discriminating against them; they were forbidden from using ordinary seats and allowed to rest only on special benches painted yellow. Far worse than the indignities suffered by those still trying to go about their daily business was the fate of the thousands of Jews who now languished in concentration camps. The family members of those being held rushed frantically from office to office trying to obtain travel documents and visas without which the detained would not be released. It was a race against time: there were reports that some of the interned had been already been executed.

Jewish-owned businesses in Munich were sold off by a form of compulsory sale order to 'Aryan' buyers, often at far less than the market price. In 1941 Jews were evicted from their apartments and houses, which were then put on the market. It was little wonder that the Gestapo were ordered to target 'wealthy Jews' when making arrests. The Nazi state – and more than a few corrupt officials – scooped up a small fortune from the expropriation of Jewish assets. These belongings were confiscated by the state through the Office of Aryanisation, which operated from the building at Widenmayerstrasse 27. Chillingly, the building had been owned by a Jewish proprietor before he was summarily forced out of his property.

In addition to stripping individual wealth, the Nazi regime imposed a colossal collective fine on the Jewish community. A 'Decree for the Restitution of the Streets' was issued. Jews were now forced to pay for the cost of cleaning up after *Kristallnacht* because, according to the official version, it was Jewish 'provocation' that had triggered the events in the first place. 'It's insane to clean out and burn a Jewish warehouse and then have a German insurance company make good the loss,' complained Hermann Göring. And in future, demanded Göring, there must be no more wasteful damage to Jewish property. The time had come, he said, to rid Germany 'one way or another' of the Jews themselves.

'Sophisticated Devilry'

Outside Germany, much of the international community expressed outrage at the terror of *Kristallnacht*. President Roosevelt withdrew the US ambassador and the Nazi regime was condemned around the world. The editorial of the *New Statesman* magazine summed up the revulsion felt by many, 'The arguments of tyranny are as contemptible as its force is dreadful,' it said, quoting the eighteenth-century philosopher, Edmund Burke, 'it is long since that the record of any great nation has been stained by a crime on so vast a scale, and carried out with such a mixture of brutality and ingenuity, as the latest persecution of the Jews in Germany.' The magazine was careful to distinguish between the government of Germany and 'the great mass of the German public [which is] ... according to reports from all quarters, aghast at the savagery which has been let loose.' Goebbels' image of an uncontrollable mob was condemned for what it was; a flat lie. The editorial concluded that 'to call the behaviour of the Nazi Government barbarism is a misnomer; it is sophisticated devilry.'

The Nazi high command anticipated that *Kristallnacht* would galvanise the German population and clear the country of Jews in preparation for war. Whether the purpose was achieved, however, is far from clear. On 11 November leading Nazis spoke to meetings around the country in a concerted campaign to explain the pogrom. In a grotesque manipulation of reality, they justified the violence as 'retaliation' against a hostile Jewish community. The hoary myth of an 'international Jewish conspiracy' was raised time and again and the lone-wolf killing of a German diplomat was presented as the first shot in an existential struggle for survival.

In fact, insofar as they could find out about the full extent of the violence, many ordinary people were shaken by the pogrom. The Nazis' own intelligence reports suggested that there was a particular revulsion in the Catholic south of the country and among those who held to a Christian tradition of loving thy neighbour. While many people had a somewhat distant relationship with Jewish neighbours, the various communities had existed side by side for decades. And whatever suspicions some may have had, this did not extend to wanting to see Jews and their families burned out of their homes and left, literally, with nothing.

One local observer in Munich saw that few people swallowed Goebbels' lie that *Kristallnacht* was the result of 'spontaneous' reaction to the murder of a diplomat or that it had nothing to do with the Nazi party. The mass detention of tens of thousands of Jews which followed was a massive logistical undertaking and few believed that it would have been possible without prior notice and planning. Munich's 'Special Court', established to deal with matters of political dissent, was, he said, flooded with cases in the aftermath of *Kristallnacht*. For example, a cobbler was denounced by SA men for saying out loud that the orgy was nothing more than robbery of Jews by Hitler. A man in a bar who, perhaps after one too many, let rip his opinion that the burning of synagogues was wrong and that all men are equal, was charged with a criminal offence. And a middle-class woman who wrote to a friend in Canada about the 'cultural disgrace' of the *Kristallnacht* had her letter intercepted and was hauled before the court.

One Munich Jew recalled that a number of friends and acquaintances expressed to him their abhorrence at the events of *Kristallnacht*. Everywhere – overtly or covertly, explicitly or implicitly – many people sought to distance themselves from the violence. A few brave souls attempted to defend their neighbours even while the pogrom was in full swing. It was assumed that there would be further attacks on Jewish property the following night (11 November) and so, recorded one local Jew, 'Aryan people, unknown to me, offered to accommodate my family for the night ... Christians behaved impeccably.' In the aftermath many showed practical concern for those who suffered losses and came to their aid; the man wrote that 'the mood of the Christian population in Munich is wholly against the action. I encountered the most expressive sympathy and compassion from all sides.'

Yet not all were so lucky. Ten days after the terrible events of *Kristallnacht,* the *New Statesman* reported to its British readers that even among those Jews who had their freedom, 'Many are in an appalling state of distress, some still wandering in the woods, others hiding with friends or trying to buy or beg food or drink which shops were forbidden to sell them.' Other individual horror stories were recorded by the Munich diarist, Fritz Reck. One woman, forced out of her home, was driven from one refuge to the next. 'Finally, deathly tired, and beyond wanting to live any more, she simply walked up into the mountains on one of the first freezing nights of this autumn. After days of searching, we finally found her: she was dead.'

In another incident, Reck recorded how an actor, well connected with the Nazis, coveted an apartment owned by an old Jewish woman on the swish Maximilianstrasse. When he insisted on taking the property, the old woman knew that she had no hope of remaining in her home. A friend helped her to obtain some potassium cyanide so that the old lady could commit suicide. 'With her tearful thanks for the poison,' the old lady 'had still one more request: would the friend sing Brahms *Ernste Gesringe* [*sic*] before they parted? The friend, who is a singer, complied.' And so the old lady died with the music in her ears and the impatient actor fretting at the front door. 'I have now lived more than fifty years, have been forced to descend into certain dark places and I have emerged with one piece of wisdom,' reflected Reck. 'No harm that I have ever done has not caused me pain later on, even if it took decades ... I wonder: is there now and then in the cocktails which [the actor] enjoys in his apartment acquired in this way the taste of potassium cyanide ... and through the march music resounding out of his radio, does he not perhaps, at times, hear something like the *Ernste Gesringe* [*sic*]?'

Refugees, 'Forest and Savannah'

While criticism within Germany was muted by fear, the Nazis were stung by the lash of international criticism. Goebbels unleashed a war of words in response. Nazi propaganda insisted that the German policy was merely confined to excluding Jews from public life. This was contrasted with the oppression of British imperialism, which was described as 'inhuman' and a 'bloody terror'. Some of the Nazi press claimed that British politicians such as Winston Churchill and Clement Attlee were behind the von Rath murder in an attempt to whip up tensions in Germany.

Questions were raised in the House of Commons. Labour MPs demanded to know what response the government would make to such Nazi hostility. The answer, effectively, was none. Despite well-intentioned condemnations and hand-wringing, critical questions remained. What would the international community do in the face of Nazi barbarity and which countries would step forward to offer the German Jews safe haven from their oppressors? A conference was organised in the French spa-town of Evian in the summer of 1938. Thirty-two countries and a handful of voluntary organisations met to discuss the issue, but the conclusions were not encouraging and the practical solutions few. Hitler would support any international scheme to remove German Jews; or so he claimed. But where could the Jews of Munich and elsewhere go?

In the aftermath of *Kristallnacht*, an answer to that question was now extremely urgent and the MP Daniel Lipson took up the challenge (ironically, Lipson sat as an Independent Conservative following an

anti-Semitic smear campaign within his official Tory constituency party).
On 21 November Lipson pressed the prime minister to say what progress
had been made to help German Jewish refugees following the Evian
meeting. Chamberlain's reply would have been familiar to modern ears.
Since 1933 the UK had taken just 11,000 men, women and children from
Germany. A key point of contention was who should pay for the refugees.
'The extent to which countries can be expected to receive emigrants,'
Chamberlain said, 'must depend very largely upon the conditions in
which they are able to leave their country of origin.' In other words,
German Jews could only expect help if they were able to pay their own
way – an impossibility given that they were now being systematically
asset stripped by the Nazi regime. And with high unemployment, the
government would not welcome large numbers of immigrants arriving
to swell the labour market. But while the British government was coldly
indifferent, other countries were positively hostile to the plight of the
refugees. When asked how many Jews it would accept, the Canadian
prime minister, Mackenzie King, famously replied that 'one would be
too many'.

Despite its sprawling Empire, Prime Minister Chamberlain could
see no space for German Jews anywhere on British imperial soil because,
he said, 'there is no territory ... where suitable land is available for
the immediate settlement of refugees in large numbers,' although he
conceded that in 'certain territories small-scale settlement might be
practicable. The Governors of Tanganyika and British Guiana have ...
been asked to state whether, without detriment to native interests, land
could be made available.' He insisted, however, that even in this case,
voluntary organisations would have to 'undertake full responsibility for
the cost of preparing the land and of settling refugees.' British Guiana,
he confessed, was 'sparsely occupied land, consisting mainly of forest
and savannah.' Quite what members of a cultivated, urban Jewish
community from cities like Munich were supposed to do (if they ever
got there) without immense support from outside was a question which
went unresolved. Finally, the prime minister dismissed Palestine as a
destination because 'that small country could not in any case provide a
solution of the Jewish refugee problem.' The *New Statesman* magazine
concluded that Britain and the USA offered the best hope and that action
was needed swiftly because 'in the present temper of the Nazis, delay may

mean an even more horrible fate for their victims.' Tragically, little action followed these prophetic words.

With the advent of war, the Jewish Question was of even less concern to most people in Germany. The preoccupation was with personal survival and that of loved ones or what one historian has called the 'retreat into personal sphere'. For many people, any daily personal contact with Jews had been minimal even before 1933. As we have seen, the Jewish population of Munich and the surrounding area was tiny. Following their marginalisation and then disappearance from the city, concern for the welfare of Jews seems to have faded in the fog of war. There was a weary resignation, shrugs and sighs as the trauma of *Kristallnacht* faded from popular consciousness. Perhaps for many (not Jews, of course,) it was enough that something which should never have happened was not repeated, at least not in the streets they walked or outside the homes in which they dwelt. Insofar as Munichers asked any questions at all, the flimsy evidence suggests many people had little difficulty in forgetting who Jews were, let alone what the Jewish Question was. For the remaining Jews, however, it was a very different story.

From Munich to Auschwitz

When the Nazis took power in 1933, Munich's Jewish community numbered some 10,000. By the time American troops arrived to liberate the city at the end of April 1945, the number who remained could be counted on the fingers of two hands. It was a fate which none could have contemplated on the morning of 10 November 1938. But appalling as *Kristallnacht* was, life for Munich's Jews became even worse thereafter.

From April 1939 it was forbidden for Jews and non-Jews to live in the same apartment blocks. In the following months some 900 Jewish-owned homes were confiscated in Munich and the inhabitants moved forcibly into 'Jew Houses' ghettoes. The Jewish houses were handed over to 'deserving party comrades', functionaries and hangers-on, while the city's remaining 4,000 Jews themselves were herded into cramped quarters. In the spring of 1941, gangs of forced Jewish labour completed the building of barracks-style accommodation on a 15,000m² site in the north of the city at Milbertshofen. The conditions were cramped and squalid. Nearly 1,400 people were squeezed into buildings that had only been designed for 1,100. No longer allowed to pursue their previous occupations, the Jews were assigned humiliating tasks or sent on 'work parties'.

In the summer of 1941 a whole new raft of measures was implemented to make Jewish life even more intolerable. Access to phones or the press was prohibited. The food they could eat became even more limited as they were banned from public markets, and milk, meat and fish were struck off their ration cards. And from now on they would be forced to identify themselves by wearing a yellow star on their clothing.

With the onset of winter 1941, hundreds of the Munich Jews were herded onto trains – 'evacuated' according to the Nazi euphemism – waiting in the freight yard at Milbertshofen. From there they were transported to extermination camps, such as Auschwitz and Theresienstadt in the north east. By the summer of 1942 there was hardly anyone left and the Milbertshofen camp was eventually abandoned. By the end of summer 1943 almost all remaining Bavarian Jews were swept up in the Holocaust of European Jewry: dead, murdered by the Nazi terror groups (the *Einsatzkommandos*) or in extermination camps. By mid-1944 there were less than fifteen thousand Jews left in the whole of Germany and the fate of the victims was sealed by the Holocaust.

After the war the Milbertshofen camp was pressed into action again. Ironically, the devastation of the war led to a labour shortage in Germany which could only be remedied with immigrant workers. Italian immigrants who came from the other side of the Alps to work at the BMW car plant were housed in the camp at Milbertshofen. Today, the area is best known as the site of the massive sports complex which was built to house the 1972 Olympic games. The fate of some individuals who passed through the camp is being marked by what are called *stolpersteine* or stumble-stones. These are small brass-coloured cobbles set into the pavement outside the former house or workplace of a victim of the Nazi regime. They record the name, date of birth, and fate of the victim.

The pogrom did not, as the Nazis hoped, result in a raised 'racial consciousness' or acceptance of a new approach to the 'Jewish Question'. But nor did the popular disgust at the excesses in the immediate aftermath of the brutality gain sustained traction. Critical questions have been asked since the Second World War of ordinary Germans: how much did they know? How much ought they to have known? To an extent seldom faced by any other generation, they have been put in the dock of history. But the evidence of wholesale guilt or complicity is inconclusive and the controversy continues. The Nazis raised the 'Jewish Question' in their propaganda but were never confident enough to brag about their 'Final Solution', the Holocaust. The Nazi high command was never explicit about the extermination programme. They never judged that public support was either wide enough or deep enough, despite years of anti-Jewish propaganda. Yet it remains impossible to believe that an entire community could have simply disappeared from Munich without those that remained drawing the obvious, logical and bitter conclusion about what was happening.

Today, there are some 10,000 Jews living, working and contributing once again to the city of Munich. But this community is new. Any historic or family link with the community of old was shattered by the Holocaust.

Chapter Eight

Through Dachau to National Socialism and the Third Reich

'Arbeit Macht Frei' were, perhaps, the three most chilling words in the German language during the period of the Third Reich. The phrase meaning 'Work Sets You Free' was the slogan over the main gates of the Nazi concentration camps, the centres of terror and degradation which now have a special place in history. The first of them was located in **Dachau**, on the outskirts of Munich.[1] The camp was an essential cog in the Nazi machine and used from the first days of the Third Reich to isolate and silence opposition to Hitler. People from almost every community in Germany and every walk of life had members detained in concentration camps. Dachau subsequently spawned a vast network of camps, but as the first of its kind, generated a special fear neatly summed up by a ditty of the time:

> *Lieber Herr Gott mach mich stumm*
> *Dass ich nicht nach Dachau komm*
> (Dear God keep me dumb
> So I don't end up in Dachau)

Dachau was opened within weeks of the Nazis coming to power and was first used to incarcerate Hitler's political opponents. Homosexuals, the disabled, gypsies, Jews, common criminals and others soon followed and Dachau became a model for other concentration camps across the country. The route that many victims tramped from the local railway station to the Dachau camp is now clearly marked by the town authorities and is called the **'Path of Remembrance'**.[2] On the site itself some of the camp's remaining buildings now house an excellent information centre. Today, Dachau's gates are wide open and a visit is essential for those who seek a deeper understanding of the integral role played by concentration camps in the horrors of the Third Reich.[3] As one Nazi deputy in the Reichstag wrote, 'Through Dachau, to National Socialism and the Third Reich!'

1933: The Organisation of Terror

Hitler's appointment as chancellor of Germany on 30 January 1933 was the result of a political fudge. He was head of a coalition government apparently dominated by right-wing conservatives who were happy to support the new chancellor if he could curb the rising threat from the communists and the left. It was a fatal misjudgment. The rapidity and brutality with which Hitler lashed out to suppress all opposition caught his partners by surprise. Far from being able to control Hitler, they were unable to recover from the shock, let alone restrain him. Less than a month after Hitler took office, the German parliament building was torched by an arsonist and gutted by fire (see Chapter 5). The Nazis claimed that the blaze was part of a plot to overthrow the government and passed an emergency law allowing detention without trial. With this measure the foundations of the dictatorship were cemented and opponents could now be locked up at will in order to 'protect' the German state.

The Nazis then began to seize political control of the police and Heinrich Himmler was appointed chief of the force in Munich. He swiftly politicised security and the SS were handed powers of arrest. A round-up of political opponents began almost immediately and, initially, detainees were taken to the imposing *Polizeipräsidium* (police headquarters) at Ettstrasse 2 in central Munich. Soon, however, Himmler and his team scarcely had space in which to work. The interrogation rooms overflowed with opposition politicians, trade unionists, journalists and others who had spoken out against the Nazis. The stairwells and corridors were clogged with files and paperwork. To relieve the congestion Himmler decided that a much larger holding camp was needed. He settled on an old gunpowder factory in the Munich suburb of Dachau, to the north west of the city centre.

An 'accommodation for 5,000'

On 21 March 1933 an official notice from Himmler's office appeared in the *Munchener Neusten Nachristen* newspaper. It announced that, as from the next day, 'The first concentration camp will be opened in the vicinity of Dachau. It can accommodate five thousand people. We have adopted this measure, undeterred by paltry scruples, in the conviction that our action will help to restore calm to our country and that it is in the best interest of our people.' Himmler then held a press conference and told journalists that suspects would be held in 'protective custody'. This was not to protect the individual being but to protect the German state from the 'subversive' individual. How long 'protective custody' might last was now anyone's guess. Much evidence had been confiscated from raids on homes and political parties, all of which needed to be sifted through. The camp was intended to 're-educate' prisoners, though none could say when the programme would be complete and it was clear that questions from friends or relatives would be futile. 'The police,' said Himmler, 'will simply be delayed in this process if they are constantly being asked when this or that person in protective custody will be set free.'

The first prisoners lived in ten stone barracks, which had been part of the old factory complex, and their immediate task was to make the buildings habitable. Some had been converted into workshops while others were abandoned. Even Himmler described the compound as 'very run down'. Worse still, the Dachau suburb had been built on a swamp and the foggy, damp climate was inclement at the best of times. In subsequent years the camp mushroomed to accommodate an ever-increasing population. By 1938 another thirty-four new blocks had been added to the camp. Most of the barrack blocks were demolished in the early 1960s but one terrace has been left as a permanent reminder of what the buildings looked like.

Eventually the camp occupied an area 300m wide and 700m long. An adjacent complex was used to train and house the SS guards. To ensure that the inmates understood why they were incarcerated a huge sign was erected on the roof of the main building with a bleak message: 'There is a way to freedom. Its milestones are obedience, honesty, sobriety, industry, order, martyrdom, truthfulness and love of the fatherland.'

The guard room, kitchen, laundry, storage rooms and showers were on the ground floor of the main building. There was even a library stocked with books that had been confiscated from the prisoners themselves and, heavily vetted, they were allowed to read in the little free time allowed. Inmates must have been reminded of the black-humour anecdote in which a prisoner goes into the camp library and asks for a book by a certain author, 'Sorry,' says the Kapo in charge, 'we do not hold that book. But we do have the author.' The offices of the camp administrators and the Gestapo were on the first floor. Paths led from the main block to the dreaded punishment block called the 'Bunker' (see below).

In front of the main block was a large open square where roll-calls were taken twice a day. On clear days, inmates could catch a glimpse of the open fields surrounding the camp and the freedom which they had so recently enjoyed beyond the walls. Escape was virtually impossible although one of the first detainees did manage to get away. Hans Beimler was a Reichstag deputy for the Communist Party before being imprisoned in Dachau within days of the camp opening. He strangled a guard with his bare hands before slipping through the perimeter security and eventually fled to Spain. Three years later he was killed helping to defend Madrid against General Franco's army in the Spanish civil war.

Such escape attempts, however, became increasingly rare. As the camp developed, security became more elaborate. The entire compound was surrounded by an electric barbed-wire fence, a wall and a deep, wide ditch. Watchtowers cast a long shadow over the perimeter and the SS machine guns were ready to kill any who attempted to escape. As Himmler explained to a gathering of army officers, 'The control towers are manned day and night with fully loaded machine guns so that any attempt at a general uprising – an event for which we must always be prepared – can be immediately suppressed. The entire camp can be strafed from three towers.' Some sought death as a welcome release and threw themselves at the fence. It was a sure form of suicide to escape the hell of confinement.

Organisation at Dachau was strictly hierarchical. The camp commandant was responsible for the overall running of the camp with the day-to-day routine enforced by subordinates. The most infamous of the camp commanders was Theodore Eicke who was discharged from a psychiatric hospital to take up his post in June 1933. Eicke subsequently used the Dachau model for other camps rolled out across Germany and became the Inspector General of the entire system. The precise structure changed over the years, but a permanent fixture was the presence of the SS guards, who were responsible for all concentration camp security.

Two of the most notorious criminals to pass through Dachau were Adolf Eichmann and Rudolf Hoss. Eichmann was an author of the 'Final Solution'; the Holocaust. He escaped to Argentina after the war, where he was tracked down by Israeli agents, abducted, tried for his crimes in Jerusalem, found guilty and hanged. Rudolf Hoss became camp commandant at Auschwitz. He gave damning evidence at the Nuremberg trials of 1946 (see Chapter 9) and was hanged in 1947. The SS also relied on prisoner assistants. Known as 'Kapos', these collaborators were often despised by the other inmates. The term of abuse has continued down the decades. In 2014 the then Italian prime minister, Silvio Berlussconi, provoked uproar in the European parliament when he taunted the German leader of the socialist group as a 'Kapo' and was later forced to correct his remark.

Why Are We Here?

Himmler's plans for a camp that would hold just five thousand prisoners were soon out of date. Over the next decade the camp was swamped with new arrivals and the prison population swelled to well over twice the planned total. After 1940 the number of inmates ballooned again with the arrival of prisoners detained in territory now occupied by German troops. Just days before the end of the war, in April 1945, there were over 30,000 in the main Dachau camp with another 37,000 working in Dachau's satellite camps. By the end of the war it was estimated that some 200,000 inmates had passed through the gates of Dachau since it first opened. Although it was not an extermination camp, around 31,000 people were registered as having died there during that time. A definitive figure would certainly be much higher but will never be known for sure.

Dachau was a 'feeder' camp for a network of smaller camps that sprang up across southern Gemany and where prisoners were sent to work. As a consequence, wholly accurate numbers are difficult to pin down because the population of Dachau was not static. People came and went: some were transferred to the other smaller satellite camps, sent to concentration camps in other parts of Germany, or 'hired out' to private companies. The work done by Dachau prisoners in the different centres varied but was mainly focused on the munitions industry. In every case they were used as forced labour to sustain the very regime that held them as slaves. Dachau was also part of the wider network of concentration camps that sprang up across Nazi-occupied Europe. Prisoners were moved between camps as the demands for labour shifted. The travelling conditions between the camps could be atrocious. In November 1942, for example, a detachment of 900 Russian and Polish prisoners left from another camp in Poland for Dachau. Each prisoner had a food ration of just two days and 300 died on the long journey. When the survivors arrived at Dachau, witnesses were horrified to see that some, crazed with hunger, had survived by gnawing at the corpses of the dead.

The first group of Dachau inmates were socialists, communists and other political inmates detained following the Reichstag fire. But over the next decade many others were swept up by the Nazi terror. Doctors, school teachers, lawyers, journalists, administrators, priests, Jehovah's Witnesses, gypsies and Jews: the list was varied and seemingly endless. What each of these individuals had in common, however, was their opposition to Hitler. For some reason or other – politics, religion, social position – they had resisted the Nazi regime. As no specific charges needed to be brought, let alone being tried by an independent court, some never discovered the precise reason for their detention. One baffled priest was detained with twenty others and later wrote, 'Why exactly did they arrest us? That was the first question we asked each other. The Gestapo never gave us a reason for our arrest. No accusation was ever read to us in those five and half years. We were never examined; they did not tell us why we were there.'

Others were incarcerated not for political opposition as such but because they simply did not fit in with Nazi ideals of the 'good citizen'. 'Anti-social behaviour' was one of the accusations levelled against people, but as this was seldom defined there was no hope of a mounting a defence. Some of the disabled prisoners were subjected to a programme of euthanasia. The work-shy were another target. Himmler was irritated when a woman who had lost both her legs in an accident tried to cadge money off him in a Munich street in 1937. He ordered a complete clean-up of the city so that around 2,000 tramps and vagrants found themselves being rounded up and sent to Dachau.

When the German army began to overrun other European countries, mass deportations from the newly invaded territories began. There was an influx of political prisoners into Dachau and the dozens of different nationalities turned the camp into a hellish version of the tower of Babel. The biggest group remained German, but there were also large numbers of Belgians, Croats, Czechs, French, Hungarians, Italians, Lithuanians, Poles, Russians, Slovenes, Rumanians and others. A dozen or so Swiss nationals strayed from the safety of their neutral homeland and were incarcerated in Dachau. Some 600 Spanish republicans passed through the camp. One may have been the former prime minister, Largo Caballero. Like others, he had fled over the Pyrenees in the closing days of the Spanish Civil War to what he expected would be a safe haven in France. All their hopes were dashed when the Germans invaded France in 1940 and they were handed over to Franco or to the Nazis. It was even recorded that there was one Persian and one Chinese person in the camp.

In this bewildering array, inmates were easily muddled one with another. The SS authorities attempted to resolve the confusion of identification by categorising the prisoners. Each was forced to wear a chevron-shaped badge which colour-coded the reason for their internment. Political prisoners wore red badges, green was for criminals, black for the work-shy or anti-social and violet for religious objectors. Pink was for homosexuals, 600 of whom were held in the camp by 1945. The prisoners' nationality was indicated by a letter inked inside the triangle. And those serving a second sentence had a bar drawn above the triangle.

Jews were forced to wear yellow stars. Following the events of *Kristallnacht*, thousands were rounded up and held in Dachau (see Chapter 6). The youngest was just thirteen, the oldest eighty- six. Over the following months they were able to 'liberate' themselves if they paid exorbitant 'voluntary donations' to the Nazi regime and promised to emigrate. Around 700, however, perished in Dachau.

'Welcome to Dachau!'

New inmates were stripped of any personal possessions which they might have been carrying when first detained. The process of dehumanisation then continued apace. The SS guards' sardonic cry 'welcome to Dachau!' was accompanied by beatings and kickings. Newcomers were stripped of their own clothes and given the camp uniform of striped drill cloth and wooden shoes. The prisoner's hair was shorn, not by trained barbers but by other prisoners using old, blunt razors. It was a painful process. Photographs were taken and personal details recorded on endless lists and index cards. The inmate would be obliged to repeat the information several times over, but for many it would be the last time. From now on they would be known by the assigned number, not their name. As one inmate recalled, 'Anyone who has never had to undergo such an ordeal can scarcely imagine how degrading all this can be, even more painful than the closed fists which buffeted my face.'

Thereafter the prisoner was entirely subject to the rules of the camp authority. Inmates were expected to know the camp layout and regulations without fail. The stipulated form of how to march, greet and report had to be observed. German songs had to be learned. Orders – even those of the lowest SS orderly – were to be obeyed without question and instructions carried out to the letter. The art of survival in Dachau consisted in keeping a low profile and the head firmly down.

Work was key to Dachau's existence; 'Arbeit Macht Frei', as the message on the gate insisted. Inmates were assigned to arduous duties as part of a rigorously structured day, which began with a camp wake-up call, often at around 5am. The first roll call of the day was at 6am with an evening roll call followed by lights out and sleep from nine in the evening. The roll calls were an essential part of the fixed routine every day of the year, whatever the weather. Even in the depths of winter the prisoners were forced to assemble in the main square and stand to attention until all had been counted as present and correct. When numbers did not tally the consequences could be dire. One inmate recalled a snowy night in January 1939, which was, he said, 'Unforgettable for those that experienced it.' Two prisoners were unaccounted for and so, 'A thousand others had to stand the whole night until eleven am (the following day) on the square, bare-headed; they dared not make the slightest movement to warm themselves.' Men froze to death where they stood and 'seven dead bodies had to be carried off the square'.

In between roll calls the inmates fell into gangs and began their march to work at set tasks. Some were engaged in digging ditches or farm work. The worst assignment was the gravel pit. Surrounded by SS guards with ferocious Alsatian dogs, the men descended into the pit with picks and shovels to dig the gravel, which then had to be brought up onto wooden carts. Hands bled and limbs ached but any slacking was punished by kicks or blows from a rifle butt. The drudgery continued through freezing winters and boiling summers in a scene which reminded one of Dante's phrase about hell: 'abandon hope all ye who enter here'. Another feared duty was the roller used to keep the parade ground, roads and paths level. The weighty roller was of the kind which might have been pulled by a team of horses but in Dachau those harnessed were prisoners. SS guards and Kapos beat the pullers with bullwhips if the pace slackened. Those unable to continue working were finished off by a programme of euthanasia or simply allowed to die. Ironically, the Second World War brought a little light relief for some prisoners. As the conflict dragged on, detachments of Dachau inmates were sent to work in munitions factories where conditions were a little better. At least prisoners could work alongside civilians, who were generally more cheerful, and they were free from the close scrutiny of the SS guards.

Punishment was an ever-present threat in Dachau. Slacking at work, making disparaging remarks about the regime, organising meetings or infringing any number of other rules was heavily castigated. The punishment block was called the 'Bunker' and the punishments meted out there would have been familiar to a medieval torturer. The stake, or 'the tree', involved the prisoner being held with his hands around his back. His wrists were then tied with an iron chain which was used to winch then man up off the ground for an hour or more. Other prisoners were strapped to a table called 'the trestle', where prostate victims were lashed with water-soaked leather whips by SS guards. One prisoner recalled that some of the more sadistic derived 'real pleasure ... when the prisoners screamed, sobbed, cried or fainted from pain'. The prisoner was obliged to count the number of strokes aloud. If he failed or miscounted in his agony the guards declared that they too had lost count and began the torture again.

Solitary confinement of up to forty days was a common sentence, sometimes enhanced by the prisoner being held in a wholly blacked-out cell for the duration. Worst of all, however, was 'standing confinement' with the prisoner being held in a space narrower than a telephone kiosk for three days and nights and fed only bread and water. Every fourth night they were released to eat and sleep with the other prisoners. But then they were returned to the isolation of the 'standing confinement' for another three days, and so the punishment went on. Some prisoners never emerged from the 'Bunker'. An unusually high number were reported by the SS to have committed suicide and this may well have been true in some cases.

Medical Experiments: Low Temperatures, High Altitude and Malaria

Another building that terrified many inmates was, ironically, the infirmary. By every convention of medical care, the camp hospital should have been the first refuge for the sick. But it was not. Some of the research and the experiments conducted there challenge our comprehension of life in Dachau even eighty years after the event. One inmate described how a camp physician wanted to test a remedy for malaria. This could easily have been done in the tropics where the disease is rife, 'But why go to such trouble? One could make everything more convenient in a concentration camp.' The doctor had the mosquitoes imported and let them bite over a thousand camp inmates so that, 'He first *made* his patients [sick] but he was then unable to *heal* them.' As a consequence, many were tormented by malarial attacks for the duration of their confinement and, if they survived, for the rest of their lives.

These patients, however, were fortunate in comparison to others used as guinea pigs in tests for the German Luftwaffe. With the development of the jet engine and planes able to fly at ever-higher altitudes, the military needed to know more about the effects of speed and compression on their pilots. Dachau prisoners on death row or deemed unfit for work were used to find out. In a series of hideous experiments, individual prisoners were strapped into chambers and subject to rapid changes of compression and decompression to discover the limits of their tolerance. Most did not survive the torture but only died after being driven insane by the most excruciating pain. Some seventy victims perished in this way.

Luftwaffe chiefs were also concerned that, as the Second World War went on, an increasing number of their pilots were being shot down and forced to bail out over the sea. They wanted more information about the reaction of the human body to low water temperatures temperatures and the doctors at Dachau set about finding an answer. In this case the victims were dressed in flying jackets before being lowered into baths of icy water. Their body temperatures were checked meticulously every ten minutes until they became immobile, unconscious and then died from hypothermia. Nearly one hundred victims died in these experiments.

The doctor who carried out these tests was eventually executed, but not as retribution for the suffering of his victims. Along with his wife, he was shot by other members of the SS shortly before the camp was liberated in 1945. This was on the direct orders of Himmler, who was apparently furious to discover that the tests had not been conducted with sufficient scientific rigour. Despite all the suffering it seems that the doctor had falsified some of his lab reports.

The Prisoners of Dachau

Until 1944 Dachau was a male preserve and women were detained in other camps. But in the last year of the war around 1,000 women were transported to Dachau and used as forced labour. Amongst the women held and executed at Dachau were four members of the British Special Operations Executive (SOE). These extraordinarily brave agents had volunteered to be dropped into occupied Europe and faced certain death if they were captured. Noor Inyat Khan was an Indian princess, born in Moscow to an American mother and largely brought up in France. She studied music at the Sorbonne and the Paris Conservatory. Her language skills made her an ideal SOE agent but the work must have tested her naturally shy character, which made her subsequent courage all the more remarkable. Working alone, she transmitted clandestine radio reports to the Allies but was eventually captured by the Gestapo just outside Paris. Khan was detained, along with three other young multilingual women agents: Yolande Beekman, Elaine Plewman and Madeleine Damermant. All were tortured by the Gestapo, but refused to do more than lie to their captors. In September 1944 the four women were taken to Dachau where, kneeling and holding hands, they were executed outside the crematorium. Two other British intelligence officers were caught by the SS in Holland at the outbreak of the war and spent much of the duration in Dachau as 'special prisoners'. They were fortunate to survive the experience and were liberated in 1945.

All the victims of the camp deserve to be remembered, but the biographies of just a few illustrate the broad spread of Nazi terror.

Status, nationality or wealth were no guarantees of protection against persecution in the Third Reich. Non-Nazi politicians across the political spectrum – from communists to nationalists – were victims in Dachau. Perhaps the most high-profile was the former Bavarian president, von Kahr, who had refused to back Hitler during the 'Beer-Hall Putsch' of 1923 (see Chapter 3). Both he and the journalist Fritz Gerlich, who had exposed the Nazis in opposition, were killed in Dachau during the Night of the Long Knives (see Chapter 5).

Other political opponents included Kurt Schumacher, the youngest Social Democrat (SPD) deputy in the Reichstag when first elected in 1930. A fierce opponent of the far right during the turbulent years of the Weimar Republic, he had little more time for the revolutionary left and apparently described the communists as 'red-painted Nazis'. Schumacher was arrested in July 1933. He spent a decade in Dachau, only to be rearrested in 1943 and sent to another concentration camp. Schumacher's health was wrecked by incarceration – he had a leg amputated in the late 1940s – but, nevertheless, returned to active politics after the war as a leading social democrat.

Dr Alois Hundhammer served in the First World War and then with the ultra-right wing *Freikorps*, which put down the Marxist 'Republic of Bavaria' after the war (see Chapter 4). He then began to campaign for the rights of Bavarian farmers and completed two doctoral degrees at Munich's Ludwig Maximilian University on the history of agricultural labour. But Hundhammer's work and free-thinking led him to a full-fronted clash with the tenets of National Socialism. Along with other members of the catholic Bavarian People's Party (BVP), he was arrested and sent to Dachau. He was fortunate to be released after a few weeks, but stripped of all his posts, he opened a shoe-repair shop to earn a living. This too was closed down in 1937 by Gestapo chiefs, who suspected that it had become a meeting point for clandestine dissidents. From now on Hundhammer kept his head down and mouth shut, apparently for the sake of his wife and children. After the war he emerged to draft the Bavarian state constitution and take a leading role in the region's politics.

Another associate of the BVP detained in Dachau was Philipp Held, not for anything he had done directly but because his father, Heinrich Held, had been the Bavarian prime minister. Heinrich Held attempted to resist Nazism in Bavaria but was thrown out of office at the beginning of

March 1933 and fled. When Held junior refused to divulge his father's whereabouts the Nazis detained him instead.

Whilst the first Dachau inmates were German, the camp quickly swelled with prisoners from conquered territories. The invasion of Austria in 1938 led to the arrival of Austrian dignitaries and politicians. The sons of the Archduke Ferdinand, whose assassination in Sarajevo triggered the First World War, were two Austrian nationalists taken to Dachau as a form of preventive custody so that they could not lead further resistance. The Mayor of Vienna, where Hitler had once lived, was an ardent anti-Nazi. He spoke out loudly against Hitler during the 1930s and was only silenced by being sent to Dachau, where he remained until 1945. The occupation of the Czech Sudetenland in the autumn of 1938 was the green light for a political cleansing of that region. Some 2,000 local social democrats and communists were rounded up and sent to Dachau. Towards the end of the war the French resistance became increasingly active in occupied France. The Nazi authorities responded with a crackdown of suspects, including General Charles Delestraint, who had once been De Gaulle's commanding officer. He resisted Gestapo torture and was eventually shot in Dachau in April 1945. In total, around 100,000 French people were deported to concentration camps; some 15,000 to Dachau.

What Did the Outside World Know?

Himmler encouraged members of the *Wehrmacht* to visit the camps; it would be 'extremely instructive', he told army officers. 'Once they have seen it they are convinced that nobody has been sent their unjustly ... [only] criminals and freaks. No better demonstration of the laws of inheritance and race ... exists than such a concentration camp. There you can find people with hydrocephalus, people who are cross-eyed, deformed, half-Jewish and a number of racially inferior subjects.'

Several sanitised visits were laid on for international observers. The tours showed clean facilities and cheerful prisoners. The German Red Cross representative even managed to convince some international colleagues that prisoners were better off inside the camp because, 'For the mass of prisoners hailing from the proletarian milieu, their material standard of living is better than they knew in civilian life.'

Astonishingly, some Swiss Red Cross inspectors who visited the camp largely swallowed the lie. Much effort went into disguising the true nature of the camps from foreign visitors. The food laid on for prisoners during a visit, for example, was more plentiful than the normal rations. Then, once the visitors had departed, prisoners returned to an even more meagre diet for a few days to even out the brief bonanza. Former British prime minister, David Lloyd George, visited Dachau and came away impressed by some of the land reclamation being done in the marshy fields around the camp. But by that time the political skills that the 'Welsh Wizard' had deployed to become one of the most effective politicians of the twentieth century had long since deserted him (see Chapter 8). As international tensions heightened, however, the invitations to inspect Dachau and other camps dried up, and after 1939 there were no more visits. When foreign observers returned to Dachau at the end of the Second World War it was impossible to disguise what had really been going on behind the ditches and barbed wire.

Liberation: 'The Gate of Freedom Opens'

As American troops pushed on towards Munich in April 1945, Himmler instructed that Dachau be shelled and burned; along with all the inmates. While various records of the crimes committed at the camp were destroyed, the order to carry out further mass murder was ignored. Instead, prisoners were evacuated from Dachau, and on 26 April a chaotic convoy set off for the south Tyrol in the Alps. Some clambered aboard trains and trucks, but around 7,000 prisoners were forced to make the journey on foot. One thousand died from exhaustion during what became known as 'the Death March'.

American troops entered the camp and 'opened the gates to freedom', as one put it on the 29 April. The surviving prisoners were ecstatic, but their joy was in grim contrast to the sight that greeted the liberating US troops. Despite years of fighting, nothing prepared them for what they found. A typhus epidemic had raged unchecked through the compound for months. The camp stank of squalor, disease and degradation. Emaciated figures wandered amongst piles of skeletal corpses (around 3,000) so that it was hard to distinguish between the living and the dead. Some American soldiers unleashed their fury on the

SS guards who remained and shot around fifty on the spot before their commanding officer managed to rein them in.

Justice followed swiftly, however. At the end of 1945 the US army staged a series of trials at Dachau using the camp setting to underline the appalling abuses that had taken place under the Third Reich. Some of the accused had been officials in Dachau and several, including the commandant, were hanged. Other hearings investigated war crimes committed by the German army elsewhere.

Ironically, some of the last occupants of Dachau were Germans. One of the biggest mass migrations in history occurred at the end of the Second World War. Millions of Germans who had lived in territories outside the country to the east were now forced west. These German refugees were often transported in the same trains that had been used to deport Jews and others to death camps. When they arrived in Germany, a country in which they had never previously lived, they had no homes. In the acute housing crisis of the post-war era – many homes had been destroyed by Allied bombing – the vacant concentration camp of Dachau provided some basic shelter for German families until it was finally closed in the mid-1960s. It was a bitterly ironic comment on both the existence of the camp and the utter failure of the Third Reich.

Chapter Nine

'Peace for our Time': Berchtesgaden and the Munich Crisis

O n 15 September 1938 the British prime minister, Neville Chamberlain, clambered aboard a small Lockheed plane at Heston airport just outside London. The journey was a novelty for the septuagenarian statesman who, apart from a spin around the airfield in his native Birmingham, had never flown in his life before. Yet Chamberlain had little choice and time was of the essence. He was at the centre of one of the gravest political crises of the twentieth century and on his way for urgent talks with Adolf Hitler. The German chancellor was threatening to launch an assault on Czechoslovakia and so shatter the fragile peace of Europe. Chamberlain was determined to stop him; at almost any price. The natural location for a conference of such magnitude might have been the German capital, Berlin. Instead, Hitler insisted that Chamberlain travel to the far south of Germany and meet him at his home at **Berchtesgaden**[1] in the Bavarian Alps.

For the next two weeks Hitler's mountain retreat became the centre of feverish activity and power politics while leaders struggled to resolve what became known as 'the Munich Crisis'. An agreement was reached and the triumphant Chamberlain returned to London, where he declared that he had struck a deal which would ensure 'peace for our time'. Hitler, meanwhile, remained in Berchtesgaden, brooding and preparing his next steps towards all-out war.

From Rustic Retreat to Centre of Power

With the idyllic Königsee lake and stunning alpine scenery, the small town of Berchtesgaden had long been a favourite retreat of the Wittelsbach monarchs of Bavaria. In the nineteenth century the area also began to attract artists and tourists (walking and rock climbing remain popular activities for many visitors to the area). A mountain called the Unterberg dominates the town and provided a mystic touch: according to folklore, the Holy Roman emperor Barbarossa is asleep inside the mountain until the day comes when he will awake at the call of the German people. It is no coincidence that Hitler's assault on Russia in June 1941 was given the codename 'Barbarossa'.

In the mid-1920s Adolf Hitler was one of those who sought out the tranquility of Berchtesgaden to escape the stresses of running the Nazi party and the rough and tumble of his meetings in the beer halls of Munich. It was here that he relaxed, wrote the second edition of *Mein Kampf*, and had a peculiar affair with one of the local girls. The liaison came to nothing but Hitler was so smitten with the region that he began to rent a small, rustic retreat called *Haus Wachenfeld* in an area known as the Obersalzberg, just above the town.

Haus Wachenfeld was typically Bavarian, with a long, sloping roof – from which the heavy snow would slide in winter – to a veranda from which to enjoy the long summer evenings. Hitler's favourite architect and acolyte, Albert Speer, recalled the 'bogus, old-German peasant style' of the house that was furnished with a 'brass canary cage, cactus and rubber plant'. Hitler subsequently became wealthy enough from the sales of *Mein Kampf* to buy the house and later embarked on a conversion in which any vestiges of 'peasantry' were stripped away entirely. By this time he was Führer and the hefty cost of renovation was paid for by the German state.

The new building was complete with lofty rooms hung with fine Gobelin tapestries and massive fireplaces surrounded by red Moroccan leather chairs. The vast reception room was anything but snug. The main talking point was a gargantuan picture window that looked out over the sweeping valley towards Salzburg. As Hitler began to spend more time here, other leading Nazis such as Hermann Göring and Martin Bormann elbowed out local landowners to acquire plots nearby and plant their chalets in the valley. Owners reluctant to part with their property were sent to Dachau for a spell where they were given time to reconsider. Such a concentration of the Nazi hierarchy required greater security. A **local hotel** was seized to become the base for an entire detachment of SS bodyguards.[2] Later, a vast a vast system of **underground bunkers** was constructed to shelter the Nazi top brass from attack. Many of these fortifications survived the war and are open to the public today.[3] By the late 1930s Hitler preferred to spend so much time at the Berghof that he had established an official 'Reich Sub-Chancellery' close to Berchtesgaden. Functionaries were now summoned there from Berlin when the Führer could not be troubled to travel to the capital.

Later, to celebrate the Führer's fiftieth birthday, an elaborate tea house called the **Kehlsteinhaus** was built high on a pinnacle above the Berghof. Better known to history as the '**Eagle's Nest**', the construction was overseen by Martin Bormann. In reality, the building was something of an unwanted gift. Hitler suffered from claustrophobia in the access lift that ascended to the Kehlsteinhaus up a shaft carved out of solid rock and, once there, he felt vulnerable to attack. (In fact, British intelligence did hatch a plan for a sniper to kill Hitler at the Berghof but logistical difficulties, amongst others, led to the operation being aborted). As a consequence, Hitler seldom visited the tea house, which today functions as a bar and restaurant.[4]

Soaking up the Alpine air and gazing at the views, Hitler claimed that life at the Berghof had an almost magical effect on his psyche. According to one source, he gushed, 'It is in the broad horizons of the land around Berchtesgaden and Salzburg, cut off from the everyday world, that my creative genius produces ideas which shake the world. In those moments I feel no longer part of mortality, my ideas go beyond mortal frontiers and are transformed into deeds of great dimensions.'

None of this activity involved the kind of routine which other 'mortals' lived by, however, and Hitler's work schedule remained as chaotic at Berghof as it did elsewhere. A summons to join Hitler at the Berghof could turn out like the invitation to a weekend house-party from hell. Guests were expected to fit in with Hitler's quixotic lifestyle and irregular timetable. Margarete Speer, wife of architect Albert, recalled, 'The phone rings [for lunch]. It might be two, three or even four o'clock. A friendly male voice: "the Führer requests your presence at table". I've been ready for a long time, sitting around waiting. Albert and I are fetched.' In the evening, dinner was followed by a film or two and then Hitler would talk ceaselessly until three or four in the morning while those around him fought to stay awake through the marathon monologues. Not surprisingly, even the loyal Speer described social life at the Berghof as 'agonizing' and 'a waste of time'.

'The George Washington of Germany'

Hitler did not enjoy physical exercise but took short strolls. Below the Berghof, the Führer's post-prandial walks began to attract large crowds for Nazi propaganda to exploit as part of the leader cult. When he was known to be in residence, multitudes gathered in the surrounding fields and paths where – under close supervision of the SS guards – they waited patiently to get a glimpse of their Führer. Hitler would occasionally appear and go on what might now be called a 'walkabout' to acknowledge their fealty. His mere presence was enough to trigger reverence bordering on quiet hysteria among the faithful and one bemused commentator recorded that 'afterward bewitched females swallowed the gravel where his feet had trodden.'

Yet there was one drawback with the spectacular setting and life at the Berghof: Hitler complained that he could only see the land of his birth with binoculars. What he wanted was to erase the border so that the German Reich would be one seamless state. The unification of all German-speaking people was the ultimate goal of the Nazi project. It was the first point of the party programme drawn up in 1920 and remained the most cherished from then on. Where Bismarck had been unwilling to complete the total unification of all German-speaking peoples in the nineteenth century, Hitler intended to carry the project through in the twentieth. Exactly how that could be achieved was a question that dominated much of Hitler's thinking at the Berghof.

Having secured the authority of his dictatorship in Germany, Hitler was emboldened to expand his foreign policy, and in the autumn of 1937 he spent a good deal of time at Berchtesgaden to work out the details. More guests, such as the Aga Khan and the Duke of Windsor, came and went but Hitler was mainly preoccupied by thinking, scheming and planning his next steps. Like a malevolent chess grand master, he passed long hours in the Berghof strategising the many possible moves by Germany and counter moves by powers such as Britain, France, Russia or Poland, who might attempt to thwart his plans. There was one crucial element of the puzzle he could not yet know: what would other European powers do to stop German expansion, if anything?

Using the Berghof as a base for his singular brand of public diplomacy, Hitler sounded out opinion formers in other countries. Lord Rothermere, owner of the *Daily Mail*, was one enthusiastic guest to the mountain retreat and in his diaries Goebbels recorded how, while there, 'Rothermere pays me great compliments ... Enquires in detail about German press policy. Strongly anti-Jewish ... After lunch we retire for a chat.' Former prime minister, David Lloyd George, was another British visitor to the Berghof, in September 1936, and gushed that he had just met 'the George Washington of Germany'. In an article for the *Daily Express*, Lloyd George brushed aside reservations about the wholesale elimination of German democracy to endorse the Hitler revolution. 'Whatever one may think of his methods,' he wrote, 'there can be no doubt that he has achieved a marvellous transformation in the spirit of the people, in their attitude towards each other, and in their social and economic outlook.' Whether the old statesman's mind was spinning from the Alpine views or whether he was simply losing it altogether is difficult to tell, but his catastrophically misplaced analysis concluded, 'Those who imagine that Germany has swung back to its old Imperialist temper cannot have any understanding of the character of the change. The idea of a Germany intimidating Europe with threats, that its irresistible army might march across frontiers forms no part of the new vision.'

Appeasement and the Path to War

Yet that, of course, was exactly Hitler's plan. The Nazi leader's calculations were proved correct as other European powers shied away from confrontation; a policy known as appeasement in Britain. The horror of the First World War was ever present and few leaders were prepared to risk repeating the catastrophe. There were also strong economic reasons for Hitler's growing audacity. The worst of the recession – which had played a part in bringing the Nazis to power – was long over and the German economy was growing apace. As Lloyd George observed, Germany was riding high under the hand of Hjalmar Schacht, the country's talented finance minister. Unusually, Schacht was not a member of the Nazi party and had an ambiguous relationship with Hitler: although a passionate German nationalist, he nevertheless resiled from other parts of the Nazi programme. Even more unusually, he was eventually detained by both the Gestapo and then the Allies. In 1944 Schacht was arrested as a suspected associate of the plot to assassinate Hitler and sent to a concentration camp.

At the end of the war he was then arrested by the Allies and put on trial at Nuremberg, where he was one of the few defendants to be acquitted (see Chapter 10).

Schacht was clever, devious, scheming and lucky. During 1933 the German economy benefited from strong tail winds and began to pick up. Firms hired cheap labour as desperate and unemployed workers accepted low wages and restocked with low-priced raw materials. Leaders of the Weimar Republic had renegotiated Germany's debts from the First World War so these repayments – or reparations – were now less onerous. Schacht then launched a massive programme of public investment. This was paid for by borrowing, and directed towards heavy industry; especially armaments and supplies for the Nazi war machine.

As the domestic economy expanded, unemployment fell rapidly and by 1936 Germany was approaching full employment. Given the dire condition of the German economy in 1932, this was an impressive turn-around. Productivity, though, remained surprisingly low, the quality of goods could be poor and, with Trade Unions smashed, many workers' wages stagnated. The real German miracle would only happen after the Second World War with the *wirtschaftswunder*, or economic miracle, of the 1950s and 60s.

Still, as other countries floundered during the 1930s, Germany appeared to flourish by comparison. And as the German economy grew, so did Hitler's confidence. Whilst UK unemployment still topped ten per cent in the late 1930s, the Nazi economy grappled with a labour shortage. Hitler was quick to brag and taunt his opponents about his success and their failure. In a speech at Nuremberg he told the party faithful, 'If this is interpreted as a welcome sign of economic weakness in the Third Reich we can bear that weakness and leave the strength of unemployment to the democracies.' The leftist British *New Statesman* magazine commented anxiously, 'They [liberal democracies] may point to the other disastrous weakness of the Reich but they have no good answer to this particular "crack" … In finding an answer, Socialism has very little time to waste.'

But neither socialists nor the Conservatives in Britain, or any of the other liberal democracies, did have an answer to Germany's growing economic and political strength. Hitler's dissembling to enhance German power earlier in the decade went unchecked and his defiance of international agreements went unchallenged. When Hitler withdrew from the League of Nations, occupied the Rhineland, reintroduced conscription, remilitarised the Germany army, or blatantly meddled in the Spanish Civil War, there was no serious attempt to stop him. He learned that with enough bravado it was surprisingly easy to cock a snook at international political norms and treaties that were meant to bind Germany. In the autumn of 1937 Hitler retreated to the Berghof, where he mused further on how he could exploit the weakness of the international community and strengthen the Reich.

The Hossbach Memorandum 1937: A Signpost to War

On 5 November 1937 a tight-knit cabal of officials met in Hitler's office at the Chancellery in Berlin. The Führer wanted to share with them his deliberations over the autumn at the Berghof. His conclusions were so profound that he decided not to share them with his full cabinet, but instead only with a group that included his foreign minister, the war minister and the commanders of the armed forces (army, navy, air force). The meeting became known, not by the name of any of the luminaries present, but by that of the adjutant who took notes and produced a memo of the meeting. His name was Hossbach and the 'Hossbach Memorandum' became one of the most important documents for the prosecution case at the Nuremberg trial after the war in 1946 (see Chapter 10).

The matter in hand which the Führer wished to discuss was *Lebensraum*. This was, of course, a well-worn theme. Hitler had long argued that demographic and economic constraints hampered national development and the Germans needed more living space or *Lebensraum*. But many of these claims had previously been formulated in general terms. Never before had Hitler spelt out his plans in quite the detail he explained to the group that afternoon.

Other European powers, he argued, had acquired colonies. This imperial expansion allowed them to secure more territory and access to raw materials and food. But because of two 'hate-inspired antagonists' – Britain and France – Germany had been prevented from becoming an imperial power. And British naval dominance of the high seas meant that Germany was permanently constrained in what she could and could not do across the oceans of the world. More seriously still, Hitler fretted about the lack of land to feed the population 'even when harvests were good', a deficiency which, 'grew to catastrophic proportions with bad harvests.' In a mangled version of Malthusian economics, Hitler concluded that 'the only solution was to acquire extra territory in the east.'

Aggressive, territorial expansion would carry a risk of war, but it was one that he was prepared to face. That was decided. Having determined the direction of travel, the big questions that Hitler wanted to share with the small group was not 'if' but 'when' and 'how'. Hitler declared that it was his 'unalterable resolve to solve the German space problem' with a military strike as soon as possible and by 1943–45 at the latest. But where? This too he had worked out during his time reflecting in the Berghof. 'Our first objective ... must be to overthrow Czechoslovakia and Austria simultaneously in order to remove the threat to our flank.' This would both add more vital territory to the Reich and establish a large buffer zone between a hostile Soviet Union and the German heartland. The Czechs in particular were in his cross sights; the descent upon Prague would need to be carried out 'with lightning speed'. Hitler gambled that neither Britain nor France would intervene because neither had any appetite for another war with Germany. Both, he said, had 'tacitly written off Czechoslovakia'.

Several of the military commanders were clearly rattled by what they heard that afternoon. General airy comments about *Lebensraum* in the Führer's speeches were one thing; being ordered to plunge into an all-out war within a few months to achieve it was quite another. The memorandum records timid attempts by army chiefs to put a break on the Führer's plans. They did not share his insouciance about the weakness of other countries nor his confidence in the strength of the German military. Over the next few days some of the group – Germany's most senior military chiefs – met Hitler for one-to-one meetings to discuss the fine detail of his plans and press their concerns. The former corporal would have none of it. Irritated, he abruptly left Berlin and returned to sulk and brood in Berchtesgarden until the middle of January 1938.

As Hitler biographer Alan Bullock commented, 'Reasoned criticism of any kind always aroused Hitler's anger: he hated to have his intuition subject to analysis.' Thus, in February 1938, the Führer testily dismissed around sixty of his senior commanders. Then he sacked the vacillating foreign minister. Even this minor purge, however, did not put an end to criticism from within the military. In the summer of 1938 Hitler invited some twenty or so younger officers to the Berghof and talked them through his plans for German expansion, but was peeved that they too failed to express sufficient enthusiasm. A whispering campaign about how to remove Hitler if he tried to force Germany into war began amongst senior officers and continued into the autumn.

There has been extensive debate about the extent to which the Hossbach Memorandum revealed Hitler's real aims at this time. Much was made of it at the Nuremberg trials where the prosecution argued that it was effectively a blueprint that demonstrated the intention to trample over international law (see Chapter 10). Other historians have questioned whether it was a definitive plan as none of the scenarios envisaged by Hitler in late 1937 ever came to pass; he did, of course, wage aggressive war, but not according to the scenarios outlined in the Hossbach Memorandum. Perhaps the most acute assessment is that of historian Piers Brendon who concluded, 'If less than a blue print, it was much more than a daydream.'

Whatever his exact intentions were in November 1937, Hitler's resolve to expand the Reich crystallised over the next few months. In February 1938 Hitler told the Reichstag that he wanted to reunite 'over ten million Germans who live in the states adjoining our frontier'. The message was clear. Both German-speaking Austria and the Germans living along the Czech Sudetenland border with Germany would be absorbed into the Third Reich.

Act One: *Anschluss* and the Rape of Austria – Spring 1938

After the First World War the sprawling Austro-Hungarian Empire, a cornerstone of the European order for centuries, simply collapsed. The emperor abdicated and the ancient House of Habsburg, which had been at the centre of European politics for some 500 years, was no more. In 1919 the Treaty of Versailles redrew European boundaries to produce new, independent states from the dismembered corpse of the old Austro-Hungarian regime. A new Austria was created but the fledgling state was dogged by political instability throughout the 1920s and the country stumbled from crisis to crisis.

In 1932 an authoritarian right winger, Engelbert Dollfuss, became Chancellor. Dollfuss assumed dictatorial powers and trumpeted a belief in

'Austrofascism', a totalitarian creed which leaned more towards Mussolini than to Hitler. In particular, Dollfuss robustly rejected any idea that a powerful Nazi Germany might swallow up Austria. In the summer of 1934, Austrian Nazis – egged on by Berlin – barged into the chancellor's office in Vienna, assassinated Dollfuss and attempted to seize power. The coup failed and the assassins were hanged, but Nazi ambitions to take control of Austria and absorb it into the Third Reich did not die with them.

A new chancellor emerged called Kurt Schuschnigg. Like his assassinated predecessor, Schuschnigg too was every inch an 'Austrofascist' who resented Nazi meddling. The tensions between Berlin and Vienna grew as Hitler growled about 'holding back the Nazi tiger from the red meat of Austria'. In 1936, under extreme pressure, Schuschnigg signed a memorandum with Hitler. He agreed that Austria was a 'German state' in return for a fatuous guarantee of independence. Meanwhile, Austrian Nazis stepped up their boisterous campaign of 'agitprop' in Vienna, once again threatening the law, order and unity of the Austrian state. By 1938 the German Führer could scarcely contain his frustration at continued Austrian independence.

In February 1938 Hitler asked Schuschnigg to visit him in Berchtesgaden. It was an invitation which the Austrian Chancellor could scarcely refuse, but not one which looked forward to. When Schuschnigg entered the salon he apparently attempted to break the ice and flatter Hitler with complements about the Berghof. 'This room with its wonderful view has doubtless been the scene of many a decisive conference, Herr Reichskanzler,' said Schuschnigg. 'Yes,' snapped Hitler in reply, 'in this room my thoughts ripen. But we are not here to speak of the fine view or the weather.'

The hapless Schuschnigg was told that his country was effectively to be liquidated as an autonomous state. Hitler gave him an ultimatum: include the Austrian Nazis in his government and release all Nazi prisoners or face an immediate invasion by the German army. The Austrian leader, virtually a prisoner now in the Berghof, had little choice but to comply with the dictat. Within days the Austrian Nazi leader, Arthur Seyss-Inquart, was appointed interior minister and a general amnesty was extended to all imprisoned Nazis. The imperiled Schuschnigg did try to push back. He publicly insisted on national sovereignty and, in March 1938, organised a plebiscite to let the Austrian people express their view. Popular resistance in Austria to German Nazism was widespread (for example, it subsequently formed the plotline to the hit musical *The Sound of Music*). But Hitler did not want to hear the voice of the people. He immediately demanded that the Austrian government call off the referendum. With German troops massing on the Austrian border and little sign of international support, Schuschnigg had little option but to comply and resigned.

The following day the Nazi satrap, Seyss-Inquart, became chancellor of Austria. The German army immediately marched unopposed across the border and some six million Austrians woke up to discover that they were now Germans. On 14 March an emotional Hitler returned to the land of his birth. The powerful, noisy pro-Nazi lobby turned out in force to laud his entry into Vienna. He was cheered through the very streets that he had wandered as a vagabond artist just over two decades before. Others, however, were quickly on the run. Political opponents were swiftly rounded up while those who could, fled the country.

Firmly in control, Hitler decided that he could now risk a plebiscite. On 10 April the pro-Nazi puppet regime installed in Vienna called a referendum and Austrians went to the polls. The result purported to show an astonishing change of heart: 99.3% of voters apparently now supported union with Germany. The Nazis heralded the result as a triumph and called it the *Anschluss*, or connection. Winston Churchill, however, summed up the misgivings of many around Europe when he described it as 'the rape of Austria'. And as Churchill warned, worse was to follow.

Act Two: Munich Crisis and Death of Czechoslovakia – Summer/Autumn 1938

Having effectively seized Austria, Hitler now moved on to his next objective which was to split Czechoslovakia. Once again the resolve of the international community was tested, and once again found wanting. The events marked a watershed in twentieth-century history and became known as the 'Munich crisis', though much of the drama was played out at Berchtesgaden as well as in the city. At issue once again was the way in which Europe had been sliced up after the First World War. A new state – Czechoslovakia – was created from the central European territory where the Habsburg emperors had once ruled. The country was something of an artificial construct. It encompassed a mixture of Czechs, Slovaks, Germans and Hungarians, all with different languages, cultures and ethnic roots. The famous Czech writer, Franz Kafka, personified the cosmopolitan brew: a native of Prague, Kafka was Jewish and spoke German as a first language. Some of the different groups rubbed along in the fledgling state, bound together – just – by a sense of Czech nationalism. Around twenty-five per cent of the population, however, was German and far less integrated.

Early in 1938 the increasingly aggressive Hitler began to tug at the fragile threads that held Czechoslovakia together. At issue was the fate of the millions of people who lived in the Sudeten region of Czechoslovakia on the border with Germany. The *Sudetendeutsch* (Sudeten Germans), as they were known, were people who generally spoke and felt themselves to be German, but found themselves living in the new Czechoslovakia. Hitler aimed to bring them back into Germany, but he did not intend that the people should move; he was going to move the border.

The German *Anschluss* with Austria in the spring of 1938 left the western half of Czechoslovakia now effectively surrounded on three sides by Nazi Germany. One famous cartoon of the time portrayed the Czechs as being effectively trapped in the jaws of a wolf. Apprehensive, the government in Prague and the international community held its collective breath: it would only be a matter of time before Hitler moved in to claim the Sudetenland.

In April 1938 the Sudeten Nazi leader, Konrad Henlein, abruptly demanded complete autonomy from Czechoslovakia. He was supported by the vast majority of the *Sudetendeutsch* and his Sudenten German Party (SdP) was the second biggest in Czechoslovakia. The Czech government in Prague offered to devolve more powers to the region but the SdP simply responded by stepping up its noisy agitation for total separation. There were protests throughout the summer of 1938, some of which led to violent clashes between *Sudetendeutsch* separatists and Czech security forces. Casualties were reported with alacrity by the Nazi press and propaganda minister Goebbels seized on every incident to crank up the tension. In reality, pro-Nazi agitators clandestinely financed by, and under orders from, Berlin stoked much of the trouble. Meanwhile, the pro-Nazi *Sudetendeutsch* leader Henlein went on a charm offensive abroad. He met opinion formers in London, peddling the romantic myth that the Sudetens were an oppressed minority who simply wanted more autonomy from Prague. Some of the more gullible commentators and politicians were taken in and became vocal converts for the cause of Sudeten 'self-determination'.

Tension reached boiling point as local elections loomed in May 1938. German troops began to mass on the Czech frontier ready to support the *Sudetendeutsch*, by whatever means. While Hitler was eager to gamble on the use of force, however, many within the military remained jittery about the prospect of triggering conflict. German generals feared that a rash attack on the Czechs would provoke all-out war because France, Britain and Russia might come to the defence of Czechoslovakia. Such an escalation would rapidly mean Germany having to fight a war on two fronts: in the east and the west. The military high command feared that the military was not yet prepared and would be overwhelmed by a superior force. Hitler's audacity had paid off so far, but an attack on the Czechs would surely provoke a catastrophic war and defeat. It would be 1918 all over again.

Over the summer of 1938 there was a flurry of political and diplomatic activity. The French and British governments in particular made various attempts to calm the situation, but failed. Meanwhile, Hitler's preparations for conflict stepped up a gear. German troops were sent to the Czech border regions in ever larger numbers. Military spending – especially on the German navy – and plans for war increased apace.

At the beginning of September 1938 the Czech Nazi leader, Henlein, was summoned to the Berghof for talks. Ten days later Hitler launched a scathing, inflammatory attack on the Czech government in his speech to the annual Nazi rally in Nuremberg. The 'oppressed' Sudeten Germans, he claimed, were in danger of being 'annihilated'. He promised that Germany would defend them; 'and not just with words'. In Prague, President Benes prepared to put up a fight and ordered a mobilisation of the well-trained Czech army. What Benes required most of all, however, was backing from powerful allies like France and Britain. He knew, as they did, that without support Czech resistance to Nazism would be crushed.

Benes had good reason to expect that his call would be answered. After the First World War the French had agreed to defend the fledgling

Czechoslovakia should it ever be attacked 'without provocation'. In a separate agreement, Britain had agreed to defend France if the latter was attacked, although Britain had no direct commitment to help Czechoslovakia. Nevertheless, a domino effect was abundantly clear: if Czechoslovakia were attacked the French would side with the Czechs and the British would side with the French. British intelligence left Chamberlain in no doubt that Hitler was ready for war over Czechoslovakia. Conversations with Paris, however, made it equally clear that the French were not. And if the French would not act, neither would the British. According to Winston Churchill, 'The British and French cabinets at this time presented a front of two overripe melons crushed together; whereas what was needed was a gleam of steel.'

Far from threatening war, the British prime minister, Neville Chamberlain, sought to de-escalate tension and resolve the conflict by negotiation. In September 1938 he made the first of what would be three trips to Munich in as many weeks. In subsequent decades the phrase 'shuttle-diplomacy' entered the language to describe the to-and-fro of seasoned diplomats trying to assuage international tension. For the British premier in his seventieth year, with little experience of foreign affairs, the task of restraining Europe's most aggressive dictator without tipping the entire continent into war was a daunting task.

Act Two, Scene One: Chamberlain, Hitler and the Berghof

On 15 September Chamberlain took off from Heston airport just outside London and went to meet Hitler at Obersalzberg the following day. Chamberlain described the visit in a letter to his sister. After a brief stopover at Berchtesgaden's Grand Hotel, the British party was taken by car to Hitler's Berghof:

> The entrance to the house is on one side opening to a sort of terrace, from which a flight of steps descends to the road. Half way down these steps stood the Führer, bare headed and dressed in a khaki coloured coat of broadcloth with a red armlet and a swastika on it, and the military cross on his breast. He wore black trousers, such as we wear in the evening, and black patent-leather lace up shoes. His hair is brown, not black,

his eyes blue and his expression rather disagreeable, especially in repose, and altogether he looks entirely undistinguished. You would never notice him in a crowd and take him for the house painter he once was.

The two then made their way to what Chamberlain described as 'the celebrated chamber' of the reception room, 'one end of which was entirely occupied by a vast window'. Chamberlain was somewhat disappointed to note that clouds obscured much of view which 'must be magnificent but this day there were only the valley and the bottom of the mountains to be seen.'

The two men quickly got down to business and a one-to-one discussion with only an interpreter present. According to a Foreign Office note, dictated by Chamberlain, Hitler told the British prime minister that he had from his youth been 'obsessed with the racial theory'. All Germans, he asserted, were of one blood and so were one people. Nevertheless, Hitler said he was willing to draw a line between the possible and the impossible and he recognised that there were places where it might not be feasible to bring Germans into the Reich. But where Germans lived on the frontier – as was the case with the three million *Sudetendeutsch* – that was a different matter. Hitler felt 'that those Germans should come into the Reich. They wanted to and he was determined that they should come in.'

Chamberlain was puzzled by Hitler's apparently modest claim and interjected, 'Hold on a minute: there is one point on which I want to be clear … you say that the three million Sudeten Germans must be included in the Reich: would you be satisfied with that and is there nothing more that you want? I ask because there are many people who think that is not all; that you wish to dismember Czechoslovakia.'

At this, Hitler embarked on long-winded speech in which he insisted that he wanted only racial unity, 'He did not want a lot of Czechs. All he wanted was Sudeten Germans.' When Chamberlain attempted to clarify how this might work in practice and raised further questions, Hitler became testy and cut him short. The German leader complained that details were 'academic' and launched into another lengthy tirade. He alleged that 300 Sudetens had been killed and vowed to 'avenge' further deaths, 'The thing has got to be settled at once: I am determined to settle it: I do not care whether there is a world war or not: I am determined to settle it and to settle it soon and I am prepared to risk a world war rather than allow this to drag on.'

At this point, Chamberlain became exasperated. If Hitler was determined to settle the Sudeten question by force and without discussion, the British PM snapped, 'I have wasted my time,' by coming to Berchtesgaden at all. In a more emollient tone, he assured Hitler that, in his personal opinion and in principle, he had, 'nothing to say against the separation of the Sudeten Germans from the rest of Czechoslovakia, provided that the practical difficulties could be overcome.'

After three hours the meeting adjourned with the outline of an agreement. Border areas with a high concentration of *Sudetendeutsch* could be transferred to Germany, if Hitler would agree to guarantee the independence of what remained of Czechoslovakia. A flurry of diplomatic activity followed the Berghof meeting. Chamberlain returned to London to brief his cabinet while various countries voiced their views about how far they might go – or not – to protect the integrity of the Czechoslovak state.

Ironically, there was one group that neither the French nor the British wanted to consult too closely as these events unfolded; the Czechs themselves. Prague was effectively told that whole chunks of the Sudetenland were to be handed over to Germany without a fight. War had been avoided with the price paid by the Czechs: Benes and his people were about to be betrayed. Following the Berchtesgaden meeting Britain and France pressured the Czechs to give up the Sudetenland. Reluctantly, but without any alternative, Prague agreed on 21 September.

Act Two, Scene Two: Hitler Doubles the Stakes

The following day – 22 September – Chamberlain, relieved that the crisis had passed, flew to Germany for a second meeting with Hitler, where he expected to 'seal the deal.' The two met at the spa town of Bad Godesberg, but there was nothing relaxed about this summit. To Chamberlain's astonishment, Hitler now reneged on the possible accord that had been outlined at Berchtesgaden. Emboldened, the Nazi leader simply doubled the stakes. Map in hand, he produced a further list of territorial and other demands which he expected the hapless Czechs to accept. If his terms were not agreed in full by 1 October – just over a week – Hitler promised that there would be war. Chamberlain was dumbfounded. Nevertheless, the British prime minister promised to put Hitler's proposals to the Czech government.

Chamberlain then returned to London, where he briefed his sombre cabinet in Downing Street on the latest, unwelcome development. Once again, Europe seemed to be staggering inexorably and thoughtlessly towards war, just as it had in 1914. Czech and German troops began to mass on either side along the Sudeten border. French reservists were sent to reinforce the units stationed along the Maginot line, the defensive fortifications between France and Germany in the west. The British navy was put on alert and trenches were dug in Hyde Park. At a huge rally at the Sportspalast in Berlin, Hitler whipped himself and the crowd into a frenzy of indignation. 'The Czech state began with one single lie ... that there was a Czechoslovakian nation [but] there is no such thing as a Czechoslovakian nation,' he shrieked, before concluding ominously, 'In relation to the Sudetenland Germans my patience is now at an end.'

From across the Atlantic, President Roosevelt urged European leaders, 'For the sake of humanity ... to find a peaceful, fair and constructive settlement to the question at issue.' But, tellingly, at no point did he suggest that the USA might be prepared to intervene. In Downing Street Neville Chamberlain solemnly addressed the British people on the wireless. Weary and dispirited, he lamented that the nation was on the verge of another European war. It was all, he said, in a bewildered tone, because of 'a quarrel in a far-away country between people of whom we know nothing.'

The Final Act: Munich and the Reprieve

Then, at the eleventh hour, when conflict seemed inevitable, came a reprieve. On 29 September Chamberlain took off from Heston airport bound yet again for Munich to meet Hitler for a third and final time. These negotiations took place in the Führerbau, the Nazi HQ in Munich, followed by an informal meeting at Hitler's flat in Prinzregenstrasse (a fuller account of the chaotic meeting is given in Chapter 4).

Central to the discussion and signatories to the final agreement were Hitler, Mussolini, the French premier, Daladier, and Neville

Chamberlain. Talks began at midday and went on for fourteen hours, with an agreement finally reached in the early hours of the following morning, on 30 September. The final accord handed Hitler most of what he demanded: Czech evacuation of the Sudetenland was to begin the following day, 1 October. The process was to be completed over the following ten days and an international commission would determine exactly where the final frontier was to be fixed. Despite the conference being about their country, no representative of the Czech government at any level was present. Nor were the Russians invited, although they too had a stake in Czech sovereignty. When leaders of the Czech government finally arrived in Munich they were presented with a *fait accompli* and told to sign the document. There was no Plan B. The clear winner was Hitler; Chamberlain's policy of appeasement had almost reached its apogee. There was still one final scene to be played out, however. It was the one by which history would record the whole sorry episode.

Weary but pumped with adrenaline, Chamberlain rose early to meet Hitler at his home in Munich's Prinzregenstrasse the following morning. The elderly British premier was anxious to try and build on the accord arrived at a few hours before. Ambitiously, he sought to reset the whole relationship with Germany to try and avoid any similar crisis arising in the future. Chamberlain prevailed on Hitler to sign a memorandum in which both leaders declared their mutual desire to settle any future differences through consultation in order to preserve the peace of Europe. It was this paper that Chamberlain flourished when he flew back to a triumphant reception in England. It was, he proclaimed, 'symbolic of the desire of our two peoples never to go to war with one another again,' and later said that it guaranteed 'peace with honour … peace for our time.'

Chamberlain's declaration met with a rapturous reception. The Munich crisis had taken Europe to the brink of war and there was a palpable sense of relief that conflict had been avoided. But there were also vocal critics who expressed their dismay. In the front rank of the sceptics was Winston Churchill who thought the accord was delusional and reportedly told Chamberlain, 'You were given the choice between war and dishonour. You chose dishonour, and you will have war.'

When the House of Commons was convened to debate the agreement days later on 5 October, Churchill expanded on his view that the agreement finally reached in Munich was a sham. Despite Chamberlain's weeks of shuttle diplomacy, he concluded that the prime minister had been hoodwinked. Churchill asked what the differences were between the positions reached at Berchtesgaden, Bad Godesberg and Munich. 'They can be very simply epitomized ... £1 was demanded at the pistol's point. When it was given, £2 was demanded at the pistol's point. Finally, the dictator consented to take £1 17s. 6d. and the rest in promises of goodwill for the future.' Left on their own and without intervention from Britain and France, Churchill mocked, the Czechs could have negotiated better terms than those agreed for them. He closed his speech with another important point. The Munich agreement laid bare a fundamental division between ideas and not between peoples: 'The Prime Minister desires to see cordial relations between this country and Germany. There is no difficulty at all in having cordial relations with the German people. Our hearts go out to them. But they have no power.' The issue, he insisted, was between competing visions: 'There can never be friendship between the British democracy and the Nazi Power, that Power which spurns Christian ethics, which cheers its onward course by a barbarous paganism, which vaunts the spirit of aggression and conquest, which derives strength and perverted pleasure from persecution, and uses, as we have seen, with pitiless brutality the threat of murderous force. That Power cannot ever be the trusted friend of the British democracy.'

Churchill's reservations were shared across the political spectrum. Just days later an editorial in the left-wing *New Statesmen* magazine commented despondently, 'The bitter fruits of the Munich ultimatum have begun to ripen fast. We shall soon, if Mr Churchill proves right, discover the terrible price that Britain has paid. For the moment we watch with horror the torment and destruction of Czechoslovakia.'

The Shadow of Munich

As events turned out, the eventual destruction of Czechoslovakia just months later was only one of the many dire consequences of Hitler's triumph. The meetings at Berchtesgaden and Munich in September 1938 cast a shadow that stretched over the rest of the twentieth century and into the twenty-first. One immediate effect was to silence Hitler's critics in the German military. The whispering campaign of the summer and all talk of a coup d'état to overthrow him ceased abruptly. The audacity of his diplomacy and the ease with which he had outmanoeuvered other international statesmen meant that the Hitler regime was now unassailable within Germany. Hitler's invincibility was mirrored by the Czech president Benes' vulnerability. Just three weeks after the invasion of the Sudetenland, Czech president Edward Benes fled Prague and found refuge in London. He made his home by the river Thames in suburban Putney and from there he helped lead the Czech resistance in the Second World War.

In March 1939 Germany invaded Prague. Hitler's guarantees of Czech sovereignty proved, predictably, to be wholly worthless. Other neighbouring countries – Hungary and Poland – also took a share of Czech territory, descending, in Churchill's words, like 'vultures on the carcass of Czechoslovakia'. The Nazi regime had effectively removed an entire country from the chessboard of European politics without firing a shot. Emboldened, Hitler now prepared for further invasions and war.

The policy of appeasement was now in shreds. Scarcely has any policy so central to a government's purpose been discredited in so short a time. The ignominy of appeasement followed Chamberlain to the grave and left an irredeemable stain on his reputation. Even in our own time accusations of 'appeasement' or of being 'an appeaser' have a special, negative connotation almost without parallel in the extensive lexicon of British political insults. The charge of 'not having learned the lessons of Munich' remains a grave one indeed for any politician to answer.

Yet within a short time Hitler's triumph at the Berghof lay in ruins. He left his mountain retreat in July 1944 and never returned. In April 1945 the entire Obersalzburg complex was heavily bombed by an Allied air raid. Many buildings on the surface were badly damaged although the underground bunker complex was relatively unscathed. American ground troops liberated the area and, along with locals, stripped the Berghof of its contents, many for souvenirs. In the early 1950s what remained of the Berghof, by then a shell of a building, was blown up to avoid it becoming a Nazi shrine. Today, the area once occupied by the building is largely covered by woodland and a forest path runs across what was once the patio. The only visible remains are fragments of the foundations.

While walking the path it is impossible not to reflect on the characters who once shaped European history there: the hoodwinked statesmen, the conniving fellow-travellers and, of course, the cavorting Nazis. But perhaps the final word should go to one whose country was betrayed at

Berchtesgaden. In one of the greatest movies of the war, *Casablanca*, Victor Laszlo is a Czech resistance fighter on the run. When the apparently cynical nightclub owner, Rick (Humphrey Bogart), questioned the point of resisting the Nazis, Laszlo's reply summed up the feelings, not just of the Czechs but of millions of others at that desperate time, 'You might as well question why we breathe. If we stop breathing, we'll die. If we stop fighting our enemies, the world will die.'

Chapter Ten

Nuremberg: The Triumph of Justice Over Power

In November 1945 a small group of men were led into the dock of courtroom 600 of the *Justizpalast* (Palace of Justice) at Nuremberg.[1] They were all leading players from what remained of the Hitler elite and they knew the city well. For nearly two decades Nuremberg had hosted the annual Nazi rallies, the swaggering displays of pomp which, more than any other, encapsulated the arrogance and aggression of the Third Reich. Yet now the parade grounds lay abandoned. Many of the city's medieval buildings were in ruins, and the Nazi satraps were on trial for their lives. Nowhere was the vaingloriousness of Nazism more fully displayed, or the degradation of the regime's crimes more ruthlessly exposed, than in Nuremberg. Just an hour or so from Munich, even a day in the city can help the modern visitor understand much about the crucial events that took place here during the Third Reich. No other city in Europe is so associated with the basest instincts and noblest aspirations of human nature. This chapter will explain why Nuremberg assumed such prominence under the Nazis; and the vital role it played in helping to bring justice for their victims.

Nuremberg: 'the most German of all German cities'

Had there been a capital of the Holy Roman Empire, Nuremberg would have been a contender for the title. The city was a hub of medieval power and wealth, renowned for fine craftsmanship and innovation. Today, a stroll around the city's streets and along the river Pegnitz helps us to understand why it was such an important centre of European culture many centuries before the Nazis came to power. Although the medieval city was extensively damaged in the Second World War – almost half of it was destroyed by Allied bombing between 1943 and 1945 – it has since been rebuilt with some of the narrow streets reconstructed to look as they did before the war. It was here that the rulers of the Holy Roman Empire, which covered the German-speaking world and more, had a secular power equal to that of the Pope's spiritual authority in Rome. The emperors travelled incessantly across their fiefdom, but so frequently were they in Nuremberg that it became known as the 'unofficial capital' of the empire. All new kings paid homage to the city's pre-eminence by holding their first assembly in Nuremberg. The imperial court worshiped at the main church, the Frauenkirch, while the emperor's regalia – imperial crown, holy lance and ceremonial sword – were held permanently in the city.

A massive imperial castle dominates the city and is a very solid reminder of its importance during the Middle Ages. From then on, artisan guilds nurtured artists and fine craftsmen such as the city's most famous son, Albrecht Dürer. The metalworkers of Nuremberg developed an unrivalled reputation and a culture of manufacturing excellence which continues in Germany to this day. Composer Richard Wagner also reflected some of the artistic tradition when he used the city as the location for possibly his most famous opera *Die Meistersinger von Nürnberg* (the mastersinger of Nuremberg).

This long, rich history led to an official description of Nuremberg under the Nazis as 'the most German of all German cities'. Yet, paradoxically, it was this reverence for Nuremberg's outstanding contribution to European culture that led to some of the city's darkest years. The Nazis used Nuremberg as a stage for their notorious annual gatherings. They built a messianic complex on the outskirts of the city to host these rallies, much of which survives today. The area is easily accessible and now has an excellent **visitor information centre** which explains the history of Nazism in the city.[2]

Banners and Blood: Nazism on Parade

The first Nazi rally at Nuremberg took place in 1923. With good transport links and a sympathetic local police force, it was conveniently located as a centre where party members could gather. Hitler himself stayed at the Hotel Deutscher Hof, opposite the main railway station, where he took the salute of endless march-past parades from the window of his room. Nuremberg's connection with the Holy Roman Empire was an added symbolic bonus. The annual rally in September eventually became a fixed event in the party calendar. As each year passed the gathering became more sophisticated and soon would last for several days. It also involved ever more people. After 1933 mass rallies were held and huge encampments of tents were constructed for participants. By 1938 some half a million people flocked to Nuremberg for the rally, though this turned out to be the last. The rally of 1939 was given the title of 'Rally of Peace' as a signal of Germany's desire to live in harmony with her neighbours. It was cancelled with just a few hours' notice when Hitler abruptly declared war on Poland.

Although different in character every year, each rally was a carefully orchestrated theatrical event with music, visual effects and speeches. Initially the columns of the SA drummed their way through the narrow streets of the city while the medieval buildings provided a perfect backdrop for Hitler's speeches to the Nazi ranks. Then, when the Nazis came to power, there was a step change in the organisation of the rallies, which now took on a new and enhanced importance. An entire new complex of buildings was planned to host all party events in Nuremberg. Albert Speer, the chief Nazi architect, was responsible for the overall project, with much input from Hitler, who had once yearned to be an architect himself. This pharaonic exercise was intended to cover an area of 11km² and included the massive open arena, a closed 50,000-seat auditorium and any number of memorials and pantheons. Much of it was never completed and what remains today is only a fragment of the whole project. Nevertheless, it is enough to provide a clear idea of what was intended.

Famed for their scale and spectacle, the rallies were used to showcase German nationalism and a new order for the future. Some yearned for deliverance from the past and, above all, security. The Nuremberg gatherings embodied the Nazi belief of a racial–national unity in which the individual was only important as part of a greater whole. Artifacts such as the 'blood banner', stained with the blood of those who died in the *putsch* massacre of 1923, were solemnly paraded. A temple was built to Nazi 'martyrs' and their names read out as a roll of honour. More than mere assemblies, the rallies became quasi-religious ceremonies in which participants venerated sacred Nazi principles and expressed their adulation for the Führer. Like a messiah he walked alone through the massed ranks of uniformed followers up to the high-alter of the speaker's rostrum. Then, swept up by the manipulative use of thundering, rhythmic music and powerful arclights, Hitler's hypnotic demagogy took hold on thousands of minds.

For those who could not be there in person, the rallies were filmed in meticulous detail by a talented film director, Leni Riechfenstal. Her documentary of the 1934 rally, for example, called *Triumph of the Will*, was shown in cinemas throughout Germany and was one of the most successful propaganda films ever made in the Third Reich. Even today the immediacy of Reichfenstal's documentaries from the period have a disturbing power to shock and they are the subject of huge controversy. On the one hand, they are pure propaganda: designed to enhance the prestige of the Nazi regime and inspire adulation for Hitler, any right-thinking person will condemn them for what they are. On the other hand, their technical brilliance and immediacy enables the viewer to better understand – or even feel – the full force of Nazi power projected at Nuremberg. The debate about how far it is possible to respect the form of Riechfenstal's work while condemning the content continues to this day.

Others attempted to describe the rallies in words. American journalist William Shirer attended the 1934 rally and recorded, 'Two hundred thousand party officials packed in the Zepplin field with their twenty-one thousand flags unfurled in the searchlights like a forest of weird trees … And there in the flood-lit night, jammed together like sardines in one mass formation, the little men of Germany who have made Nazism possible achieved the highest state of being; the shedding of their individual souls and minds … until under the mystic lights and the sound of the magic words of the Austrian [Hitler], they were merged in the completely Germanic herd.'

Hitler's speech-making is discussed elsewhere (see Chapter 2). It was at Nuremberg, however, that his oratory was given full rein. In 1938 a correspondent of the *New Statesman* reported from Nuremberg where, he said, he 'felt like an invisible intruder at a savage tribal ceremony'. Like a modern-day rock concert, there was frequently a long wait and a warm up before the main act:

> For twenty minutes before the speech began we were worked
> up to a complete emotional surrender. The Wagnerian ecstasy
> of drums and soaring brass enveloped speaker and audience in

a thick atmosphere ... [An] acolyte announced the presence of the man-god, and at last he spoke. Once again, the strangely feminine contralto voice fumbled for the mood of the audience. As usual, for the first quarter of an hour Hitler spoke hurriedly, halting often and swallowing in the middle of his sentences. "National Socialism ... 1921 ... workers ... spiritual leadership", the general drift was clear – the miraculous growth of the party. But he was still feeling for the right note and the audience was faintly restive. Then Hitler hit his stride and his voice shrieked with invective against Germany's enemies and how they had been overcome, before the crescendo, "Now world democracy and Bolshevism try to strangle our people – but again we will prevail." As if beckoned by a conductor the chorus responded with a ponderous "Seig Heil" of tribal hate.

But not all observers were impressed by Hitler's style. British journalist Sefton Delmer covered one of Hitler's mass meetings and rapidly concluded that he was a 'crackpot'. Others must have wearied of the rallies too. The parades, marches and displays went on for a week with different themes and groups involved – for example, military, farmers, mothers, youth, etc. – but in the end the message was always tediously identical and amounted to the same thing: blind loyalty to the Nazi revolution and Hitler. Any sign of ennui would have been fatal, though some participants surely were bored by the end. Beyond the arena and away from the town, much of the spectacle met with sheer indifference. Clandestine diarist Victor Klemperer recorded walking into a bar where the owner had dutifully tuned to a radio transmission of the rally in 1938, 'But no one was listening. I could barely understand the broadcast because a couple of people were playing cards, striking the table with loud thumps, talking very loudly. One man was writing a postcard, one reading a newspaper and one writing in his order book ... Truly not one in a dozen people paid attention to the wireless, not even for a single second. It could just as well have been transmitting silence or a foxtrot from Leipzig.'

Closer to Nuremberg, others became disillusioned with the gargantuan stadiums. Vast resources were sucked into building the complex and this set off grumbling amongst the local workers. They wanted building materials used for better housing with proper sanitation to replace some of the city's medieval slums, not a vast Nazi theme park on the edge of their city. Both the scale and cost of the building work were enough to trigger silent protests. Several of the most valuable granite blocks to be used in the construction of the Party Congress Hall were deliberately damaged by some of the 900 local construction workers with the result that the building could not be completed on time. Then the Second World War intervened to consume both workers and resources so that the full project was never realised and remains unfinished today.

The Nuremberg Laws 1935: Are they not Jewish?

Anti-Semitism was a cornerstone of Nazi ideology and quickly incorporated into German law. In September 1935 Hitler convened a meeting of the German Reichstag in Nuremberg – the one and only time it met outside Berlin – to ratify the 'Reich Citizenship Law' and the 'Law for the Protection of German Blood and Honour'. Herman Göring explained that the new laws would ensure that, in future, 'citizens of the Reich would include only those of German blood or blood of similar races.' Together, these measures became known as the 'Nuremberg Racial Laws'.

The most visible change introduced by the new regime was symbolic. The Nazi swatiska would now officially replace the old black-red-and-white German flag as the emblem of the state. Most Germans could have been forgiven for thinking that the substitution had already been made. From now on, the symbolism of the Nazi movement and the German state were as one. The new Nuremberg race laws would now synthesise what it meant to be German. Since Hitler's rise to power in 1933, Jews in German society had been subjected to arbitrary discrimination, designed to make their lives uncomfortable. Jewish businesses were boycotted and their livelihoods threatened. Bullying and beatings by SA thugs were an ever-present threat.

The Nuremberg Laws, however, went much further in marginalising the Jewish population from mainstream society and began to regulate even private matters such as relationships. Under the new code, a Byzantine system was concocted to define an individual's ethnicity and determine whether or not a person was Jewish. Being a Jew no longer depended on an individual's personal beliefs or religious practice; it was now solely determined by genetics, ethnicity and Nazi ideology.

According to the scheme, a person with four Jewish grandparents was easy to categorise: the current generation was one hundred per cent Jewish. But a person with three Jewish grandparents, or even just two Jewish grandparents, but who was religious or married to a Jew, was now deemed to be one hundred per cent Jewish too. Various levels of Jewishness could then be calculated according to a formula. Anyone categorised as a Jew was automatically stripped of their German citizenship, disenfranchised, and forbidden to marry or to have any kind of sexual liaison with a non-Jew. To limit the possibility of such couplings, for example, the law forbade any Jew from employing a female servant under forty-five years old.

Many people, not necessarily wholly Jewish, were now startled to discover that the new law deemed them to be a *Mischling*, or part-Jew. Once again, the new scheme determined how Jewish a person might be: two Jewish grandparents made you a first degree *Mischling*, while one Jewish grandparent resulted in a second degree categorization. These definitions meant that over 1.5 million people in Germany were considered either full Jews or *Mischlinge* in 1935; approximately 2.3 percent of the population. Many people who did not believe in Judaism, never practiced Judaism or had only the sketchiest contact with the Jewish community now found themselves in a sort of ethnic limbo. Whilst they might consider themselves ethnically German, the law declared that they were not. In a Nazi state founded on gene theory, the Nuremberg laws obviously mattered a great deal. In addition to the practicing members of the Jewish community, many other innocent victims were also swept up in the drive for racial purity and declared members of supposedly inferior, distinctly non-German alien groups. A couple of months later, in November 1935, the Nuremberg law was extended. It now became a criminal offence for Roma or people of black ethnicity to have relationships with gentile Germans.

The Nuremberg Laws marked a menacing and sinister shift in Nazi racial policy. What began with malicious words in *Mein Kampf* a decade before now moved up a notch towards the biggest pogrom in history. Occasionally there was a let up in the application of the Nuremberg laws. During the Berlin Olympics, for example, in the summer of 1936, when the world was watching the Nazi regime closely, there was some respite for the Jewish community and other minorities. But after the closing ceremony was over and the international guests departed the hounding of the Jewish community and other minorities began again.

In September 1936, the Jewish Telegraph Agency reported Hitler's speech from Nuremberg in which he said, 'The German nation will attempt once and forever to give a secular solution to the Jewish problem,' before adding, ominously, 'Should this attempt be unsuccessful, then revision of the entire Jewish problem will be made.' Within a decade millions of Jews were dead, swept up in the demonic lunacy of the Holocaust. For many, whether they lived or died was effectively decided at Nuremberg. As one commentator noted, 'For many, the categorizations of Jewishness established in the Nuremberg Laws were pivotal in determining their ultimate fate.' With the code as a point of departure it was only a short journey to death camps such as Auschwitz and Buchenwald as the ultimate destination.

The Nuremberg Trials: the Tribute of Power unto Reason

By the summer of 1945 the once-beautiful medieval city of Nuremberg lay in ruins. Many thousands of its citizens were dead. Those who remained survived as best they could in buildings, ninety per cent of which had been damaged by Allied bombing. But Nuremberg was, of course, not unique in its misery. Six years of war had left sixty million people dead. Families had been destroyed, whole communities had disappeared and entire populations were uprooted. If the Nazi leaders who had wrought this havoc on humanity were not guilty of some crime it was difficult to understand how the word had meaning. But exactly who could be indicted? On what charges? And where? The answers to these and many other questions were decided in the sombre, wood-panelled courtroom 600 of Nuremberg's Palace of Justice.[1]

Nuremberg and the International Military Tribunal

The unprecedented events of the Second World War called for a new type of court and so the Allies set up an International Military Tribunal to try the Nazi leaders. These hearings, known as the Nuremberg trials, broke new legal ground in 1946. Before the war it was a generally agreed principle that states should not meddle in one another's domestic affairs. This was known as the Westphalian principle. It dated back to the sixteenth century when Europe had been pulled apart by the devastating Thirty Years War, in which several European states waged war with one another to protect religious minorities in neighbouring states. The result was a bloodbath. For the next 300 years the Westphalian principle helped to maintain some degree of stability on the continent by obliging states to mind their own business and refrain from interfering in the internal order of another. The agreement did not, obviously, eliminate conflict completely, but whenever war did break out the subsequent peace treaty normally included an amnesty for combatants. Bygones were bygones and each returned to their own.

The Treaty of Versailles dented the Westphalian notion of immunity and then the Nazis tested the principle to destruction. The Nuremberg trials of 1946 put an end to the idea that the government of a country enjoys unlimited sovereignty to do as it will within their own borders or in times of war. The court at Nuremberg was a milestone on the path to the idea that government should be held accountable if its actions violate some basic but universal principles of human rights. Nuremberg became a dividing line in the history of jurisprudence, a place which gave its name to a 'before' and an 'after'. The Nuremberg trials marked an almost revolutionary leap forward in the scope of international law.

Leipzig and the Trial of 'Kaiser Bill'

Cracks began to appear in the principle of untouchable Westphalian sovereignty in the aftermath of the First World War. The victorious allies demanded reparations from Germany in the Versailles treaty, which became a cornerstone of the post-war settlement. Less well known is that they also demanded recognition of individual guilt, because the normal rules of war had been flouted as never before in the carnage. The Allies sought to make an example of (German) perpetrators. They wanted politicians, military commanders and some ordinary soldiers to stand trial before a national or international tribunal. A court was established in the central city of Leipzig to conduct the trials, but there was a fatal flaw because the process was left in German hands to try their own. Not surprisingly, there was a marked lack of enthusiasm on the part of prosecutors to bring the culprits to book and there was much legal confusion about exactly what crimes had been committed. As a consequence of the foot-dragging and uncertainty, the Leipzig hearings lumbered on for six years and achieved almost nothing. Of the 900 or so people indicted just a handful ever faced trial. Most of the accused were found not guilty or handed down risibly lenient sentences. Even then, hardly any of the convicts served out their full term. The ultimate authority of the German war machine, Kaiser Wilhelm, never came anywhere near the court. Wilhelm successfully fought extradition from Holland and never appeared at Leipzig, so the man who, perhaps more than any other, personified German militarism escaped scot-free.

At Nuremberg, the defendants also claimed that the international court had no jurisdiction, or right, to try them. Göring complained noisily that he would 'only acquiesce to trial by a German court'. But *force majeure* prevailed. The Allies were not going to make the same mistake twice.

Court Room 600: a Special Tribunal

The Allies were aware of some – though by no means all – of the barbarity being committed by the Nazis even during war and discussed how it might be dealt with after victory had been achieved. Top level meetings in London, Moscow, Tehran and Yalta discussed retribution, but at first there was little agreement. Stalin pressed for the summary execution of 50,000 or so Nazi staff officers at the end of the war. President Roosevelt was appalled and sarcastically suggested that killing just 49,000 Nazis should do the trick. Winston Churchill insisted that shooting just 100 German leaders would be enough. Other voices, however, argued that the due process of law must be observed and eventually, in the summer of 1945, the four victorious Allied powers agreed to establish a special criminal court to try the Nazi leaders.

Nuremberg was the location of choice for the Allies, both for practical and symbolic reasons. On a functional level the massive Palace of Justice in the city suburbs had, miraculously, survived the air raids more or less intact. This meant that the city was one of the few with a physical infrastructure ready to host such a trial. One observer recalled how, when he returned in 1945, he was disorientated by the devastation and felt 'increasingly confused for I could no longer get my bearings in this gigantic rubble heap ... But there in the middle of this destruction, as though spared by a miracle, stood the Palace of Justice. How often had I driven past it in Hitler's car.' The words were those of Albert Speer, architect of the monumental stadiums used for the Nazi rallies. He was now back in Nuremberg and on trial for his life.

The contrast between the arrogant prewar rallies in Speer's grandiose settings and what was left of the Nazi elite as wretched prisoners in the dock would not be lost on anyone. The trial was staged in Court Room 600, an elegant, solemn room completed in 1913. The entrance to the court is surrounded by heavy, dark-green marble porticos adorned with figures that refer to original sin and the ancient roots of law. Adam and Eve are flanked on one side by German law carrying a sword and on the other by Roman law carrying sticks. Today, the appearance of the court is much as it was in 1946, although it was lengthened a little then to accommodate the large number of people involved in the trial. Apart from the accused, hundreds of people crowded into the court, which became hot and sweaty as each day wore on. Alongside the judges, clerks, prosecution and defence teams were interpreters (German, French, English and Russian), press and the public. Given the massive interest in the case, the public and press gallery was extended by knocking out the back wall of the court. The enlarged dock was furnished only with spartan wooden benches. The Nazi leaders were stripped of all privileges and the hard seats served to remind them that they had only the rights of any other accused in a criminal trial.

In retrospect, the Nuremberg trials – with punishment for the perpetrators and recognition for victims – seem an obvious and inevitable outcome of the defeat of Nazism. But that is not how it seemed at the time. There were several hurdles which nearly prevented any trial at all. Apart from space, the combined logistical arrangements for all the support staff – from interpreters to catering and cleaning – were complicated and difficult. The Palace of Justice had just about survived saturation bombing by the Allies, but many other buildings were badly damaged and accommodation was scarce. Security was also a worry. Although Germany had been comprehensively defeated, groups loyal to Hitler remained and nobody was quite sure how strong the resistance might be. Christine Rommel, teenage niece of the German general, worked in the library of the Palace of Justice. She told journalists that there was a serious danger of an attack on the jail by local Bavarian Nazis because 'there is so much that they do not want exposed and they are very bitter.' As a consequence, five tanks were brought up to defend the building and everyone was thoroughly searched before being allowed to enter.

The trial process was driven by the Allied powers: USA, UK, Russia and France. Each, however, had a very different legal system. Several on the American team were better versed in prosecuting financial fraud than criminal cases. Eyebrows were raised when the Russians nominated Judge Ion Nikitchenko as their representative on the bench. He had presided over Stalin's notorious Moscow 'show trials' in 1935 where most of the accused eagerly confessed to their 'crimes' to avoid further torture. And the German lawyers defending their clients were used to another set of trial rules from a very different legal tradition (even prior to Hitler).

The chances of a fair trial also seemed to be hampered by recent events. In France, for example, there was a comprehensible but near-hysterical clamour for revenge on those who had collaborated with the Nazis. Thousands of hearings were held, including that of Pierre Laval, head of the French vassal state that had cooperated with the Nazi occupation. Laval's trial descended into bedlam. Judges and jury seemed to join in with the prosecution, while there were emotional scenes in the public gallery before the former French leader was found guilty and executed in the autumn of 1945. In this context, the likelihood of blind justice producing a fair trial for Nazi leaders at Nuremberg seemed remote.

Many Germans resented the trial taking place at all. They felt that it was not just the accused but the entire nation in the dock. They regarded the process with studied indifference and dismissed it as 'victors' justice'. Many were reluctant to accept that crimes had been committed on the scale that was alleged. And even if they had, they insisted that the barbarity had nothing to do with them. One of the American prosecutors conducted a straw poll as he travelled round the country: of the one hundred people whom he asked about the trial seventy-nine did not even know it was happening. Was this indifference, a form of denial or simply the result of the daily struggle for survival in a country in ruins?

Two of most culpable Nazis – Hitler and Goebbels – had committed suicide in the final days of the war and so could not stand trial. The whereabouts of other leading figures was also unknown. Martin Bormann, Hitler's malevolent deputy, was last seen picking his way through the rubble of Berlin, trying to escape from the Russians. No one knew if he had succeeded. Witnesses suggested that he had been killed but his body was never recovered so the mystery remained. For the avoidance of doubt, Bormann was tried in absentia at Nuremberg and sentenced to death. Gustav Krupp was indicted to answer for the use that his industrial steel empire had made of slave labour in the service of the Nazi state (and his own rich profits). By this time, however, the old man was bed-ridden, senile and incontinent. The French suggested that his son or even his wife, Fraü Krupp, should be tried in his place, but this would have turned the proceedings into something like a judicial round of the game 'Happy Families'. No court can substitute defendants at will simply because it wants to convict somebody and the idea so obviously contravened basic principles of jurisprudence that it was swiftly abandoned.

Nevertheless, there were some weighty characters who could be brought to book. Eventually, twenty-two defendants were brought to stand trial at Nuremberg and, to their enormous credit, the Allies did conduct a trial in which the interests of justice were served. In his opening speech, one leading prosecution attorney – the American Robert Jackson – elegantly summed up why this had to be so. It was, he said, both a privilege to prosecute the Nazi accused but also a grave responsibility:

> The wrongs which we seek to condemn and punish have been so calculated, so malignant, and so devastating, that civilization cannot tolerate their being ignored, because it cannot survive their being repeated. That four great nations, flushed with victory and stung with injury stay the hand of vengeance and voluntarily submit their captive enemies to the judgment of the law is one of the most significant tributes that Power has ever paid to Reason.

Jackson and his fellow French, Russian and British prosecutors then began to set out their case in minute detail.

The Evidence

Most people are now wholly familiar with the atrocities committed by the Nazi regime. It is a part of our cultural understanding of the Third Reich. But until 1945 many details had been obscured by war and it was only at Nuremberg that the full facts of the terror began to emerge for the very first time. What the court heard was frequently new and often appalling. A week or so into the trial, for example, the court was shown a sickening film about the concentration camps, with graphic images of what had happened just a few months previously. One of the most powerful testimonies came from Rudolf Höss, who had been the camp commandant at Auschwitz. In session after session the court was stunned into a shocked silence by the evidence being heard or seen for the first time.

Each defendant faced a different combination of charges and each, of course, needed to be proven if the prosecution was to be successful. The bundle of evidence against each of the Nazi leaders was a thicket of fine legal detail as the prosecution attempted to establish exactly which of the accused knew what and when. Ironically and with Teutonic efficiency, the Nazis had documented the actions of every department of the sprawling Reich in astonishing detail. Thousands upon thousands of data sets, orders, instructions, regulations, comments and observations had been produced by a myriad of departments and circulated to many of the others. Entire rooms and corridors of the Palace of Justice were overrun by mountains of boxes filled with papers and files. A further complication arose because each document needed to be translated into the three other working languages of the court – English, French and Russian – with copies provided to the defence teams. A small army of support staff was required as typists, copyist and translators worked literally around the clock to prepare the documents for the trial. At times it seemed as though the entire process would collapse under the sheer weight of material.

On the floor of the court even some of the lawyers seemed overwhelmed and the threads of the legal arguments they were trying to put together began to fray alarmingly. Cross examinations became unwieldy so that it became unclear which charge the prosecutor was actually trying to prove. Bundles of documents were dumped on the judges, who were left wondering about how they fitted into the overall case and against whom. It was as though they were having to put together the case for the prosecution. Time after time the increasingly testy judges demanded to know what relevance the evidence offered had to a particular charge; or even which charge was being addressed.

Some of the evidence pointed in a direction which it might have been better to avoid. The other prosecution teams were startled, for example, when the Russians suddenly insisted on including evidence about the massacre of Polish army officers captured in the forest of Katyn. The annihilation of much of the Polish officer corps was certainly a war crime – one of the most notorious of the Second World War – but most assumed that it had actually been committed by the Soviets themselves rather than the Nazis.

Each document was classified by a code number so that all the participants – prosecutors, defence lawyers, witnesses and judges – could be certain that they were discussing the same paper at any one time. If, however, a new statement was inserted into the bundle this upset the classification of the rest and so more time was lost while the series was reordered. An extract of just one exchange between the British prosecutor Sir David Maxwell-Fyfe and Hermann Göring, from 21 March 1946, illustrates the heavy jurisprudential seas through which the trial had to navigate.

> Maxwell-Fyfe: Do I understand this document to say that a man who escapes will be handed over to the Security Police? ... Wasn't that the condition which obtained from 1941 up to the date we are dealing with of March 1944?
>
> Göring: I would like to read the few preceding paragraphs so that no sentences are separated from their context
>
> Maxwell-Fyfe: My Lord, while the witness is reading the document might I go over the technical matter of the arrangement of the exhibits? When I cross-examined Field Marshall Kesselring I put in three documents UK-66 which now becomes Exhibit GB-274; D-39 which now becomes GB-275; TC-91 which becomes GB-276 so that this document will become GB-277. [Turning to the witness.] Have you had an opportunity of reading it, Witness?

Göring: Yes, I have.

Maxwell-Fyfe: Then I am right, am I not, that the Soviet prisoners of war who escaped were to be, after their return to the camp, handed over to the Secret State Police. If they committed a crime, they were to be handed over to the Security Police, isn't that right?

Göring: Not exactly correct. I would like to point to the third sentence in the first paragraph. There it says, "If a prisoner-of-war camp is in the vicinity, then the man who is recaptured is to be transported there."

Maxwell-Fyfe: But read the next sentence, "If a Soviet prisoner of war is returned to the camp" – that is in accordance with this order which you have just read – "he has to be handed to the nearest service station of the Secret State Police." Your own sentence.

Göring: Yes, but the second paragraph which follows gives an explanation of frequent criminal acts of Soviet prisoners of war, et cetera, committed at that time. You read that yourself; that is also connected with this Paragraph Number 1.

And so the trial ground on, day after day. The prosecution teams from the four different countries attempted to demonstrate the responsibility of each of the accused while each constructed their own defence and the interpreters tried to keep everyone abreast of what was being said.

The Accused

Each of the defendants was arraigned in the court because of their individual complicity with crimes against humanity. But they were also chosen to represent various professions which had sustained the Nazi regime: leading politicians, military, industrialists and judges all found themselves in the dock. The intention was to demonstrate how a broad spectrum of German society had been directly involved in sustaining the Nazi terror.

Each of the accused was arraigned on different combinations of four different charges: (1) conspiracy to wage aggressive war; (2) crimes against peace; (3) war crimes; and (4) crimes against humanity. On 19 October the accused were individually handed a copy of charges they would face. The young officer who went from cell to cell serving the indictments on the Nazi leaders was British. His name was Airey Neave. He had been held captive as a prisoner of war and then escaped from the notorious Colditz Castle. Neave went on to become a Tory MP and was murdered when his car was blown up by the IRA in the Palace of Westminster car park in 1979.

The prison regime was unpleasant but, with regular food and health checks, it was better than anything experienced by the inmates of Dachau or Buchenwald. Previous status or rank now counted for nothing and no prisoner was given any privileges. The defendants were held alone in small, spartan cells on one wing of the jail. Each prisoner was observed every thirty seconds round the clock through an observation hatch in the door. Every morning they were led from their cells via a covered walkway to the court house where they sat on the hard wooden bench for another day in the dock. In the evening they were allowed thirty minutes exercise in the prison yard. The jailers lived with a constant apprehension that an attempt may be made to rescue the prisoners or that they might attempt suicide, as both Hermann Göring and Robert Ley managed to do.

Time in custody and the humiliation of defeat took its toll on the prisoners' physical appearance. When they were led into the dock the American journalist William Shirer, who had covered Germany during many years of the Third Reich, scarcely recognised them. There had, he wrote, been 'a metamorphosis. Attired in rather shabby clothes, slumped in their seats fidgeting nervously, they no longer resembled the arrogant leaders of old. They seemed to be such a drab assortment of mediocrities. It seemed difficult to grasp that … such men … could conquer a great nation and most of Europe.'

The most important of the living Nazi leaders in the dock was Herman Göring (1893–1946), a powerful personality who seized on any opportunity to dominate the proceedings. The American prosecutor Robert Jackson all but lost control during his cross examination of Göring, which allowed the Nazi leader to use the court as a soap box. Göring was born in Bavaria, though his parents had married in London, where his father was a consular official at the time. The young Göring became a pilot in the First World War and flew with the von Richthofen formation. When the fabled 'Red Baron' was killed, he was promoted to squadron leader. After the First World War Göring enrolled at the University in Munich, where he met Hitler in 1922 and became a Nazi convert. A year later he was badly wounded in the fracas of the *putsch*. He began to use frequent shots of morphine to control the pain and this led to a lifelong addiction. In office, Göring's ego and power swelled along with his waistline; he had a gargantuan appetite for food and coveted any valuable object he could get his hands on, from Gobelin tapestries to entire houses. When the Nazis came to power Göring was named as Prussian Minister of the Interior and ruthlessly purged senior officials who were not sufficiently pro-Nazi. Göring contemptuously dismissed one young state prosecutor, Robert Kempner, screaming that he 'never wanted to see his face again'. But now, in courtroom 600 at Nuremberg, Göring did see Kempner again. Exiled to America, Kempner had become a US citizen. He adapted his legal skills, perfected his command of English and, in 1946, returned to help prosecute those who had tormented him just a decade before. Göring was condemned to death at Nuremberg but escaped the hangman's noose. On 15 October 1946, just two two hours before he was due to hang, Göring bit into a capsule of cyanide and died within minutes. How he came to obtain the deadly poison has been debated ever since. One theory is that his American guard was bribed. Another suspect was the German prison doctor, the last person to visit Göring. His body was cremated and ashes scattered on the river Isar which flows through Munich.

Admiral Karl Dönitz (1891–1981) was the final leader of Nazi Germany. When Hitler committed suicide on 30 April his last will and testament named Dönitz as his successor. He did not bear the burden of office for long. He was arrested in May 1945 and given a ten-year sentence at Nuremberg. Dönitz had the dubious honour of being the only head of state to be tried by an international criminal court for well over half a century, until Charles Taylor of Liberia joined the blacklist in 2012.

Rudolph Hess (1894 -1987) was originally number three in the party hierarchy after Hitler and Göring, and by the time he was taken to Nuremberg had already been imprisoned for almost three years. Hess made an extraordinary exit from Nazi Germany on 10 May 1943.

After taking tea at his home in Munich with his wife, Hess left, saying that he would be away for some time and not sure exactly when he would be back. As it turned out, he never returned. Hess went directly to a nearby airfield where he took off in a Messerschmitt 110. An accomplished pilot – he had once aspired to fly solo across the Atlantic – Hess then headed north west on a 900-mile journey across Europe until he landed at Eaglesham, near Glasgow in Scotland. His arrival was seen by pitchfork-wielding farmers who rushed to his plane and then escorted him to the nearest police station. He was taken to London where he tried to negotiate with Churchill, who dismissed him out of hand.

At Nuremberg, Hess cut something of a pathetic, rambling figure and in the early days of the trial he even claimed to have total amnesia. He evidently had difficulty in following all that was going on around him; at times he sought refuge from reality and sat in the dock reading a novel. The contrast with the bright young student that he had once been – he had once hoped to go to Oxford University – could not have been starker. Yet none of this could disguise his criminal participation in events well before the war. Hess was sentenced to life imprisonment. Like Göring, he finally committed suicide, but this was in 1987. By then Hess was aged ninety-three.

Two other Nazi veteran bosses, Alfred Rosenberg and Julius Streicher, who had played leading roles in the party from the earliest days, were arraigned. Alfred Rosenberg (1893–1946) had briefly been leader of the Nazi organization while Hitler was serving out his sentence following the Beer-Hall *Putsch* (see Chapter 3). He was found guilty and executed. Julius Streicher (1885–1946) was originally a primary school teacher who became a *gauleiter* and known as the 'Beast of Nuremberg', notorious for his depraved sadism. He was found guilty and hanged.

Joachim von Ribbentrop (1893–1946) was Hitler's foreign minister. One of the most careerist Nazis, Ribbentrop ran a wine and champagne company after marriage into the wealthy Henkell wine family. His upper-class lifestyle and carpet-bagging ambition was resented by other senior Nazis, who dubbed him 'Ribbensnob'. By the time he arrived at Nuremberg the preening was long gone. The journalist William Shirer described how 'at last shorn of his arrogance and his pompousness, [he was] looking pale, bent and beaten.' As Hitler's foreign minister he was author of the Molotov-Ribbentrop pact between Nazi Germany and the USSR in 1939 one of the most cynical agreements in the history of diplomacy, which sealed the fate of Poland. He was instrumental in organising the transportation of Jews in the Second World War. Ribbentrop was found guilty and executed.

Several of Hitler's military commanders were indicted and found guilty on various charges. Alfred Jodl (1890–1946) and Wilhelm Keitel (1882–1946) were the senior operational commanders of the army and ever-willing to do Hitler's bidding. Both were found guilty and executed. Naval commander Erich Raeder (1876–1960) escaped with a life sentence and was later released early on grounds of ill-health.

Others who had been instrumental in executing plans for the aggressive Nazi expansionism were in the dock. Ernst Kaltenbrunner (1903–1946) and Arthur Seyß-Inquart (1892–1946) had connived to undermine Austrian independence and then terrorised populations throughout Europe. Both were executed. Dr Wilhelm Frick (1877–1946) was named 'Protector' of the Czech provinces of Bohemia and Moravia. It was an ironic title for a man who subjected the local populations to some of the worst atrocities of the Nazi regime. He was found guilty of war crimes and crimes against humanity at Nuremberg and executed. Fritz Sauckel (1894–1946) held the ornate title of Plenipotentiary for the Allocation of Labour, which meant he effectively organised systematic slavery. Sauckel oversaw the forced deportation of some five million able-bodied men and women from France and the occupied territories in eastern Europe. He was hanged at Nuremberg for his crimes. Hitler Youth leader, Baldur von Schirach (1907–74), was given a twenty-year sentence for his part in the crimes against humanity. Dr Robert Ley, the head of the Nazi labour organisation, which replaced Trade Unions, might have been given a similar sentence but avoided the court's verdict by strangling himself with a towel in his cell on 25 October.

Other leaders of the German government were fortunate to escape from the Nuremberg trials with their lives. Dr Hjalmar Schacht (1887–1970) was the finance supremo who piloted the German economy out of recession; without undue modesty he described himself as the 'economic Napoleon of the twentieth century'. But he later fell foul of Hitler and had been held in a concentration camp since 1944. Schacht was acquitted at Nurnberg but later sentenced by another denazifaction court to eight years in a work camp. In fact, he was released in 1948 and returned to civilian life as a financial adviser. Walter Funk (1890–1960), a second-line minister in various roles, was sentenced to life imprisonment but released on grounds of ill-health in 1957. Konstantin von Nürath (1873–1956) German foreign minister from 1933 until 1938, was given a fifteen-year prison sentence but was released early on grounds of ill-health. Franz von Papen (1879–1969) had preceded Hitler as chancellor and continued to serve – not always willingly – in various roles during the Nazi years. Von Papen was acquitted at Nuremberg but subsequently sentenced to eight years by a German denazification court in 1947. He served just two years before being released.

Perhaps the most controversial defendant was Albert Speer, Hitler's favourite architect, who designed many emblematic buildings of the Third Reich (1905–1981). Speer was appointed to a pivotal role in the Nazi war machine but then intrigued against Hitler. At Nuremberg he went some way to apologising for his part in the crimes committed during the Third Reich and was jailed for twenty years (the Russian judge wanted to hang him). Speer remained a highly divisive figure up to the time of his death in London in 1981.

Although a journalist and leading commentator on German radio, several observers were unsure about why Hans Fritzsche (1900–1953) had been selected to stand trial. The court dismissed the charges and he was acquitted.

The Verdict and After

The initial trial at Nuremberg set a new precedent but was not the end of the process, which continued for years after. Hearings continued until 1949 and hundreds of people were brought before the court to answer for their crimes. Trials were also held in other centres, such as Dachau, and continued as part of the international clean up. In 1961 the Israelis kidnapped Adolf Eichmann from his hideout in Argentina and put him on trial in Jerusalem for his leading role in organising the 'final solution' of the Holocaust. In 1965 a German prosecutor broke new ground by using German state law – rather than international law – to arraign former concentration camp personnel in what became known as the Auschwitz Trials.

Since then, the scope and depth of international criminal law has continued to expand apace. Leaders such as Slobodan Milosevic, Radovan Karadzic and Charles Taylor have found themselves in court to face international justice. Crimes against humanity continue to be committed by regimes around the world, of course, and much wickedness goes unpunished. But some is prevented. Brutal dictators now need to look over their shoulders and think twice before deciding to act, or not. And what they see – whether they know it or not – is the long, dark shadow of the Palace of Justice in Nuremberg.

Notes

Chapter 2: Hitler's Early Life in Munich: From Bohemia to Germania

1. Schleissheimerstrasse 34 (Hitler's first address in Munich).
2. Ludwigstrasse 16 (Bayerische Staatsbibliothek).
3. Platzl 9 (the Hofbräuhaus).
4. Corner of Amalienstrasse and Theresienstrasse (Café Stefanie).
5. Odeonsplatz.
6. Elizabethplatz 4 (Hitler's army training centre).
7. Lothstrasse 29 (Hitler's barracks).
8. Kaiserstrasse 46 (Lenin's flat).
9. Corner of Kardinal-Faulhaber-Straße and Promenadeplatz (Karl Eisner memorial).
10. Wiener Platz, Innere Weinerstrasse 19 (Hofbräukeller).
11. Tal 54–55 (Sterneckerbräu keller).
12. Thierschstrasse 41 (Hitler's address in Munich).
13. Gentzstrasse 1 (the Hanfstaengl home).
14. Corneliusstrasse 12 (Nazi party offices).
15. Petersplatz (Café Neumayr).
16. Nymphenbergerstrasse 4 (the Löwenbräukeller).

Chapter 3: The Munich *Putsch* 1923: From Bürgerbräu Keller to Landsberg Prison

1. Odeonsplatz (*Putsch* memorial).
2. Viscardigasse (Shirker's Alley).
3. Rosenheimerstrasse 29 (site of Bürgerbräukeller).
4. Nymphenburgerstrasse 4 (Löwenbräukeller).
5. Ludwigstrasse corner with Shöenfeldstrasse (Bavarian war ministry).

6. Maximilianstrasse 14 (von Kahr's office).
7. Marienplatz (Munich Town Hall).
8. Ludwigsbrücke bridge (route of march).
9. Türkenstrasse 17 (army barracks.)
10. Residenzstrasse, Residenz (site of the massacre).
11. Blutenburgstrasse 3 (*Putsch* Trial building).
12. Blutenburgstrasse 18 (Hitler detained here).

Chapter 4: From Failed *Putsch* to Absolute Power: The 1920s and 30s

1. Thierschstrasse 11 (Publishing house of *Mein Kampf*).
2. Corneliusstrasse 12 (Nazi party offices).
3. Bürgerbraükeller (venue of Nazi relaunch).
4. Schellingstrasse 50 (Nazi party offices).
5. Schellingstrasse 39 (*Völkischer Beobachter* office).
6. Schellingstrasse 56 (Shelling Salon).
7. Schellingstrasse 62 (Osteria Bavaria).
8. Englishergarten (Englishergarten park).
9. Schellingstrasse 2 (Memorial wall).
10. Galeriestrasse and Ludwigstrasse (Café Heck).
11. Maximilianstrasse 17 (Four Seasons hotel).
12. Printzregentplatz (Hitler's flat).
13. Frauenplatz 9 (Bratwurstglockl bar).
14. Amalienstrasse 25 (Heinrich Hofmann studio).
15. Isabellastrasse 45 (Eva Braun birthplace).
16. Hohenzollernstarsse 93 (Eva Bruan family home).
17. Max-Mannheimer-Platz 1 (NS documentation centre and visitor centre – see below).
18. Köningsplatz (Nazi book burning site).
19. Arcisstrasse 12 (Führerbau visiting possible – see below).
20. Briennerstrasse corner with Arcisstrasse (Temples of Honour).
21. Prinzregentenstrasse 1 (Hause der Kunst gallery visitor centre – see below).
22. Galeriestrasse 4 (Hofgarten cultural centre visitor centre – see below).

Visitor Centres

17. NS Documentation Centre, Max-Mannheimer-Platz 1 (former Brienner Straße 34), T:+49 89 233-67000, E:nsdoku@muenchen.de, open Tue-Sun 10am-7pm (including bank holidays).
19. Arcisstrasse 12 is the old Führerbau building which now houses a music conservatoire. Visitors may be admitted to view the building at the discretion of the door porter.
21. Hause der Kunst, Prinzregentenstrasse 1, hausderkunst.de, open daily 10am-8pm (Thu 10am–10pm),
22. Hofgarten Cultural Centre at Galeriestrasse 4 (Am Hofgarten), which housed the Degenerate Art Exhibition, now hosts various events. T:+49 89 200 011 33, kunstverein-muenchen.de, open Tue-Sun 11am-6pm.

Chapter 5: Operation *Kolibri* (Hummingbird): The Night of the Long Knives

1. Hanslbauer Hotel site. The original hotel was demolished in late 2018, Bodenschneidstraße 9, 83707, Bad Wiessee. Bad Wiesee has spectacular mountain views and the beautiful lake Tergensee – it a popular spot for breaks to get away from the hustle and bustle of Munich. The town is due south of Munich. The journey by car takes around one hour along the A8 auto route. Tourist information: Lindenplatz 6, 83707, Bad Wiessee, tegernsee.com

Chapter 6: Sophie Scholl, Georg Elser and the Nazi Resisters

1. Rosenheimer strasse 29 (Hilton Hotel/GEMA).
2. Türkenstrasse 59 (Elser workshop).
3. Türkenstrasse 94 (Elser lodging).
4. Briennerstrasse 20 (Gestapo HQ).
5. Platz der Opfer des Nationalsozialismus (Memorial to victims of Nazism).
6. Georg Elser Platz, on Türkenstrasse between Schellingstrasse and Blutenstrasse (memorial to Elser).
7. Geschwister-Scholl-Platz (Platz in honour of the Scholls).

8. Profesor-Huber-Platz (Platz in honour of Prof Huber).
9. Franz-Joseph-Strasse 13 (Scholl's Flat).
10. Leopoldstrasse 38 (White Rose print shop).
11. Museumsinsel 1 (Deutschmuseum).
12. Prielmayerstrasse (Justiz Palast).
13. Stadelheimerstrasse 12 and 24 (Prison and cemetery).
14. Nuehauserstrasse (St Michael's church and Bürgersaal Crypt).
15. Frauenplatz 12 (Frauenkirche).
16. Altheimer Eck 13 (Münchener Post).
17. Sendlinger Strasse 6 (Fritz Gerlich office).
18. Ettstrasse 2 (Police Headquarters).

Chapter 7: *Kristallnacht* and the Persecution of the Jews

1. Marienplatz, Altes Rathaus and Neues Rathaus (Old and New City Hall). The square is dominated by medieval Gothic town hall and the tower of the Neues Rathaus (new town hall). Note the plaque on the wall in German and English which recalls the events of *Kristallnacht*.
2. Munich City Museum (Münchener Stadtmuseum) and site of the Jewish-owned Uhlfelder, St-Jakobs-Platz 1, Metro Marientplatz, muenchner-stadtmuseum.de
3. Munich Jewish Museum, St Jakobs Platz 16, Metro Marienplatz, juedisches-museum-muenchen.de. Open Tue-Sun 10am-6pm. Plans for a Jewish Museum in Munich were first hatched in 1928 when a small group of individuals decided to try and document the history of the community in the city.

Chapter 8: Through Dachau to National Socialism and the Third Reich

1. Dachau is a suburb of Munich and easily accessible on public transport. Many people who live here make their daily commute into the city centre. From Munich's city center, take the S-Bahn S2 line in the direction of Petershausen. You need to get off the train at Dachau station; the journey time is around 20mins. Once at Dachau station there are plenty of signs to the 'Concentration Camp Memorial Site'. Buses 724 or 726 go to the camp, marked 'KZ-Gedenkstätte', at the end of the line.

2. The Path of Remembrance is 3km long and takes about 45mins to walk. It begins at the railway station and there are twelve information panels at various points along the route which explain what happened. You can follow the route and make a virtual tour of the camp on the official website, kz-gedenkstaette-dachau.de
3. Visitors' Center Dachau Memorial Site, Pater-Roth-Str. 2a, D - 85221 Dachau, T+49 (0) 8131/66 99 70. Open daily 9am to 5pm. Closed 24 December. Entry free.

Chapter 9: 'Peace for our Time': Berchtesgaden and the Munich Crisis

1. Berchtesgaden is 150km to the south east of Munich. As an excursion from Munich the town can be visited in day but is well worth a night stop over for a less pressured visit. To get there by car follow the A8 and exit at Bad Reichenhall or at Salzburg Süd to Berchtesgaden. From Berchtesgaden follow the Obersalzberg road to the Hintereck parking area at Obersalzberg. Journey time: 1hr 40mins. Trains leave Munich for Salzburg with one change at Freilassing. The journey time is between 2½ to 3hrs.
2. Hotel Zum Türken, Hintereck 2, Berchtesgaden, 83471 Tel: (+49) 8652 24 28. The Hotel is currently closed for renovations.
3. Documentation Centre Obersalzberg, Salzbergstr. 41, Berchtesgaden, 83471, T +49 (0)8652/947960, obersalzberg.de. Open daily 9am–5pm. Last admission 4pm. An excellent visitor centre which aims to educate, inform and remember the victims of National Socialism. There is a permanent exhibition alongside special exhibitions, lectures and events.
4. The Kehlsteinhaus (Eagle's Nest), T +49 8652 2029/656 5070, kehlsteinhaus.de. Open daily May to mid-Oct 8.30am-4.50pm. Bar-restaurant with views as spectacular as its history is sombre. It is open to the public and no reservation is needed for individual visits. Get there by bus from Hintereck parking area to the Eagle's Nest parking area. It is also possible to hike from Ofneralm up to the Eagle's Nest parking area (1½ to 2hrs) or hike from Scharitzkehl parking area to the Eagle's Nest parking area on a trail that offers beautiful panoramic views (2 ½ to 3 hrs).

Chapter 10: Nuremberg: The Triumph of Justice Over Power

1. Nuremberg Trials Court Room and Visitor Centre, Palace de Justiz, Bärenschanzstraße 72, 90429 Nuremberg, T +49 (0)911 321 79 372, museums.nuernberg.de. Court Room 600 and the information centre is open to visitors when it is not being used for criminal proceedings. Direct trains to Nuremberg from Munich take 1hr 15mins.

2. Nazi Party Rally Grounds and Documentation Center, Bayernstraße 110, 90478 Nuremberg, T +49 (0)911 231 75 38, museums.nuernberg. de. Open Mon-Fri 9am-6pm, Sat, Sun and holidays 10am-6pm. The former Nazi Party Rally Grounds are freely accessible. Information in German and English is provided at 23 locations all over the grounds. For a first short tour, you should plan about 90 mins. You may buy a map in English at the Documentation Center ticket office.

Index